Henry Noble Day

**Elements of Mental Science**

Being a comprehensive exposition of the phenomena of the human mind

considered in its general characteristics, in its particular functional activities, and as

an organic whole

Henry Noble Day

**Elements of Mental Science**
*Being a comprehensive exposition of the phenomena of the human mind considered in its general characteristics, in its particular functional activities, and as an organic whole*

ISBN/EAN: 9783337370459

Printed in Europe, USA, Canada, Australia, Japan

Cover: Foto ©Thomas Meinert / pixelio.de

More available books at **www.hansebooks.com**

# ELEMENTS

## OF

# MENTAL SCIENCE

BEING A COMPREHENSIVE EXPOSITION OF THE PHENOMENA OF
THE HUMAN MIND CONSIDERED IN ITS GENERAL CHAR-
ACTERISTICS, IN ITS PARTICULAR FUNCTIONAL
ACTIVITIES, AND AS AN ORGANIC WHOLE

BY

## HENRY N. DAY

AUTHOR OF "PSYCHOLOGY," "ÆSTHETICS," "LOGIC," "ETHICS," "PHILOS-
OPHY OF THOUGHT AND BEING." "ENGLISH LITERATURE,"
"ART OF DISCOURSE," ETC.

COPYRIGHT, 1886, BY

IVISON, BLAKEMAN, TAYLOR, & COMPANY
*PUBLISHERS*
NEW YORK AND CHICAGO

# PREFACE.

THIS text-book in Mental Science is designed
to be a compact but comprehensive presentation
of the facts of the human mind in scientific
method and form. The science is treated as one
of observation, not of speculation. Little space
accordingly is given to metaphysical discussions.
The design is rather to prepare the beginner in
mental studies for an appreciative understanding
of the history of philosophic thought in the
past and of the speculations and discussions in
this field of investigation at the present, as he
may prosecute these studies in the lecture-room
or in private reading.

The science is carefully defined in its proper
province and comprehension, and is mapped out
into departments that are determined by lines of
demarkation appearing in the nature of the mind,
so that the treatment may be recognized as exact,
orderly, and exhaustive.

The outer boundaries of mental science, it is
believed, are now determined beyond reasonable
question ; and the leading divisions with their respective organic relationships are also as clearly

ascertained.   The progress of the science, hence-
forth, will be in the line of the investigation of the
more specific phenomena of mind in their respective natures, and their relations to one another
and to the universe of object with which the human mind is in interaction.

Two leading peculiarities in this present treatment of the subject may be specified here.   They
are, first, the separate formal presentations of the
three comprehensive functional forms of mental
activity—the functions of form, of knowledge,
and of choice on the one hand, and of their several objects—the beautiful, the true, and the
good on the other.   The active subject and its
object are exhibited each in its own proper character and laws, so that light from each side is
thrown upon the other.

Secondly, the facts of the mind viewed as an
organic whole, and accordingly as more than a
mere aggregation of specific functions, are presented under the two like complementary views
of rational activity—subjective and objective.

In addition to those peculiarities of method
may be mentioned many peculiarities in special
doctrines, as touching the place and office of the
imagination and of memory in mental phenomena,
the nature of knowledge, the genesis of our ideas
of time and space and of so-called *a priori* truths,
and others.

Free use has been made of the author's previous works in this field of knowledge, his " Psychology," " Æsthetics," " Logic," " Ontology, or Philosophy of Thought and of Being." MULTUM MAGNORUM VIRORUM JUDICIO CREDO : ALIQUID ET MEO VINDICO.

*New Haven,* 1886.

# CONTENTS.

## INTRODUCTION.

## BOOK I.

### GENERAL ATTRIBUTES OF MIND.

## *BOOK II.*

### THE SENSIBILITY.—I. SUBJECTIVE VIEW.

THE INTELLIGENCE.—II. OBJECTIVE VIEW.

## *BOOK IV.*

### THE WILL.—I. SUBJECTIVE VIEW.

# INTRODUCTION.

§ 1. MENTAL SCIENCE in the larger sense comprehends the four subordinate sciences of Psychology, Æsthetics, Logic, and Ethics. It is the proper province of *Psychology* to set forth the facts generally of the human mind as learned from observation; of *Æsthetics* to exhibit the laws and generic forms of the particular function of mental activity known as the Sensibility and the Imagination; of *Logic* to present the laws and forms of the Intellect; and of *Ethics* those of the Will.

Mental Science will properly embrace these four subordinate sciences, but will view them from its own single point of observation and with a single method also peculiar to itself, while each of the others will have its own separate starting point and develop itself by its own method. It will thus be more comprehensive than psychology, as now generally understood, while it will avoid entering into the technical details and peculiar methods of the other three. Its aim will be to present in a general view the entire field of mental states and operations in their organic relations and interdependencies, preparing the student in this way to enter more intelligently into the investigation of the manifold questions that present themselves concerning the phenomena of the human soul and the nature and regulative principles of truth, of beauty, and of morality, as well as also the deeper and broader speculations of metaphysical philosophy.

§ 2. In dignity and importance no science can outrank the science of mind. The mind is " the self," the conscious, proper self; and sound wisdom indorses the familiar maxim that "the proper study of mankind is man." The most important thing for one to know is himself—his own rational nature, its powers, its conditions, its final destiny as determined by a wise use of this self-knowledge. All other sciences found their claims to interest in this and from it derive their shaping and validating principles. " To know and understand itself," says Sir William Hamilton, speaking of the human mind, " and thus to establish its dominion over the universe of existence—it is this alone which constitutes man's grand and distinctive pre-eminence." No study affords a better means of discipline, as no science—at least no science of observation—can put forth a better claim to certitude and exactness of method, and none certainly is better fitted to train to those habits of reflective contemplation on the phenom-

ena of human existence which characterize the
man of truest and highest practical wisdom, and
thus to effect the fullest and fastest growth of
the essential excellencies of personal character.

§ 3. The science of mind and the science of
matter—Mental Science and Physical Science—
constitute the two great branches of science divided in reference to its subject-matter. If,
however, Space and Time be assumed to be true
realities, since we observe that the logical attribute of quantity has in them its most fundamental applications, Mathematical Science may
not improperly be ranked as a third co-ordinate
science with those of mind and matter. The
three comprehensive divisions of human science
would accordingly be : (1) Mental or Spiritual ;
(2) Physical ; and (3) Mathematical.

Mental Science is properly ranked among the
so-called Inductive Sciences. It begins with
observation of particular facts, not with general
truths. From one or more of such observed
facts it induces to others of a like nature, so that
a single observation may suffice to give a trustworthy knowledge of an indefinite number of
facts of the same class. One observation, or at
least a few observations, thus, will afford a knowledge of the essential nature of all exertions of
thought, or of imagination, or of will. So the observation of the character of one man's feelings,
or thoughts, or purposes will acquaint us with the
character of those of other men generally in like

relations. Still farther than this: as guided by inductive thought, Mental Science conducts us from observations of one department of mind to other co-ordinate and complementary departments, just as the comparative zoologist is enabled to determine from the bony structure of an animal what its cellular, its muscular, its nervous systems, what its size, its food, its habits of life must have been, and even the character of other animal and vegetable life around it, as well as its general climatic environment. Mental Science, thus, is built up chiefly and characteristically by the application of the methods of inductive thought. The co-ordinate movement of thought—the deductive—which proceeds from the whole class or the composite attribute to a subordinate grade, and so on to the individual or to the simple, as also the secondary logical processes of classification and of analysis, are much and freely employed in aid and furtherance of induction, but rather in subordination than predominance.

§ 4. The facts of mind, which first through observation and then by means of induction, with its auxiliary processes of thought, are developed into the full form of a science, are discovered first and mainly by direct introspection. The mind is enabled to look inwardly upon itself, upon its exercises and affections, to distinguish one from another, to mark the respective qualities of each, to note their relations to one another and their interdependence, and thus to gather up into its comprehensive observation the facts which enter into and constitute the science.

But in addition to this, the thoughts, the feelings, the determinations of other men are also revealed to our view in the various ways in which the mind of man is accustomed to reveal itself.

Still a third important field in which are to be observed the facts of mental science, is that of language, in the formation and the use of which men unite, dropping aside for the time what is peculiar and abnormal and expressing thought and feeling in so far as they are common to men as a class. Language is the grand social revelation of the facts of mind in which there is agreement and consent of many minds, and so is peculiarly trustworthy and authoritative.

While in manifold other ways the mind of man reveals itself to our observation, as in the arts, in government, in social customs, and science will not overlook any of those revelations, still it remains that the great commanding sources of fact for mental science are these three : —1. Introspection ; 2. Observation of others ; 3. Language.

§ 5. From a careful survey of these several fields in which the facts of mind are presented to our observation, and in these facts, we learn that there are certain appearances or phenomena which are traceable to one common source or ground, and which in one particular selection and

grouping we call the peculiar characteristics
of mind. These characteristics or attributes of
mind, which are thus observed to be common
to mind, constitute the subject of mental science.
The science or knowledge of these attributes is
the science or knowledge of mind, since the
science or knowledge of an object is nothing but
the science or knowledge of the attributes of that
object considered in themselves and their relations. The object itself, indeed, is none other
than the complement or concrete whole of its attributes ; and it is known solely in and through
its attributes.

Attributes are divided into two great classes,
the essential and the relative. The essential
attributes are intrinsic to the object and make
it to be what it is in itself ; the relative attributes
are extrinsic to the object and make it to be
what it is by reason of its relations to other objects. The roundness, and the brightness, and
the gravity of the sun are among its essential
attributes ; its being the center of motion to the
other bodies of the system is a relative attribute.
It becomes thus the one object of mental science
to gather up these attributes of mind, distinguishing the essential from the relative, to
arrange them in their due order of importance
and dependence, and then unfold each in its
proper fullness and bearing.

We shall find that the mind possesses one
essential attribute which so far outranks and

transcends all others that it has often not improperly been regarded in its divers modifications
as constituting the one comprehensive fact of
mind, and thus the one topic to be considered in
mental science : it is the attribute of *activity*.
This attribute, because of this pre-eminent, if we
do not more truly say exclusive, importance, it will
be convenient to exhibit, first, in its divers subordinate forms and modifications, and, secondly,
as one organic whole. Our method will accordingly be to consider, in the First Book, the
GENERAL ATTRIBUTES of Mind ;

In the Second Book, the first subordinate department of the essential attribute of mind, just
named, its activity, viz. :—Its FUNCTION OF
FORM, otherwise known as the Function of the
SENSIBILITY AND THE IMAGINATION ;

In the Third Book, the second special department of mental activity, THE INTELLIGENCE ;

In the Fourth Book, the third special department, THE WILL ; and—

In the Fifth, the attributes of mental activity
as an organic whole, under the appellation of
THE REASON.

# BOOK I.

## GENERAL ATTRIBUTES OF MIND.

---

## CHAPTER I.

### THE ESSENTIAL ACTIVITY OF MIND.

§ 6. THE first glance turned inward on our mental nature discovers to us the prominent fact that it is an essentially active nature. We discern the mind, in truth, only in its operations. Even what we call the states of mind are active states. Our thoughts are active; our imaginings are active; our determinations are active. They all bear the character of change, of motion from one form or condition to another. Our feelings are the feelings of active natures; they are not like impressions on stones, or inactive substances; they are the affections of active beings. So striking is this fact that by some philosophers the feelings have been denominated the active powers of the mind.

Observation of other minds corroborates this testimony given by the inspection of our own inward being. They make themselves known to us indeed only as they act or move and as by such action or motion they impress our minds. The universal language of men confirms the fact:—the human mind is essentially active. This is its first, great, comprehensive attribute. There is no actual or possible revelation made of mind that does not reveal this as its ever present and its predominant attribute.

It is by this characteristic that mind is distinguished from all other real or supposed natures. It is primarily and sharply distinguished from matter by this. Matter is recognized as inert, inactive ; as motionless and formless, except as moved and shaped by something extrinsic to itself. Whatever hypothesis may be entertained in regard to the nature of matter, whether as a real, peculiar entity in itself, or whether as a mere " center of force," or, in the better form of this class of hypotheses, as a potentialized force, that is, as force changed from an active or living force to a mere potency—a mere capability of moving when meet occasion shall come to it for moving —whatever hypothesis may be entertained in regard to the nature of matter, it is ever and always recognized as the direct opposite of mind in this respect—that it is inert, inactive, moving only as it is moved.

In like manner, the prevalent theories of space and time, even when recognizing them as real entities, refrain from attributing to either of them any such attribute as that of activity, at

least in the narrower and more generally accepted
sense of that term.  They may be recognized as
active positively in determining our cognitions,
and negatively in certain limitations of real
objects and actions.  It is after all only the
niceness of metaphysical speculation that recognizes activity as a mark of space or of time.

This grand attribute—activity—,then, we recognize as entering into the essential constitution
of mind.  In exact statement, indeed, activity
constitutes the very essence of mind.  We are
not to think of the mind as a something existing back of this activity, and from itself putting
forth the activity.  The activity is its very self,
in the sense that the whole constituting attribute
of an object is the object itself.  As will appear
hereafter when the nature of thought or of
knowledge is unfolded, there is no *substratum* to
be supposed as a necessary support for the attribute, in which the attribute may be said to inhere
while yet distinct from it.  The substance, so far
as an actual being, is the same as its constituting
attribute; the mind is the same as its attribute
of activity ;—mind and active substance are the
same.  This will more fully appear in the sequel.

Activity being thus the very essence of the
mind, the beginning studies of mind should be
led to recognize it as having this character.  Our
more familiar view regards the mind as a substance with certain attributes, a view which in
itself shuts out the notion of mind as a cause;

whereas, subject to the restrictions of the meaning of that term to be given hereafter, the mind should far more properly be viewed under this latter relation of thought—as a cause, and so as active. The exposition of the nature of mind suffers much from this inconsiderate treatment of it, as a mere inactive substance. A chief difficulty in the study of mind springs from the difficulty of conceiving it as essentially active. From the start, therefore, the study should aim to regard the mind as an essentially active nature; and every conception of it in any of its particular modifications, should keep steadfastly in view this essential attribute of its nature: THE MIND IS ESSENTIALLY ACTIVE.

# CHAPTER II.

## THE UNITY OF MIND, WITH A THREEFOLD DIVERSITY OF FUNCTION.

§ 7. THE human mind is, in the proper sense of the statement, a unit—it is single or individual, one by itself. The phrase—the human mind—may be used abstractly to denote the aggregate of the attributes of mind; but when we speak concretely of the mind of a man, we speak of it as a unit, existing distinctly and separately from all other beings, as one among many.

The decisive proof of this singleness or individuality of the human mind is derived from experience and observation. So positively does every one know as from his own personal knowledge of himself that he is truly himself a distinct and separate being, that the statement of the truth seems a truism. He unintentionally and unavoidably makes this interpretation of his conscious experiences, that he is himself and not a part or a mode of the existence of any other being ; and that his mind, his soul, the being within him that thinks and feels, is as distinct from other minds as his body from other animal bodies. He feels himself, accordingly, to be responsible for much at least of what he thinks and purposes. All the records of human experience present uniform testimony in confirmation of this utterance of individual consciousness. There is a plurality of minds; each human mind is one of this plurality.

§ 8. Much less is the human mind to be regarded as identical with its object. As an activity it implies an object upon which or toward which it is exerted ; and to account for the interaction of mind with its object, to account, for example, for the mind's apprehension or thought of an object, it has been supposed by some that thought and object must be one and the same. But the common sense of men rejects this supposition as in contradiction of all its strongest and deepest convictions—of convictions that could have only grown out of uniform experiences.

That mind and its object are distinct is a truth of simple observation. This dualism in existence, implied in the fact of mental activity exerted upon some object distinct from itself, is thus a truth fundamental to all true philosophy,—to all philosophy that builds not on groundless assumption, but on solid fact as presented to human observation. Mental action and object imply each other and are real correlatives in thought ; and the speculation would seem to be idle that should seek to reduce the one to the other, or indeed to subordinate the one to the other. The remotest conclusion which any such speculation could legiti-

mately reach would be that mind ever acts upon
mind as object—upon some other mind, or upon
itself in some one of its own departments of
being.

§ 9. The human mind is also simple. It is not
made up of a number of constituents of diverse
nature put together so as to form a mere aggregate
or accumulation of elements. It has divers functions, performs divers acts, but it remains in all
the same simple nature. The sun both warms and
illuminates ; but it is the same sun that acts in
both heat and light. So the human mind with
its diversity of functions is one and simple, and
cannot be decomposed into different things, one
of which discharges the function of thinking,
another that of feeling, and a third that of purposing.

§ 10. With this singleness and simplicity of
essential nature, we yet can easily distinguish
three different modes of mental activity ; and accordingly we say that the human mind has
three different functions. If thus we take up an
orange and bring it near the sense, we find that
it makes certain impressions upon us; we feel, for
instance, its softness through the sense of touch.
The function of the mind thus is feeling ; and
this function of feeling is technically called the
*sensibility*. Then we perceive that some object
impresses us and gives us a feeling of this one of
its attributes—its softness ; and we know that this
object is soft. Another function of the mind

thus is that of knowing; and this function is called *the intelligence.* Still further, we may determine to hold fast the orange, to press it upon the hand, to move it before the eye, to smell or to taste it. We discover thus a third function of the mind, that of determining to do something; and this function of determining is called *the will.*

All the discoverable modes of mental activity are reducible to one or the other of these three— feeling, knowing, willing. No other is conceivable. They are organic functions belonging together to the same being, each implying the other. We may notice more one or the other at different times; one function may predominate and give a general character to the whole mental act or state. But the functions all go on together just as respiration and circulation of the blood and muscular contraction go on together. When we feel the softness of the orange which we hold in our hand, we may also perceive that it is soft, and determine to hold it or cast it away. The perceiving and the willing may not, in fact, come up into distinct consciousness, but we find that if we direct our attention upon either of those functional exertions, we may be conscious of its presence as entering into every mental act, provided at least that the mental action be on a scale sufficiently large to be discerned by our intellectual vision.

As stated in the Introduction our method will lead us to consider in separate books these three several functions—the mind as feeling, as knowing, and as willing—and to devote a separate book to the consideration of the action of the mind as an organic whole. For reasons which will then appear, this last view of the mind will be represented under the appellation of the REASON, a term equivalent to *the rational nature* as it is distinguished from the animal or bodily nature of man.

# CHAPTER III.

## THE CONTINUOUSNESS OF MIND.

§ 11. THE very notion of action involves that of continuousness. In so far as active, consequently, the human mind must be recognized as more or less continuous. Every specific feeling, every thought, every purpose, has a beginning and an end and a continuity from beginning to end that constitutes it a single identical action or affection. This bond of continuity extends through the experience of the same mind during the entire period of its existence. Mental life is thus more than a chain made up of separate links; it is more than an ever-flowing river which bears along the particles of water from the original spring down to their union with the sea; it is the continuity of a living thing. The river may in its course part with every particle that left the primitive source, from the effect of evaporation or other displacement, and yet maintain its continuity and thereby its unity and identity by receiving successive supplies from rainfalls or from tributary streams that may indeed more than replace what it has lost. The life of mind flows on, never parting with anything of its true

2

essence; relaxing its vigor, it may be, from time
to time, and changing its current, but maintaining
the unity and identity of a living nature that is
far closer and more persistent than belongs to
any merely inorganic thing. Every specific act of
mind, every change or modification which it suffers, is bound by the bonds of a life to that which
precedes and to that which follows. Any conception or reasoning which treats the mind as
discontinuous, as at best only an aggregation of
unconnected events or phenomena, as a mere
succession or successions of changes, having no interior vital bond of unity, is radically at fault.
It is hazardous to truth, even, ever to keep out
of view the grand fundamental fact in regard to
mind that its activity is continuous, never broken
during its entire existence.

There is, of course, no proof of discontinuous-
ness. It would be a strange thing for a man to
set up the claim that his present inner being of
to-day has taken the place of the other and entirely different inner being of yesterday. The
presumption is irresistible at the outset that his
being of to-day has not been utterly disrupted
from that of yesterday. The undeniable fact of
observation that each specific action or affection
of the mind has a certain continuousness of its
own leads as irresistibly to the belief that the activity prolonged through days, or years, or through
life, has suffered no interruption, has leaped no
chasm separating different lives. Universal con-

sent, indeed, of itself establishes the truth so fully
and surely that formal proof seems well nigh
inept, certainly needless. But there are certain
very important facts or truths of mind which are
so closely connected with this attribute of continuousness in mind, that they are both proofs of
the attribute and, also conversely, are proved by
it. They are of such a character as to justify
particular consideration.

§ 12. Men generally believe in the personal
identity of each individual mind. Each one be-
lieves that he is the same man to-day that he
was yesterday. The belief is warrant for the belief in mental continuousness; for certainly there
could be no personal identity without personal
continuousness. If the flow of my life has been
broken, my present self is not the same self as
that of yesterday, even if we should allow the
hardly allowable supposition that the same current of feelings and actions had been reproduced
in the present self that the self of yesterday
would have had if its continuousness had not
been broken off. No conceivable power could
make one, lives or selves once divided and separate.
We need to take a still higher view. Not only
is it to be believed that the mind as a whole continues, but we are constrained to the belief that
every act and every affection of the mind abides
imperishably forever afterward, maintaining an
abiding presence in it. The mental experience
of a year ago, of a decade of years ago, is, in a

true sense, a part of the experience of to-day, shaping it, coloring it, characterizing it.   It is certain
that extraordinary experiences abide for years or
even for life ; grand  conceptions, strong feelings,
momentous  decisions  and  purposes, hold  on for
years, for life.    But  great  things  are made up
of small, and cannot subsist without them ; the
small, therefore, if the  great and  grand survive,
must also survive with  them.    They may be unnoticed, they may be beyond the  capabilities of
our finite  minds to  notice  them ; they may be
there, nevertheless.    Nothing forbids the supposition that they have not been utterly annihilated.
What, indeed, should cause them to perish ?   A
live thought—how can it utterly die ?  A living nature that has put forth itself in this  form or that
form, can never be the  same  in  all respects that
it would have been  but  for  that forthputting of
its energy.   Every act of  thought was a part of
its life and cannot be extirpated from it.    Even
such a supposed extirpation must leave the scar ;
and the scar shows  something of what was once
living there.   *My whole past lives in my present
life.*  This continuousness of my past into my present is the ground and the only proper evidence of
my personal identity.    I am the same being that
I was  long  years  ago  in  my childhood, when I
was  startled  by the  lightning  stroke  that smote
down  my  dwelling,  because that scene  is  in my
soul to-day.   I felt it then, I feel it now.    The
same feeling in the soul proves the soul itself to

be the same.   In regard to the future, the question of personal identity, stripped of all the obscurities and ambiguities of language, seems of the most fatuous character :—if I myself continue, it is myself—my identical person—that continues, whatever catastrophes befall me.

§ 13. The continuousness of mind is evidenced also *in memory* as it is in its turn the ground of this mental state.   The full consideration of this phenomenon is reserved for another place.   See Book II., c. xii.   We recognize here the fact that we remember: it is a fact of universal recognition that men remember.   But what is memory? Memory as retentive is mind holding on to acts or affections once experienced : memory as reproductive is mind bringing forth into distinct consciousness and into further use such retained acts or affections.   In either aspect there is involved in a state of memory something that is retained.   And it is preposterous to suppose that one mind has felt the affection and dropped it for another mind to pick up and transmit to a third, and so on ; that there has been a succession of heirs as in the case of an estate.   But we need to take a higher view.   Continuousness of mind is not merely the ground of memory. memory, as will be seen hereafter, is but mind itself abiding, continuing on with the form which it has taken on in some previous experience.

§ 14. Further, the continuousness of mind is evidenced in what is universally experienced and

universally recognized as *habit*—the holding on
of any specific form of mental activity. Memory,
indeed, in its aspect as an active state, is but a
form of habit. Some habits originating in childhood abide through old age; others disappear to
our limited vision, but hold on, invisibly affecting
our mental action. Habit attaches to feeling, to
thought, to will, to the whole mental life. It is
indeed a recognized law of every living thing
that it tends to continue any form of action
till the energy that prompts it ceases or other
opposing energies hinder. Men have habits of
feeling, habits of thinking, habits of purposing and
choosing. But clearly there can be no habits conceivable in what has no continuousness. Habit
is a law of mental life; it has its ground and
seat in mind as continuous. Habit finds its explanation and governing laws in mental continuousness, presupposing it, therefore, and proving it.

§ 15. Once more, the continuousness of mind is
evidenced in the fact of *mental growth*, as it is
the necessary condition of such growth and is
presupposed in it. The human mind grows.
The fact is universal and is universally recognized. It grows from puny childhood to sturdy
manhood. It grows in range of acquisition and
in vigor of capacity. It grows in every function.
Feeling strengthens and expands in continued
life and exercise. The passion of a child is
quick as it is tender and susceptible; but it is
transitory as a controlling affection, and easily

yields to new impulses, tracing only shallow
marks of its existence on the abiding soul. The
passion of adult manhood is comparatively strong
and enduring, and shapes more observably mental character. So thought grows, develops vigor
and augments its treasures of knowledge in the
continuance of legitimate exertion. And purpose
and endeavor in the same way grow in strength
and also in breadth and compass. These abstract
statements are verified in concrete life. Men are,
as a general fact, growing into fuller and more
determinate character. The portrait of the youth
can hardly be identified with the picture of the
man. The man is hardly himself, indeed, in the
fullest sense, till he has growth ; and his character is fairly represented only in the picture of advanced age, if, at least, the picture be taken before physical decline has begun its defacing work.
The philanthropist is a man of growth. He was
a child as careless and as selfish as others were ;
he has grown by his continuous life of sympathy and of kindness. The artist has grown by
continuous study and production of beautiful or
perfect form. The philosopher has grown by
protracted thinking, observing and reflecting.
The statesman, the general, all men who have
large character are the subjects of growth ; and
they are so by reason of this law of mental continuousness. Only as what has been attained is
still held, can there be any accumulation of
strength or resources. It is the grand vice in

education that the growing mind disregards this fundamental principle of growth. Skipping from study to study, from school to school, from teacher to teacher, permanent acquisition of knowledge, of thought, or of skill is impossible except on the lowest scale. If bud after bud be nipped just as it has begun to germinate, the season of education passes with no possibility of growth; and the characteristic volatility, shallowness, and imbecility of childhood mark the youth and the man. The principles of mental continuousness, which may be violated although not with impunity, allow an indefinite growth. Life begun tends of itself to grow; once started, if guarded and nourished till it has attained the stage of self-maintenance, it keeps on, itself putting forth new buds and at the same time sending back aliment to the parent stock itself. The simple condition is continuousness—continuousness to the proper stage in like direction, and under like conditions of endeavor. As there is mental growth, in fact to a degree, and in possibility to an indefinite extent, so there must be the necessary condition of this growth—mental continuousness.

The whole mind thus has a nature susceptible of indefinite growth. As the plant and every growing thing unfolds itself in its several organs, in continuously successive yet simultaneous development, from primitive life-germ to stalk and root, to trunk and branch, to twig and leaf, to flower and fruit, the whole mind grows. This growth may be stunted, or it may be fostered and quickened; it may be misguided into deformity or be wisely trained into strength and beauty. The great fact is: the mind, as a living, active nature, is the subject of indefinite growth. The fact is evidence of the great truth or principle of the continuousness of mind.

There are certain facts to be recognized which seem at first view to be opposed to this representation of mental continuousness. The mind is essentially active; but this essential activity seems sometimes to be interrupted, as, for example, in sleep. It has been, indeed, a somewhat debated question whether the mind does suspend its activity in sleep. Sometimes, at least, no sign of activity appears. Nothing is remembered on recovery of wakefulness. But the predominance of evidence in the case is altogether on the side of continued mental activity. That, on waking, we remember nothing of this action that is going on during sleep, has little weight; we do not remember much of what we know to have been in our thought, particularly of uninterested and unintentional thought. It would puzzle one to recall the total current of his lighter incidental thinking during the hour just passed; to recall even much of it. We remember, perhaps, if we are careful to attend to it, the thought that we happen to have just at the moment of waking; but the dream that has

seemed to embrace numerous events of long continuance, hours, days, years even, may have occupied only the waking moment. The oblivion
attending disease is no disproof of a suspension
of mental activity, as often recovered health brings
back what had seemed to be forgotten. The
presumption is all against the belief of such a
cessation in sleep or in disease. The life of
mind certainly continues, for memory can travel
back to previous experiences, which would be
impossible if any chasm intervened. And how
could this life of mind, which is in its very essence
active, continue unless acting? We have evidence
of this continued action in the observed restless-
ness of persons in sleep, showing a mental agitation of which, when they have awaked, they can
perhaps remember nothing.

So in the records of somnambulism it is shown
that a long, well-connected series of actions, solv-
ing intricate problems, composing letters, execut-
ing works of art, as painting, and the like, may
take place in sleep of which there is no recollection on waking. The somnambulist sometimes
seems to live two different lives. He remembers
in his normal condition nothing of his somnambulistic experience, and conversely nothing of the
latter when in his normal state. The great fact
appears in these records, that there may be simple suspension of power to recall into distinct
consciousness mental acts and affections for days
or weeks, without actual annihilation of them
in the consciousness.

# CHAPTER IV.

## THE ORGANIC NATURE OF MIND.

§ 16. THE human mind is to be recognized as having a proper organic nature. It is a part of a larger whole without itself, as it is also a kind of whole in relation to parts within itself. In each of these relationships, of part to a larger whole, and of whole to its own parts, it both ministers and is ministered to, existing and acting ever in sympathetic interaction, in respect both to outer realities and to its own inner diversified being.

The human mind is a part of a larger whole—of a universe of being around it. Obvious and simple as is this truth, it is liable to be overlooked in philosophical speculation, and error easily slips in and vitiates our conclusions. As a part it is finite. The whole of which it is a part may conceivably be, or it may conceivably not be, bounded. There is a whole, embracing all smaller wholes or parts, which is not bounded. Indeed the idea of finiteness, of bounds or limitations, attaches properly only to the notion of a part. To think of a whole as bounded is at once to make it a part. The idea of a whole in itself excludes the notion of bound, which, when it

comes in, at once makes the former whole a part.
A part is essentially and necessarily finite ; a
whole in itself, as whole simply, excludes finiteness or bound.   If bounded, an object must be
bounded by something else, and so the two are
parts of. a larger whole.   The human mind as
part is finite.   It is limited in the range of its
activity and also in the intensity of its activity.
It can compass but a part of the universe of
objects around it.   Age and growth enlarge this
sphere of its objects , but the more it takes in,
the more capacious it becomes, the more does
the sphere of objects widen and enlarge.    Its
energy too is limited.   It is ever encountering
forces which it finds itself incompetent to over-
come or resist.   Its history is at times to faint,
and quail, and yield.   Its very conquests are confessions of hopeless desires for the more that
remains to be won.    The poet sings and the
philosopher boasts : " On earth there is nothing
great but man ; in man there is nothing great but
mind ; " yet both conclude with equal truth that
this greatness " is nought but weakness and dependence."

For this very finiteness, this limited, bounded
nature of the human mind is not absolute.    As
organic, it is dependent.   Its very activity waits
to be moved at the beginning of its being by
some outward object that comes to awaken and
call it forth.   It cannot even choose its object ;
for before its beginning action it does not know

whether there be object for it, or if there be, where it may be, or what its character, or how it may be brought nigh to move the mind to its first exertion. So all along the course of its history, the human mind is dependent on things around it.

The consciousness of this finiteness and dependence may be awakened in reflection on any occasion of the mind's action on its objects. That the human soul is but a part of the universe of being; that there are, accordingly, other parts with which it exists in incessant interaction; that there is a whole greater than itself, to which it can see no bounds,—infinitely greater, with which its own being is interlinked,—these are truths rooted in the very depths of its history. This sense of dependence, it has been in truth maintained, has as a necessary correlate the truth that there is an object—an infinite whole—and other objects—other parts of indefinite extent—on which it more or less depends; but it is erroneous to suppose that the sense of dependence exists before any activity of the mind is called forth, existing as a mysteriously inborn principle. Much more erroneous, if possible, is it to suppose that any such native sense of dependence can indicate beforehand the particular character of the object on which it depends. It is accordingly an illegitimate foundation for an argument for the existence of God; for He can be known in his distinguishing attributes only as

He manifests himself. The human mind is incompetent to determine from itself, from its own nature or experiences, except in the most general way, the properties of the world of beings external to itself. As it finds in actual experience that it can exert its native activity on other objects around it, and as it finds itself thus to be a part of a larger whole, it may legitimately reason that these objects are more or less like itself, since otherwise they could not be parts of the same whole ; and that they are also more or less in sympathetic affinity to itself, since otherwise there could be no interaction between itself and them. But this sense of dependence, of relationship as a part in sympathy with the external world of being, can arise only on the actual exertion of its activity in interaction with the objects on which it depends. Its life begins with action ; and there can be no sense or feeling, if at least we leave out of the account the impression which first determines it to act, anterior to such beginning of its life.

§ 17. This characteristic of dependence involves the more positive organic attribute of sympathy. The human mind not only depends, but suffers, is passive. Its very activity is encompassed or pervaded by this sympathetic nature through which it experiences—suffers, or is passive to—the action of other realities in its universe of being. It is never purely active, nor purely passive. Any particular mental state is characterized alike in both respects, as passive and as active; yet not necessarily in equal degree. So we speak of the mind as a *faculty*, when we regard the active side, and as a *capacity*, when we regard the passive side of the experience. The mind is ever in all its states both faculty and capacity.

As one part of a universe, the human mind stands in organic, that is, in sympathetically interacting relationships to the other parts. That it should be affected by them as well as itself react upon them, according to their respective natures, is involved in the very idea of a universe. All created things, so far as we can know them, are bound up together in one, and reciprocally act upon each other. The fact of this sympathetic interaction is one of universal recognition. To be subject to this law of reciprocal action, that is, to be truly sympathetic in its nature, is one of the most fundamental characteristics of mind; one of its most comprehensive laws. Out of this characteristic in its constitution, as will be seen, are evolved the governing principles of one of the leading functions of mind. In this organic interaction with other realities, the mind evinces its sympathetic nature; it impresses and receives impressions; communicates with other realities, imparting and receiving.

§ 18. In an analogous way, the human mind possesses the character of an organic whole in relation to its own parts. It is in sympathy with them, and they with one another. The whole mind never moves, no specific function moves, but in this reciprocal sympathy—acting and reacting. The whole is affected, is characterized by each particular function, and each particular function is similarly affected and characterized by the whole organism, as well as by every other function. The whole nature of the human soul or spirit gives character to each specific act and affection ; and each feeling and thought and endeavor gives character to the action of the whole mind, just as the several functions of respiration, circulation, digestion, interact with the animal body as a whole, as well as with one another. The special functions of the mind interact in like manner with one another. Our feelings influence our thoughts ; our thoughts determine our wills. Each function is in organic, sympathetic ministry to each of the others. Farther than this, each function is an organic whole to its parts ; and the same character of sympathetic interaction is to be recognized in it. The feelings influence subordinate feelings ; the thoughts subordinate thoughts; the purposes subordinate purposes ; and all these subordinate acts or affections are in organic sympathy with one another.

Throughout the entire structure of the human mind thus do we discover this grand characteristic and attribute. Out of it we shall evolve great determining, regulative laws of mental action and affection. The human mind is an organism.

Its whole life is in sympathetic interaction and ministry in relation to beings external to itself, and also ever maintains the same organic character in relation to itself and its own constituent functions.

# CHAPTER V.

## THE SELF-CONSCIOUSNESS OF MIND.

§ 19. WE have recognized the mind as an organism with a threefold function. § 10. We have seen also that it is essential to the very life of mind that these its several functional activities should maintain a perpetual interaction with one another. § 18. Thought must act upon feeling as object and equally upon purpose ; and they in like manner upon thought and upon each other. The human mind knows thus its own feelings, knows its own purposes or determinations. It equally knows its own thoughts. "If I did not know that I knew," says Hamilton most truly, "I would not know ; if I did not know that I felt, I would not feel ; if I did not know that I desired, I would not desire." The self, the ego, would not be a true self or ego if destitute of this organic function of knowing all it does and feels. This self-knowing power possessed by the human mind is denominated *consciousness*. The etymology of this term and its use, both in familiar discourse and also in scientific discussion, indicate very exactly its meaning. "Consciousness," says Locke, "is the perception of what passes in a

man's own mind." In like manner Reid affirms,
" Consciousness is a word used by philosophers
to signify that immediate knowledge which we
have of our present thoughts, and purposes, and
in general of all the present operations of our
minds." . . . . "Consciousness is only of the
things in the mind and not of external things."
Hamilton says: "The expressions, *I know that I
know, I know that I feel, I know that I desire*, are
translated by *I am conscious that I know, I am
conscious that I feel, I am conscious that I desire*.
Consciousness is thus the recognition by the
mind or ego of its own acts and affections."

Two characteristics stand out distinct and un-
qualified in these representations of consciousness; first, that it is essentially a term denoting
knowledge ; secondly, that its sphere of knowing
in regard to its objects is exactly " what passes in
the mind itself." Consciousness, then, in mental
science, must be held ever to be characterized as
simply a knowing fûnction and is limited to the
mind's own acts and affections. It is only a loose
popular use of the term when it is said: " I was
not conscious that the clock had struck ; " "that
the sun had risen," and the like ; as if we could
be conscious of purely external objects. In the
strict technical usage of exact thought we can be
said to be conscious only of what passes in our
own minds.

The term, however, it should be observed, like
other terms of similar character, although as cor-

rectly used, ever presenting this elemental contest of self-knowing, is employed with divers specific modifications of meaning. It is variously used to denote the power or faculty of self-knowledge, the exercise of this power, and the result of the exercise. The term is also sometimes loosely used to denote the mind or spirit itself, or the spiritual nature generally, and moreover its condition or state, or what it experiences, and particularly here the abiding result of this experience. As a technical term in mental science it denotes simply self-knowing or self knowledge.

§ 20. Consciousness is to be ever recognized as being essentially of an active nature—a power or a function. To be conscious is to know. Consciousness must possess the properties and parts of knowledge generally, as we shall hereafter come to recognize them. It is of an active nature therefore as is knowledge. Only in the allowable looseness of familiar discourse, or the license of poetic and rhetorical usage, never in the exactness of science, can consciousness be truly represented as a *light*. It is a beholder in its essential meaning. Neither can it be truly represented in scientific discussion as a *condition*, in any other sense than as knowledge is a condition. It is illusive and misleading to represent it as that which must be supposed to be antecedent to all mental activity or affection, except in its loose use as a synonym of mind itself. The nature of such a supposed antecedent none can tell or even con ceive. There is not anything back of the mind's acting to be imagined as antecedent condition to its acting, to its knowing, to its knowing its own acts, except indeed, the active nature itself and some object on which this active nature is to exert itself. Out of the groundless assumption concerning consciousness as such antecedent condition to mental action, which in its mysterious nature can be filled with all sorts of properties and relations—out of such mystic imaginings can come only illusion and error. Neither can consciousness be truly regarded as a *field*, in which the active mind may employ itself. It is the cultivator, the laborer, the producer, the active power. The field of consciousness can be nothing but the field in which consciousness exerts itself—the field of internal or mental phenomena, of actual mental products. It has no existence until after the mind has felt or acted. It does not condition or determine those acts or feelings ; in strict scientific meaning consciousness only knows them—becomes cognizant of them—when existing.

Consciousness is but one form of knowledge. There is a knowledge which respects objects without the mind, objects that are presented to the mind through the physical senses and also objects that, being themselves of a purely spiritual nature, address the mind directly through its own apprehensive sense. This form of knowledge is precisely distinguished from the knowledge called consciousness or conscious knowledge, by the characteristic that its objects are external to the mind while those of conscious knowledge are entirely within the mind.

Consciousness accordingly is not to be reckoned as a fourth function of mental activity, co-ordinate with the functions of feeling, thought, and will. It is as a knowing function simply a subordinate function of the intelligence. Consciousness is one form of knowledge—knowledge confined to the self; other knowledge respects the not-self. The knowing nature in these two forms of knowledge is the same; the object which it respects only is changed. There can therefore be no more mystery in consciousness, in self-knowing, than in knowing external objects.

But farther, consciousness, strictly speaking, gives only that form of knowledge which is denominated perceptive or intuitive, in distinction from reflective knowledge. It simply observes, perceives, intuits, the mental act or affection as a phenomenon of mind. The discriminative act which analyzes the act or affection, distinguishes its characters or contents and judges what they are, follows the action of consciousness in observing. The knowledge given in consciousness is thus only immediate, inchoative knowledge, not full, completed knowledge, such as is first gained when a proper judgment emerges. Consciousness gives only perceptive or intuitive, not attributive knowledge. § 137.

Conscious knowledge, being thus immediate and of an object nearest possible to view, and accordingly exempt from the liabilities to mistake that may attend means or instruments of knowing, is of the first and most commanding order. No testimony respecting real things can outrank that of consciousness.

But while consciousness is recognized as strictly self-knowledge, its sphere being entirely circumscribed by the mind's own modifications, Sir William Hamilton contends that this immediate knowledge, given in consciousness, embraces also the external object which interacts with the mind and impresses it. "I see," he reasons, "the inkstand. How can I be conscious that my present modification exists—that it is a perception and not another mental state, and finally, that it is a perception of the inkstand only, unless my consciousness comprehends within its sphere the object, which at once determines the existence of the act, qualifies its kind, and distinguishes its individuality? Annihilate the inkstand, you annihilate the perception; annihilate the consciousness of the object, you annihilate the consciousness of the operation." He admits that it sounds strange to say, "I am conscious of the inkstand," but maintains that the apparent incongruity of the expression arises from the prevalence of erroneous doctrines of perception. The difficulty of Hamilton arises from his failure to observe the sharp distinction between apprehensive and attributive knowledge—between perceptive or intuitive and reflective. In fact, he represents consciousness as discriminative and as involving judgment and even memory. Still he holds that consciousness is an immediate knowledge and enumerates only three things as necessarily involved in it—a knowing subject, a modification, and a recognition of the modification by the subject. These three things are clearly reducible to two—the knowing or conscious power and the modification; so that it is the mental modification only of which consciousness in its simplicity takes cognizance.

Consciousness, then, as the function of self-knowledge, giving only immediate, perceptive or intuitive, and not analytic and attributive knowledge, and having for its object some modification of the mind, some mental act or affection, must be held to regard that object only as a concrete; it is the mind itself, but the mind as acting or feeling in some specific way that is regarded in consciousness, just as in the immediate perceptive knowledge given in vision the perception takes in the concrete whole—the bird flying or the fish swimming. The analytic discrimination into subject and attribute—the bird as subject and the flying as attribute—is posterior to the perception; this is an act of reflective knowledge. Consciousness takes notice of the mind as modified—as acting or feeling. It is this concrete which is its proper object. We use language in a loose, unscientific way, accord-

ingly, when we speak of consciousness as having
the pure ego, or self, irrespectively of its acting
or feeling, as its proper object. In scientific
discourse such representation is erroneous and
leads to unsound speculation. Self-consciousness in exact truth always regards the self not
abstractly, but in concrete act or affection.

But a modification of the mind, a mental act
or affection, involves an object as well as a
subject. It is ever an interaction of mind
and object, in which both meet. Consciousness takes cognizance of this interaction, which
takes place within the mind itself, with all
the peculiarities that characterize it. Its vision takes in, however, only the interaction, the
impression. The outer object in itself does
not come within its range of view, except in
its working, as a force from without actually
impressing or engaging the mind. Consciousness
may present grounds of inference as to what the
object may be ; it does not immediately observe
the inkstand. The same state of mind might
be occasioned by a mere image of the inkstand,
by internal nervous affection, by some exterior
force. It is competent to affirm perhaps thus the
reality of a world without as discerning the twofold character of the interaction : but, what the nature of that exterior something is, what its form,
its mode of working, its relations to the world
without, consciousness itself does not observe.
Here comes in the function of reflective thought.

This analytic movement of thought proper may follow so quick upon observation by consciousness, that the two acts may seem to be one. The truth remains: consciousness simply observes; it does not analyze; it gives no attributive cognition. It observes, we repeat, the mental affection, the impression, the interaction; it does not take cognizance of what produces the affection or impression; it does not observe the inkstand while yet it may observe the immediately succeeding movement of thought by which the object producing the impression is inferred to be the inkstand.

§ 21. Consciousness is variously modified, both in degree and also in range.

As is true of all mental activity the human consciousness varies in the vigor or intensity of its action. It varies with native energy, with bodily health and condition, with advance in age and experience, with growth and culture. In specific exercises, also, we speak of being " fully conscious," " clearly " or " distinctly conscious," or of being " feebly " or " indistinctly conscious "; and we speak also of being " entirely unconscious."

In like manner, the human consciousness is variously modified in respect to its range of object. While, generally speaking, all mental acts and affections lie properly within its range—and nothing but such acts and affections—in fact, only a part, a very small part, can be truly said to be at any one time in actual view. The very finiteness of the human mind involves this. It can no more truly take cognizance of all its own modifications at any one moment than it can be cognizant of all that passes in the world around it at once. There are thus what have been called " latent modifications " of the mind, acts or affections, which, although lying within the realm of consciousness, escape its notice. In this fact we find the explanation of certain mental phenomena.

# CHAPTER VI.

## THE SPONTANEITY AND SELF-DETERMINATE-NESS OF THE MIND.

§ 22. THE mind, as an essentially active nature, must begin its being in action. This beginning exercise of activity cannot of course be self-caused. It is determined by the power that created the mind itself. This activity originating thus in a source external to the mind continues on, as we have seen, never entirely superseded by the mind's power of self-control. There is no good ground for supposing that it ever ceases. We are conscious of an ever-flowing current of mental activity that we neither originate ourselves nor sustain. Often, indeed, we are but too sensible that it holds on against our express endeavor to check it. It flows on during sleep and sweeps on even during periods of unconsciousness, connecting our past experience with our present. It takes hold of our self-originated exertions and bears them on often without any effort of our own. The thought starts perhaps through an express determination of our will; it holds on by a power of its own, at least by a power that is not properly of the will itself, but rather from above and

upon it. This activity, thus primitive and last-
ing, which involves an element other than that
of mere continuousness, we call *spontaneous* to distinguish from that other activity which we recognize as coming from our own determination—from
our free-will, which is hence designated *voluntary*
or *volitional, self-determined,* and also from that
kind of activity which necessarily takes place in
us from the action of external realities upon us.
Our thoughts and our imaginings are so-called
spontaneities as distinguished from the free
exercises of the will. But these exercises of the
will themselves, after being freely put forth, also
participate in this spontaneity. We have thus only
to purpose, as to take a walk, and the purpose
is kept alive through this primitive spontaneity
of mind, and we keep on walking without any
fresh determination of will. The will continues
its action in that particular way of purposing the
walking.

§ 23. The free-will is accordingly to be distinctly recognized as a characteristic function
of the human mind, and as distinct from what
is purely spontaneous or necessary in its nature.
We are conscious of the exercises of this function. We recognize this freedom in others. We
regard ourselves as responsible for the right exercise of this determining power, and hold others
to a like responsibility for their free action. This
self-determining power is the dominant power
in our mental nature. It presides over the

mind's natural activity, controls within certain limits the direction in which it shall flow, and regulates to a certain extent the measure of its intensity. We are free thus to choose the commanding
aim and end of our lives, or direct the ruling appetency or craving of our natures and so form
and fix our characters. We to a certain extent,
also, freely control our mental growth and culture, making ourselves superior often to circumstances, making even such circumstances as are
in themselves adverse and untoward to be helpful by our triumph over them. Struggle
develops strength ; and opposition subdued is
made subservient and ministering to our over-
coming purpose. The activity of the mind,
spontaneous from its creation and ever continuous
through its existence, is also free and self-
determined. " 'Tis in ourselves that we are thus
and thus. The power and corrigible authority of
this lies in our own wills."

§ 24. Whether spontaneous or free, all mental
activity flows on towards a result—an end. It is
not to be characterized as driftless. It has a distinguishable drift or tendency, which, however
much modified by occasion or circumstance or external condition, is never utterly lost. It is not
the mere sport of circumstance, nor is it in itself
wholly without trend or definite set. Nothing
indeed " walks with aimless feet." We are sensible in ourselves that our mental activity, our
thoughts, our feelings, our purposes, our whole

mental natures, flow on in the direction in which they are set. We observe, too, that both individually and collectively men are generally sure, if undisturbed, to hold on in a course once entered upon. In fact, we recognize, from manifold views and considerations, that the mind of man has a true rational nature, imparting an end or aim or design in its being and its action. So far, thus, as the activity of the mind is rational, it is properly *telic*, ever tending to an end or result.

This general end or result of mental activity is to be recognized as good or evil. We cannot question that the creature of a wise and beneficent maker was fashioned for good, so that in the designed and legitimate direction of itself and of its powers it would finally reach a goal that is on the whole good. Endowed with freedom the creature himself may misdirect the current of his being as designed by his creator, and so, missing the good, fall into the evil. The entire current of the mental life may thus be misdirected ; and specific powers or functions also may be perverted. The fitting end, however, is ever neared ; the life as a whole trends ever to an end that is good or evil, and each specific endeavor with the different specific habits of life has a corresponding trend. The course may be arrested, the direction turned ; but the tendency, the drift, is ever present with the entire mental activity and with each specific exertion. But for this great telic characteristic of mental activity we should be powerless as to forming our characters, or shaping our destinies.

As will be seen hereafter, moreover, this telic characteristic of mind, this drift towards an end or object, gives character to certain of our feelings. Our passive nature being impressed under the influence of this natural drift of the mental life towards some object assumes the form of a craving. Its nature seeks the object towards which it thus tends or drives ; it experiences a *want*. The modifications of this feeling of want appear in the form of propensities, appetites, and desires. In this way, this drifting feature of mind determines in the passive affections of the soul an important class of the feelings.

# CHAPTER VII.

## THE RELATIVITY OF THE MIND.

§ 25. As organic part of a larger whole the human mind exists in relation both to the whole itself and to the other parts of that whole. As itself an organic whole, it exists also in relation to its own parts, and these parts exist in reciprocal relation to one another. This relativity in the existence of the mind appears at once of immense extent and immensely diversified. In the expressions, "the necessary relativity of the human mind," "the necessary relativity of human knowledge," a large diversity of specific meanings may be comprehended. It is of the first importance therefore that speculations in this field of thought should with peculiar care maintain a firm hold on the specific application of the term which is intended.

There are several forms of this relativity pertaining to the human mind, which it seems particularly needful for clearness and for security against error in our studies of mind, to specify and define. It should be noticed, at the start, that a relative attribute pertaining to an object determines nothing as to the essential attributes

4

of the object. These essential attributes, that is, the essence of the object or concretely the object itself, must exist before there can be any relationship to other things.

§ 26. In the manifold relativity of the human mind is to be recognized as first and most fundamental, the relation already intimated of real to real—of the mind as a real existence to other real existences. As organic part of a universe of real existences the human mind exists and acts by necessary implication in the relation of a real to a real. That itself is real implies that the other parts with which it constitutes an organic whole are also real. The grand fact that it is an organic part and is real itself proves that it is in relation not to phantoms, but to realities. It interacts in fact with them; and interaction involves reality. It involves activity as well as reality. The human mind can interact only with other active natures. Still farther, as a rational nature, a trifunctional organism, its interaction is with other rational natures. A function implies, as a necessary correlative, an object; and diversity of function implies a certain diversity of object. In respect to each mental function and the action of each there must be its correlative object and a fitting condition of the object in order to be affected by the action. Every specific act of one mind respects thus, exists in relation to, an affection of some other mind. Or to use a form of statement that shall avoid any implication of favor to any of the different theories as to the nature of matter, any specific energy going forth from my mind fastens upon a correlative energy in some other reality which accordingly must exist in a condition to receive the act : the active implies the passive : the imparting implies the receiving ; each with a character corresponding in some measure and way to the character of the other. We must presume, therefore, that the three functions of the human mind have their correlatives in the objects which they respectively regard. If, as the usage in philosophical discussion warrants, and popular usage abundantly supports, we designate by the term *idea* any specific act or affection of mind, then in the interaction between mind and its object idea meets idea ;—idea as specific act of mind meets idea as specific affection of mind. Nothing but strength of bias or dullness of thought can infer from this the identity of mind and object. The very statement imports the exact opposition of one to the other.

§ 27. We have then in the trifunctional activity of the mind a threefold division of ideas as active or as put forth by the mind itself or of subjective ideas—those of intelligence, sensibility, and will, otherwise named cognitive, æsthetic, and purposive ideas. The presumption now is that we shall find a threefold division of ideas as object. This division, in fact, the history of thought and the literature of the world, has recognized as

the objective division—the division into the true,
the beautiful, and the good.   These are the
three great ideas, the three comprehensive ideas,
which have come down to us through the ages.

Each of these divisions, the subjective and the
objective, has been accepted with substantially
unanimous consent.   The one is the more recent,
the other the more ancient.   The literatures of
the modern and the ancient world show corresponding tendencies of thought.   Each may be
regarded as the recognized classification of mental
phenomena, more suited to the habits of thought
in its own time, while yet equally valid for all
other times.

As the intelligence, the sensibility, and the
will make up the entirety of the mental functions,
so that we cannot conceive of the mind as acting
except through one or other of these functions, so in the object of the mind's action, we
cannot conceive of any character pertaining to it
other than these three—the true, the beautiful,
the good—at least of this order.   And as the
mind, as one organic whole, even when one function predominates, must be at the same time also
exerting its other functions, just as the animal
body carries on all its functions together, even
although one may exhibit at times greatly pre-
ponderant activity, so in every object of mental
action the three ideas ever co-exist inseparably.
However much one may predominate in a given
case, or however much one may engage our con-

templation or our thought, the others are still there in the object. Not an object can be conceived which in some respect or some degree is not at the same time true, and beautiful, and good.

§ 28. Still further, the threefold functions have each its respective object. The function of intelligence has for its object the true. This function deals with nothing else in the object but the true ; its sphere is entirely bounded by the true. The term, as used here, will be understood as a category embracing all gradations of the true—from the perfectly true to the absolutely false. So, on the other hand, the true is object for the intelligence alone—for no other function of the mind. The intelligence may be exactly defined accordingly as the function of the true.

The function of the sensibility, using the term in its full meaning as inclusive of both the active side and the passive side, in like manner has for its object the beautiful. This function deals with nothing else but the beautiful, including here, of course, the several gradations from the perfectly beautiful to the positively ugly. And the beautiful is proper object for no other function of the mind. The sensibility, including the imagination as its active side, may accordingly be defined as the function of the beautiful, or more properly as the function of form—the beautiful being only the perfect in form. § 31.

In the same way the will has for its object the

good, with its gradations from the perfectly good to the positively bad. It deals with nothing but the good in object. And the good is exclusive object for the will, which function might be defined as the function of the good.

§ 29. This twofold classification of mental phenomena into (1), the subjective, of function, as of *intelligence*, of *form*, including sensibility and imagination, and of *will*, and (2), the objective, of object, as *true*, *beautiful*, and *good*, must, it is believed, be accepted not only as true but also as beyond all comparison the most scientific that the present stage of the science of mind can receive. The correctness of the classification is corroborated by its correspondence with another classification which has been in familiar use since the days of Aristotle. In different works of his, Aristotle gives in scientific formality, with a reiteration that attests his conviction of its vast importance to science, a fourfold enumeration of causes—known in subsequent science as the efficient, the essential, the formal, and the final or telic. His efficient cause is obviously the mental energy or activity which creates or produces. The essential cause is as clearly the object produced, viewed in respect to its essence or the complement of properties congruously united to constitute it one whole, so that the intelligence may accept it as true by identifying it as a whole with its several parts or properties, and each part as congruously related to every other part or property. The formal cause is the object viewed as form or that by which it is communicable to mind, the perfect in form being the beautiful in the stricter sense. The final or telic cause, that for the sake of which the object exists or is produced, is the object viewed in respect to its end or pupose as that which may be chosen or willed, and is named from the perfect in this respect—the good. The essential cause addresses itself thus to the intelligence as the true and causes thought. The formal cause addresses the sensibility as the beautiful and causes the affection denominated by that term or the sense of beauty ; and the final or telic cause addresses the will as the good and causes volition or choice.

It may be added here that, as will appear under the proper head, we may in our thought view any object of mental activity either as substance or as cause. If we view any object as *substance*, or as that which has attributes of quality, we have the objective classification of possible mental phenomena in relation to the object of mental activity,—we have the true, the beautiful, and the good. If we view any object as *cause* in its relation to mental activity, as affecting or determining it, that is, if we view it as having attributes of action, we have the subjective classification of the possible modes of this activity—we have the intelligence, the sensibility and imagination, and the will. This classification of objects with which the mind interacts, or with which it has to do, in respect to substance and cause as the only distinctions in this respect that are possible in the nature of thought, is exhaustive. The subordinate distinctions, under the respective classes of attributes of quality and action, giving on the one hand, under the attribute of quality, that of the true, the beautiful, and the good, and on the other, under the attribute of cause, that of essence, form, and end, must each be recognized also as exhaustive. It is not possible, certainly, in the present light of science, to conceive of any addition to either. They are, moreover, in their respective subdivisions co-ordinate and congruous —neither overlapping any one of the others. Moreover, each exactly corresponds to its respective subdivision in the other. There is also the like correspondence as already indicated between each subdivision, under each of these two objective classifications with each of the respective subdivisions of the subjective or functional classification. True and essence correspond thus with the intelligence; beautiful and form with the sensibility and the imagination; and good and end with the will. As every mental act or mental affection has these two component factors and only these two, that of subject or function and that of object, we have the most decisive grounds conceivable for accepting all these classifications as true and as final for science.

We can hardly overestimate the importance of a full and clear recognition of these classifications in their exact correspondence with each other in their several parts as well as in the grounds of the classifications, for the satisfactory determination of the nature and relationships of each of the distinguishable modes of mental action and affection on the one hand, or on the other for the satisfactory prosecution of the studies of mental phenomena. Each separate function may be explored in the light of its particular object, whether viewed as substance or cause ; and the study may pass at pleasure from one to the other with assurance that the change is not from the matter under study but only from one point of view to another, a change not of object but only of light. It will be borne in mind that the study here referred to is the study only of special functions and only of special features of object. There will still remain the study of mind as one organic whole acting through and in these special functions and in relation to a corresponding organic whole of object related to mental activity in the specific forms of its addresses to the mind as subject. We find here the justifying ground for the fourfold distribution of our studies of mental action in respect to function already stated : 1, The Sensibility and the Imagination, or the special Function of Form, or of the Beautiful; 2, The Intelligence, the special Function of the Essence, or of the True ; 3, The Will, the special Function of Ends, or of the Good ; and 4, The Reason, the organic Function of Mind as one whole in relation to the universe of object.

# BOOK II.

## THE SENSIBILITY.—I. SUBJECTIVE VIEW.

---

### CHAPTER I.

#### ITS NATURE AND MODIFICATIONS.

§ 30. THE SENSIBILITY IS THE MIND'S CAPACITY OF FEELING.

We have recognized the mind in its organic nature as in sympathetic interaction with other realities, § 17,—as passive and receptive, as well as essentially active. Its activity being that of a finite and dependent nature that has a beginning of its existence, and ever implying an object on which it is exerted, can be awakened into positive action only as it is addressed and so called forth by its object. The human mind begins its action accordingly only as acted upon, receiving impression, in other words, only with feeling ; and its succeeding action is at every step and all along attended by feeling. It is prompted in every specific motion by feeling ; it is sustained in its action by feeling ; it is followed in its action by feeling. It moves ever in feeling and is ever feeling while it is acting. Every act of knowledge must be preceded by the feeling which the object of the knowledge calls forth when it is presented to the mind ; and every such act is followed by its proper reflex impression on the sensibility. The same is true of every act of willing. Only as feeling predominates and characterizes the mental state, however, is the state denominated a state of feeling—a mode of the sensibility.

The terms of the definition, it will be noticed, regard the passive side of this mental state or function. The term *sensibility* denotes, thus, in its stricter and more proper import, rather the passive than the active side. So likewise the terms *capacity* and *feeling*, as already stated, more properly point to the mind as passive, as impressed or determined. But all the terms are, in popular use, also employed in an active sense. The term *sensibility* particularly is so identified in psychological discussions with this function of the mind as one of the three general comprehensive modes of mental life, co-ordinately with the functions of the intelligence and the will, that it seems to be the fittest term to introduce to the particular study of its nature and modifications.

§ 31. In strict truth, however, this function is to be regarded as participating in the same active nature as the other functions ; and, hence, more properly it might be named the *function of form*. By *form* is meant that characteristic or attribute of the mind through which it communicates or interacts with other minds or beings. The mind exists in connection with other minds; it is moved to feeling by them and moves them to feeling ; it impresses other minds and is impressed by them ; it determines them and is determined by them ; in a word, it interacts with them. This communion and interaction is by virtue of what may properly be designated as its characteristic of *form*. We define *form*, accordingly, as that attribute of mind by which it interacts sympathetically with other realities ; by which it communicates with them, impressing and receiving impression.

But the perfect in form is known as *the beautiful*. The beautiful is exactly defined as the perfect in form. This term, however, has been properly and generally used, in scientific treatment at least, to include all modifications from the perfectly beautiful to the positively ugly, so that under it is comprehended all that is included in the term *form*. The function of form is exactly defined, accordingly, as the function of the beautiful ; it is that function of the mind which is engaged with the beautiful—the term being used in its large sense as inclusive, not only of the perfectly beautiful, but also the imperfectly beautiful and the positively ugly.

The terms *idea* and *form* are not exactly synonymous, although often used interchangeably. The former term, *idea*, is popularly used to denote any kind of expressed mental activity, whether thought, or imagination, or purpose; while *form* regards idea more specifically as inter-action of mind with mind : it is idea as in inter-action or intercommunication.

§ 32. The whole doctrine of this department of mental activity, in which the activity appears as the function of form, rests squarely on this fundamental fact in mental phenomena that the mind lives and acts within a community of minds with which it is ever interacting—impressing and being impressed, determining and being deter-mined. The mind being thus essentially *sym-pathetic*, sympathy is the basis and source of all the phenomena of the sensibility and of the im-agination. It gives the comprehensive law as it is the indispensable condition of all feeling. Only as sympathetic, as capable of communicating with other beings, as capable of being impressed or de-termined by them or by other departments of the mind's own activity, could there be feeling. And all the modes of feeling are characterized by this radical feature and are to be studied in the light of it. The term sympathy is employed in-deed in more popular usage to denote feeling as in accord with the feeling of some other being ; but it is properly and frequently employed in a more comprehensive sense, so as to include all men-tal affection determined by some other being, or the capacity of such affection. It is in this larger import the term is here used as denoting that in the nature of mind by which it can be in communion with other beings.

The terms *sympathy* and *form* thus point to the same feature in the constitution and life of mind, and differ only in presenting this feature in different modifications of the relations of the sensibility; sympathy bringing into view more the object of the affection, form confining the view more to the affection itself.

§ 33. In the interaction of minds there are two sides—an imparting and a receiving. Form is accordingly of a twofold character : it is active, as imparting or impressing—*forma formans ;* and passive, as receiving or being impressed—*forma formata.* We have thus active sensibility and passive sensibility. But we have a synonymous term in familiar use—*imagination*—denoting the same function of form and in both senses, as active —communicative of form or faculty of form, and also as passive—receptive of form or capacity of form. We have thus both the *active imagination* and the *passive imagination.* But good use justifies, and both convenience and clearness require, that in scientific treatment at least the former term —*sensibility*—be separately appropriated to the passive side of the function, so as to denote the capacity of form, while the other term—*imagination*—is appropriated to the active side, so as to denote the faculty of form.

§ 34. The sensibility proper is accordingly defined as the capacity of being impressed, and its affections or states are *feelings*. The imagination is the faculty of impressing or communicating, and its products are *forms*.

But feeling and form, sensibility and imagination, belong to the same function and are related to each other as passive and active, as the two sides in all interaction. The nature of each reflects the nature of the other; and all correct scientific treatment must keep both in view as in this inseparable connection with each other. Neither should be subordinated to the intelligence or the cognitive function, as neither has, except as co-ordinate in a common organic life, anything of the proper cognitive nature in it. Sensation and imagination, with memory, belong entirely to the function of form.

§ 35. The sensibility proper, or the capacity of form, is modified;—First, extrinsically, in respect to the object or source of the feeling; and secondly, intrinsically, in respect to purity or simplicity and to degree and intensity.

These general modifications give rise to so many kinds of feelings, with their respective subdivisions.

I. Extrinsically, or in respect to the object or source of the feeling, the feelings are distinguished into two classes :—

1. Those which flow from the general life of the soul or attend the exercise of its several functions, without particular reference to the object

awakening them, denoted by the general terms—
*pleasure* and *pain ;* and

2. Those which are determined by some specific object. Of this class there are two species,
according as the object is material or mental,—
*sensations* and *emotions.*

II. Intrinsically considered, the feelings are, in
the first place, either *simple* or *complex.* The feelings already enumerated, those of pleasure and
pain, the sensations and emotions, are properly
simple in themselves, but suffer readily complication in divers ways.

The complex feelings are of two classes according as the complication is with the object or with
other mental acts or affections. The first class
includes as subdivisions (1) the *affections*, which
simply flow out and terminate on their objects ;
and (2) the *desires*, which reach after their objects
to grasp and appropriate them to the mind's own
uses.

The second class of the complex feelings in
which the affection is complicated with some other
mental act or affection, as of intelligence or will,
are denominated *sentiments.* As complicated
with the intelligence and characterized by that,
they are *contemplative*, and as complicated with
the will, they are *practical.*

The feelings are intrinsically modified, in the
second place, in respect to *degree* or *intensity*, as
they vary from well-nigh apathetic calmness to
the fury of ungoverned passion.

§ 36. In accordance with this general analysis, the phenomena of the sensibility as the capacity of form will be considered in successive chapters in the following order, viz.:

The Feelings of Pleasure and Pain ;
The Sensations ;
The Emotions ;
The Affections ;
The Desires ;
The Sentiments ;
The Passions.

The phenomena of the Imagination or the faculty of form will be considered in subsequent chapters by themselves.

So far as thus indicated the consideration of this department of mental activity will have been *subjective*, presenting only the affections and acts of the mind itself. But mental action implies an object ; and the special object of the function of form is, as before stated, the beautiful. The science of the beautiful is known under the name of Æsthetics. Inasmuch as it has to do more exactly with beautiful objects as realized in nature or art, it has a still more definite province and method. But the science of the mental function can hardly be regarded as complete without some consideration of its object. It will, at all events, be interesting and instructive to consider this objective side of this class of mental phenomena. Following the chapters on the sensibility and the imagination, accordingly, distinct chapters will be

5

presented on the nature and the generic forms of
the beautiful considered both in respect to the
production and also the interpretation of beauty.
The method of treatment will, however, be psychological rather than properly æsthetic, being
determined from the subject—the mind—considered in itself or in immediate relation to the
object. It will be in the order of a presentation
of the function of form in the immediate light of
its object—the beautiful. Æsthetic science respects, as stated, the result or product of the
union of these two factors, and has its form and
method determined to it by this product which
appears more prominently in the two grand
divisions of *Beauty in art* and *Beauty in nature.*

# CHAPTER II.

§ 37. PLEASURE and Pain are among the most familiar phenomena of the human soul and most universally recognized. In the popular mind there is entire accord as to their general character. They are recognized universally as feelings. We feel pleasure; we feel its opposite, pain. We do not by thinking produce pleasure as the direct product of thought; we do not will it into being. Pleasure and pain are felt; they are determined to us. The soul in experiencing them is in a recipient, passive condition; it is acted upon, impressed, affected. Imagination, thought, purpose, are activities; pleasure and pain cannot be conceived as such, but only as affections of an active nature. Pleasure, taught Aristotle, is neither motion nor production; it does not move, it does not produce; it does not act. It is precisely the opposite of this; it is moved, it is produced; it is passive.

In the interaction of the mind with other active natures there are involved the impressing and the impressed; the active and the passive. The passive side of the phenomenon is, as we have ex-

plained, feeling. But in the experience of pleasure and pain, there is no such interaction necessarily concerned ; at least, none of this ordinary
character. The feelings of pleasure and pain
differ thus radically from other feelings, which
are the result of interacting parts in sympathy
with each other. I bestow a favor on a neighbor;
I interact sympathetically with him ; I am on the
active side in bestowing, he is on the passive side
in receiving ; I act, he feels. But each experiences pleasure ; I in bestowing, he in accepting.
The pleasure is not the act nor the affection in
this interaction. It yet attends upon both.
Neither he nor I create the pleasure ; it comes
to each ; is determined to us. Pleasure, then, is
properly from a source back of the interaction—
the giving and the receiving. It attaches to the
nature of the mind. The mind is so constituted as
to experience pleasure from its acts and also from
its affections. Pleasure is the feeling, the state
determined to the mind, by its creator. It
comes from him ; is communicated immediately
or remotely by him, in his ordering of our being
and condition. No will or endeavor of ours, no
endeavor of others can create it, can produce it
in any other sense than that of giving occasion
for its appearance in our consciousness.

§ 38. We find thus the universal law of pleasure, that it is the concomitant of the mind's
activity appointed in its very creation. Pleasure
or pain thus waits, in greater or less degree, on

every exertion of the essential activity of the human mind as also on every affection. As this activity can go forth only in the interaction of the mind with other natures, the more specific statement of the law of pleasure and pain is this : pleasure comes, in its fullest degree admissible in the nature of the soul, on occasion of the most perfect interaction—the freest and fullest legitimate activity on the one hand and the freest and fullest fitting condition of acting on the other. It comes, as Aristotle's keen insight recognized, not as a state pertaining to the action or existing in it, but as an end, a result, coming to it, as fruitage to bloom. It "ends out" action. Such is the origin and source of pleasure and pain—from the constituted nature of the mind ; and such is the law of its appearance—pleasure in right action and affection and favoring condition, pain in wrong action and affection and untoward condition.

This view accords with the theory concerning the creation and ordering of the universe, that happiness, pleasure in its largest and best sense, as blessedness, is the end and design proposed by its creator and ruler, the last outcome and fruitage of the whole sentient creation. The legitimate exertion of the mind's active nature in direction and in degree is, in the natural and designed tendency of things, to be followed by good ; as the wrong exercise is to be followed by evil. Human experience recognizes this law. There is pleasure in every legitimate exercise of the mind, in imagining, in thinking, in purposing. The pleasure is enhanced by the intensity of the exertion. So pain follows the wrong use of one's powers.

But as all human action is established in sympathetic relationship to surrounding things, the object of the action and the condition in which it takes place affect the pleasure or the pain. The object, if itself illegitimate, or if engaged with in illegitimate conditions, naturally brings pain. The energy, so far as free and unimpeded and flowing out toward objects nearest in sympathy, brings pleasure. Obstructed, impeded energy, directed upon objects unsuitable or repugnant, or exerted in untoward conditions, occasions pain. Difficulties are painful in so far as they impede or hinder; they bring in pleasure when surmounted by reason of the greater energy that has been called out by them.

§ 39. This general exposition of the nature and use of pleasure and pain in the human soul indicates at once the relation to these affections of what are generally esteemed to be their external objects or sources. This relation is shown to be mediate; the so-called objects of pleasure waken or produce it only in and through the soul—only through the acts or affections of the soul as determined by those objects. Pleasure is not produced directly by the object. The mind is addressed by its object and some impression pro-

duced or some action called forth ; and the pleasure waits immediately on that affection or act.
A landscape, we say, in looser language, pleases ;
it effects this by engaging the contemplative
faculty, the action of which is "ended out " by the
pleasure.  A blow pains us ; the pain is not only
in the soul but comes immediately from the
bruised or lacerated organization of soul and body,
as it is felt by the soul itself.  If the nerves of
the smitten member are paralyzed, or if the mysterious bond between soul and nervous center be
severed, no pain certainly can be felt.  Nor can
there be any sense of it until the soul itself feels
the blow ; it is from this that the pain immediately comes.  The universal law is :—*the mind
itself, acting or affected as a whole or in some functional act or affection, is the immediate source of all
pleasure and pain.*

This mediateness of relation between pleasure
and pain on the one, hand, and their objects or
sources on the other, particularly so far as they
are external to the mind, is a principle of fundamental importance both to ethical theories and
to practical life.  Pleasure is not to be sought
directly, but only in the perfection of character
and condition.  It can be produced only by putting the mind or soul in fitting relations to the
outer objects so that that mode of general activity, or those functional acts or affections on
which pleasure waits, shall be determined to it.

§ 40. Pleasure and pain are in this exposition shown to bear the peculiar character of being in themselves finalities; they are the resulting ends of mental activity and affection. They exist indeed in the world-system; they are in the stream of change. Other experiences start from them and out of them. But in themselves they look to nothing further; nothing in their nature tends to further results. They are the creator's appointed ends of action; not means.

§ 41. Pleasure and pain, further, are simple feelings. Each particular pleasure, thus, as springing from some particular mental act or affection, is not complex, but simple and integral. Pleasure is often accompanied with pleasure, it is true, and also with pain, but only as they spring from different acts or affections. We speak, sometimes, of mingled pleasure and pain; the pleasure comes from one source in the mental experience, the pain from another. We feel a certain pleasure in tragic scenes or reports; the pleasure comes from the contemplation, the pain from some sense of bereavement or some sympathy with distress. The dramatic act gratifies in exhibiting heart-rending sorrows; pleasure and pain meet, but come from different sources in the mind of the beholder. We listen eagerly to sad news; the pleasure from the action of aroused curiosity joins, while it overbears, the pain from the wounded sympathies.

§ 42. Pleasure and pain furnish presumptive but not absolute and decisive criteria of the legitimate exercise of the mental functions. If a work of the imagination pleases, it is a sign that the production has been effected in accordance with the principles and laws regulating that function. So if the conclusion that has been reached in a course of investigation and of reasoning gives satisfaction, it is supposed to be right and true. A glad conscience signifies a right act. Generally, a procedure or a habit which draws in continual satisfaction and pleasure reconciles the mind to it as right. A protracted disquiet and distress in body or mind suggest something wrong. But it would be very rash and unsafe to rely on those tests at once in respect to every act or affection which they may attend, as conclusive. While on the one hand it is true that all pleasure and pain come by a natural law as the results, respectively, of legitimate or irregular action in favoring or untoward conditions, the application of the truth as a test of conduct or of condition requires often cautious consideration. Perfect peace and blessedness can result only from perfect character and perfect condition. Right action, naturally followed by pleasure, may take place in adverse circumstances that occasion difficulty and suffering; and inviting conditions sometimes seduce to actions that torment the conscience. Further, human conduct may enlist divers functions and suffer divers affections at the same time ; pleasure may wait on one and pain on another ; there may be, as already intimated, mingled pleasure and pain. Feats of heroism filling the soul with exulting joy have been performed in mental distress or bodily disease. In fact, with man in his present state, self-sacrifice is the price of the higher pleasure; and some kind of satisfaction is the tempter in every instance of wrong. Similarly, the healing remedy for one distress often generates or aggravates another. With all these difficulties in the practical use of the experiences of pleasure and pain as tests of character and conduct, as well as of condition, these affections are in themselves, when allowed and applied in due degree and relation, legitimate incentives and guides to human conduct ; they are, partially and subordinately, trustworthy tests of what is legitimate or otherwise. Pleasure always imports something legitimate ; pain always suggests something wrong somewhere, here or there, now or formerly, in ourselves or others, in act or in condition.

§ 43. Pleasure and pain suffer divers modifications. In their own nature they vary in degree or intensity and in breadth ; and in their relation to their objects or sources, they are variously characterized.

They vary thus, in degree, from states that border on indifference to wildest excesses of exultation or of grief. They vary also in breadth as they engage the whole soul's capacity at the time or only partially, as when only a part of its functions are enlisted.

Pleasure and pain are modified also in reference to the mental state from which they spring. They are characterized thus in reference to the general condition of the mind pervading its whole being, as in calm content, or rippling cheerfulness, or jubilant joy ; or in some settled disgust, or restless *ennui*, or desperate agony.

They are characterized, further, according to the functional energy or capacity from which they arise. The pleasures or the pains that come from the acting soul differ specifically from those that come from passive affection. The particular energies breed their own delights or dislikes ; and the particular affections end out with each its peculiar joy or sorrow.

They vary also mediately and indirectly with the objects that engage these energies or affections of the mind. We speak thus of the pleasures of food, of landscape, of society, and the like. They bring pleasure to us through their interaction with our minds and by thus determining them to acts or affections which nature ends out with pleasure to us.

More directly and immediately do the conditions of our acting or our feeling, in other words, the particular shapings of the relation between outer objects and our minds, as favoring the interaction or otherwise, characterize the pleasure or pain that attends upon the interaction or its results in our minds. The favoring environment makes action pleasant; untoward conditions make it hard or repulsive and more or less painful.

# CHAPTER III.

## THE SENSATIONS.

§ 44. THE SENSATIONS are *feelings produced in the mind by physical or material objects that address it through the bodily organism.* They are the passive side of the interaction that takes place between the human mind and the material world. They must be recognized as having their seat solely in the mind itself. The impressing force is indeed present with the impressed feeling ; but the force is on one side, the feeling on the other. Seal and wax meet in the sealing ; but the impression as received, is not at all in the seal, but only in the wax. " It is surely impossible," says Kant, " that we should feel outside us and not inside us." It has been contended by some physiologists that the seat of sensation is in the nerve. If the nervous organism were to be accepted as being the mind itself or all that there is of mind, then this doctrine might also be accepted. But the generally received doctrine recognizes the distinction of mind and matter. This doctrine involves the truth that in the inter-action of mind and matter the resulting feeling— the sensation—pertains only to the mind. With

this view the general testimony of consciousness
accords.   Men never attribute the sense of pain
to a ganglion of nerves.   They are conscious that
the sense is in themselves; it is they themselves
that feel.   Nerves cannot be conscious of the
affections which they receive ; the nervous organism cannot be conscious of them.   Men with well
nigh entire unanimity refer all proper consciousness to the soul itself.   That which consciously
feels is conceived of as back of the particular
nerve impressed ; back of the nervous organism ;
back of the brain.   Mind and matter are of a
distinct and opposite character ; they exist as opposites in their correlation with each other ; as such
they interact ; and the effect of the interaction,
when the impression comes from the matter, is,
on the mind's side, sensation.   If I press my
finger forcibly on a piece of yielding wax, both
myself and the wax are affected by the interaction, but differently.   I have a sensation which is
wholly in me ; the wax has an indentation which is
wholly in it.

The philosophy of this interaction between
matter and mind cannot as yet be expounded in
minutest detail with the confidence that science
might seek.   Theories, hypotheses, are proposed ;
but how such opposite natures as those of mind
and matter can interact at all and in what particular way they do interact, involve problems
that are still unsettled.   If there was but one
nature concerned, much at least of the mystery

would be dispelled. The fact of interaction implies the exertion of force or energy ; all action implies this. And action and force imply a being that acts and exerts the force. Sensation accordingly is the result of an interaction between two beings, two entities, two realities, which must be either two different kinds of force or be charged with force. When in the interaction the impressing force is from the matter-side, the result on the mind's-side is sensation. The meeting ground in the interaction is the nervous organism of the human body. This is the sole medium of sensation with man.

§ 46. The nervous organism in man consists of an upright trunk which is surmounted by a large oval mass known as the brain or *cerebrum* lying in the skull or *cranium*, and branches out into manifold lateral ramifications. Next below the cerebrum are other smaller masses of nerve-matter, the *cerebellum* being the largest of these ; and lower still is what is called the *spinal* column passing down through the *vertebræ*. From this upright column forty-three pairs of nerves—twelve cranial and thirty-one spinal— branch out in cords that here and there swell into ganglions differing in size and figure, consti- tuting nervous centers with their respective func- tions. The matter constituting this nervous sys- tem exists in the twofold form of cells and fibers. The cellular matter is of gray color and its special function seems to be that of a reservoir where nervous force is gathered and thence sent forth. The fibrous matter is white, and its function is that of a vehicle of force. For its twofold use of transmitting force outward and inward, there are provided two different sets of nervous fibers—one called *the efferent* or *motor* nerves, the other, *the afferent* or *sensory* nerves. They are always conjoined constituting so many pairs of nerve-cords. The outer coating of the brain or *cerebrum*—its *cortex*—it should be added here, is of the cellular substance; the interior of the brain is a fibrous mass.

§ 47. A fundamental characteristic of the nervous organism is that it is throughout *functional*. It is everywhere characterized as a medium, a seat and channel of activity—of a force or energy which acts to work out a purpose and to effect an end. This we should presume beforehand; for every living nature involves ends, purposes, uses, means; and observation uniformly corroborates this presumption. Everywhere and more and more as investigation proceeds, the distinctive functional uses of the divers parts of the nervous organism reveal themselves. The twofold substance—cellular and fibrous—as already stated, imports a diversity of function. So the positions of the parts, their connections, their forms, in figure and size, indicate distinctive functions respectively.

These functional uses of the nervous organism

are threefold, as they respect the nervous system itself, the body generally, or the mind.

§ 48. First, we notice a functional activity in the nervous system as directed upon itself. It is the proper function of the cell thus to hold force for the fiber; of the fiber to receive from one cellular mass to transmit to another. It is the office of the efferent or motor nerve to carry the nervous energy from within outward—from the brain, from the several ganglions—to determine motion in respect to the outer world. It is the office of the afferent or sensory nerve to bring in force or impression from without. Each kind has thus its own special direction of nerve-current. If an electric shock be given to either, the movement will be always and exclusively outward in the case of a motor nerve, and inward in the case of a sensory nerve. Interaction between different kinds of nerve-elements is denominated *reflex action*, being the action of one element directly upon another, without intervention of the mind. This reflex action is effected not only in the brain but also in the spinal cord and in other ganglions. This seems to be the special function of these ganglions, to serve as nerve-centers or places of meeting of different nerve elements, as also to serve as connections between the several parts of the system.

§ 49. Secondly, the several parts of the nervous structure have distinctive uses determined to them from their position, connections, and

6

forms in reference to the body.  The afferent or sensory nerves proceed from the different parts of the body with a mission to report its condition to points where required.  They report thus to their proper nerve-centers; the motor nerves receive the message; and in their turn perform their office by moving the muscles as the uses of the body, or it may be of the sovereign mind, may require.  Recent physiological science, with wonderful industry and sagacity, has investigated the respective functional uses of the different portions of the nervous organism.  It now generally regards thus the pair of ganglia called the *corpora striata* lying below the *cerebrum* as the nerve-centers by which the motions of the body to a certain extent are adjusted to each other and to the states of the muscular system generally. The *cerebellum* has its co-ordinating functions; and so other ganglions.  In walking, for illustration, the will issues the general order; the nervous system receives the order and carries it out in all its detailed complications.  As one foot is lifted, the equilibrium of the body is maintained by an instantaneous co-ordination of the other muscles concerned.  In like manner, the acrobat in every new attitude that he takes makes it necessary for maintaining his equilibrium that an indefinite number of muscles should act in concert; the reflex action of the nerves effects the needful muscular adjustment.  The act of speaking, in the same way, necessitates the co-ordination of a large

number of muscular movements. All this the
nervous system takes in charge and accomplishes
the work through what is called its reflex action
without the necessary interference of the brain, or
of the mind. As the nervous organism is continuous and connected throughout, these co-ordinating movements react through the whole body—as
may be requisite for its best condition and most
effective working. These recent physiological discoveries dispose of some questions that once severely tasked the ingenuity of psychologists in
seeking to explain how the mind could consciously and intentionally reach every nerve and muscle
concerned in complicated movements of the body.
The mind does not reach them at all; it only
gives out the general order; the nerves execute
the order, attending to all the minute details
that are involved. It is true that the higher
nerve-centers may sometimes intervene; the
mind itself may intervene, arresting or modifying;
the nerves obey all orders, carrying out to the
uttermost limit of their power the last or highest order received. The extent to which this ad-
justing or co-ordinating ministry, in addition to
the more proper special function of a nerve-pair
or nerve-center, would be well nigh incredible
but for the abundance of accordant testimony of
the most authoritative character. As a single fact
in exemplification, the statement may be cited,
that if an acid be applied to the side of a frog
from which the head has been removed, the frog

will brush it off with the foot of the same side
and if that foot be cut off, it will use the other
foot.

More than this : in case a given part of the
nerve system be destroyed or impaired in its action, another portion may be deputed to perform
its function, so that the body shall suffer no harm.
This delegation of ministry is of course subject to
limitation of place and connection ; for it seems
to be settled that the special function of a nerve-
element depends on its position, its connections
and relations, rather than on its peculiarity of
structure.

There is to be observed in relation to this reflex
action of the nerves, and the observation is to be
extended to the reciprocal action of the mind
and the nervous system, that a kind of law of
habit prevails in it generally. Repetition facili-
tates and expedites nervous action ; regularity and
uniformity promote it. Responses between the
different nerve-elements, and also between them
and the mind, become by such uniformity and repetition quicker and easier. What was slow and
difficult and awkward at first, becomes in time
quick and easy, and graceful or free. The law
is of remarkable extent and force. It reaches to
the attainments of agility and strength of bodily
limb—of foot and hand, in all feats of muscular
exertion ; of finger and tongue and vocal organ,
as in musical skill ; of touch and sight and all the
special senses ; as also vigor in the involuntary

movements of the body, as in respiration, digestion, and other functions of this class ; to the in-
terpretations likewise by the mind of the messages which the nerve-vehicle brings to it and its
action back on them, both collectively and as special elements ;—everywhere the law prevails.
The whole composite nature of man is subject to
this law of habit ; the mind and the body alike in
themselves and in their interaction. The recognition of it explains manifold phenomena otherwise obscure and mysterious. A nervous movement, it is to be observed, may start from any
point in the nervous expansion that can be
reached by an impressing force, as well as at the
proper terminal points. A diseased state of the
body thus, as in case of fevers, blood-poisoning,
and the like, external agents introduced by any
means into the interior of the body, as chemical
irritants, and, it may be added, the imagination
itself, may excite a sensory nerve and so occasion
sensation in the mind itself that cannot be distinguished from surface irritations. Or, analogous
effects may result in like action of a motor nerve :
bodily movements taking place as if ordered by
the mind itself. Such affections of the nerves
originating within, are naturally interpreted as if
starting from the terminal points or sources. Pain
thus in a limb that has suffered amputation sometimes seems to come from the foot or hand that
has been. removed, when a nerve that originally
started from that member is irritated anywhere

along its course. Sounds, sights, really occasioned by these interior excitants of the nerves,
seem as real and are as naturally referred to outer
objects as when they come to the eye or ear from
these objects. We are enabled in the light of
this fact to account for apparitions and mysterious sounds, other strange sensations, as well as
for singular movements of the body, which otherwise would seem inexplicable or supernatural.

§ 50. Thirdly, the paramount functional ministry of the nervous organism is exerted in relation to the mind. To this high office all its
other functional ministries are auxiliary and subordinate. And the one comprehensive ministry
here seems to be as a medium of interaction between the mind and beings exterior to it, including the body itself. In order to such interaction
some field common to it and them seems necessary ; and such a field is furnished in the nerve-
system. This office it unquestionably fulfills.

The physical entity closest to the human
mind is the body. Mind and body participate in
a common life ; they are united so vitally that
the condition and action of the one immediately
affect the other. Health and vigor in the one
are reflected in the other, as are also disease and
weakness. Every form of mental activity reaches
out through the remotest parts of the body ; and
the afferent nerves bring back to the mind in sensation their respective messages concerning the
bodily condition from every part. Feeling,

thought, volition alike put the nerves in motion. A sense of an unworthy act sends the blood into the cheeks, or agitates the entire bodily framework; a bright thought illumines the countenance, and a perplexing thought wrinkles the brow; while the will exerts its sway over body and soul alike. So, on the other hand, even the prick of a pin in the finger or the tickling of the sole of the foot may startle or agitate the mind itself. It is through the nervous organism that this interaction between mind and body is maintained. And all other physical natures reach the mind only through the body and through its nerve-system.

Influenced apparently by the localization of the several functional ministries of the different portions of the nervous organism, particularly in the case of the special senses, physiologists have held that analogy leads to the conjecture that the brain is the instrument or organ of the higher mental activities. But the analogy utterly fails here. The nervous organism has for its comprehensive function to serve as medium between mind and external bodies, the functional ministries to the body and to other parts of the nerve-system being only subordinate and auxiliary. No such medium is required for those activities of the mind which are limited by their nature within its own sphere. Where there is no use to be subserved, it is absurd to suppose a special function. Then there is no support for the conjecture that the higher spiritual activities are localized in the brain, in any ascertained fact. Investigation has been pushed with the most industrious zeal, and most scientific method and exactness; but no limitation of any particular part of the brain to any particular form of that higher spiritual activity which lies wholly in the spiritual realm, has ever been observed. The localizations in the nerve-system of the different forms of the mind's inter-action with outer bodies, have been ascertained by recent investigations, to a truly marvelous extent. But not one fact of observation, has passed the boundary of this interaction. The purely spiritual activities of will, thought, imagination, have never been found to engage specially any portion of the brain. The arguments from the affections of the memory by diseases or lesions of the brain, all fail in the light of a true theory of the memory which denies to it the character of a special faculty of the mind. The general vital sympathy of the mind and body as parts united in the same organic whole, sufficiently accounts for other phenomena, such as the lessened circulation of the blood in the brain during sleep, without supposing an organic functional relation, except, as stated, in cases of interaction between the mind and outer bodies.

The hypothesis of a special localization in the brain of these higher mental activities which are carried on within a purely spiritual realm, is accordingly to be rejected :

First, because no fact of observation sustains it ;

Secondly, because no use in the mind's activity requires it ;

Thirdly, because the function of the nerve-system is exhausted in its office as a medium of interaction between body and mind ;

Fourthly, because the special function of the brain is sufficiently engaged in the co-ordination of the entire aggregate of nervous activities and conditions throughout the body. For this function its location and its relations, as well as its own internal structure, specially adapt it ; and in the exercise of this function its full capacity may well seem to be enlisted, so that it shall have nothing to spare for other service.

§ 51. The sensations or affections of the mind from physical forces in the animal frame itself, or from external bodies acting through the nervous organism, are conveniently distributed into four classes :

First, the sensations of pleasure and pain from bodily motions and states ;

Secondly, the sensations from the exterior conditions of the body as a living whole—those of the *general vital sense ;*

Thirdly, the sensations from affections by external agencies of general organic structures— those of the *general organic sense ;* and

Fourthly, the sensations from affections of the special sense-organs—those of *special sense.*

§ 52. The body is a source of pleasure and pain to the mind in its movements and states as truly as the acts and affections of the mind itself, for the body is an organic part of the man in the present life. § 38. A bodily movement or a bodily state, so far as normal or legitimate of itself is attended by pleasure, as its natural result or consequence; and equally, so far as irregular, and in contradiction to the law of its being, such movement or state brings in this sense of pain. Bodily health and vigor, unobstructed vital processes, as of respiration and nutrition, free and unimpeded exertion of muscles, are sources of pleasurable sensations, more or less general, more or less pronounced; the opposites of these conditions are followed under the appointments of nature by painful sensations. The mind may turn itself away from noticing them, may absorb itself with other operations or affections; but nature is ever present with her inexorable law and forces in the appointed consequence, heeded or unheeded.

§ 53. The sensations of the general vital sense are those produced by the outer condition or environment of the body. They include the sensations of heat and cold, of atmospheric exhilaration or depression, of light and darkness, of stillness and noise, and the like.

§ 54. The sensations of the general organic sense proceed from the affections by exterior agencies of one or another of the organic structures in the body, as the muscular, the cuticular, the general nervous structure. The sensations of pressure and resistance, titillations or lesions of the skin, of heat and cold from immediate contact with external bodies, are exemplifications of this class of sensations.

§ 55. The sensations of special sense proceed from certain nerve-structures specially appropriated each to its own kind of impression. These special structures are five in number, and are familiarly known as those of *Touch, Taste, Smell, Hearing,* and *Sight.*

I. The sensations of Touch proceed from the extremities of the nerves terminating in the skin particularly at the tips of the fingers, also on the surface of the tongue and the lips. They arise only from actual contact of the external body which acts mechanically upon the tactual nerves. They are closely associated with those of the general organic sense on the one side and with those of taste on the other ; and freely mingle or unite with them.

II. The sensations of Taste proceed from affections of certain nerve-structures at the surface of the tongue and soft palate with the adjacent parts. The gustatory nerves are acted upon by liquids or gaseous substances in immediate contact and only through chemical properties.

III. The sensations of Smell proceed from nerves in the inner and upper part of the nose. This sense is the weakest and the most variable of the senses. In the case of some persons it is entirely lacking. The olfactory nerves are affected chemically by odoriferous particles in the air or, perhaps, as some suppose, by an odoriferous ether after the analogy of vision as produced by a luminiferous ether.

IV. The sensations of Hearing proceed from affections of the auditory nerves seated in the ear. The impressions are made by vibrations of air on the outward ear which are transmitted by a complicated apparatus to the auditory nerves. The action is purely mechanical; and the vibrations, which by exciting the auditory nerves produce the sensations of sound, may originate not only in atmospheric waves, but also from internal causes, as from electrical excitement, from disease, from narcotics, and even from the imagination acting upon the motor nerves and so causing forcible circulation of the blood. We hear thus at times ringing sounds or even musical tones occasioned by internal affections alone. It is probable that some supposed supernatural sounds resembling cries or vocal addresses are to be accounted for by this reference to an internal origin.

V. The sensations of Sight proceed from impressions on the optical nerve-structure situated in the eye, by the undulations of light. This is at least the normal source or occasion of Sight. But impressions on the nerves of Sight may originate from within, as from electricity, from dis-

ease, from chemical irritants, from the imagination, and also from external pressure or violence.
The action on the nerves is mechanical. The
sensation will of course be variously modified by
the modifications which the nature of light or the
character of its undulating movements may suffer.

# CHAPTER IV.

## THE EMOTIONS.

§ 56. THE EMOTIONS *are feelings awakened in the mind by immaterial or spiritual objects.*

These objects or sources of emotion may reach the mind by direct and immediate address or indirectly and mediately. The acts and affections of the mind itself are immediate objects of emotion. The mind becomes object thus to itself, and when standing in this relation it is designated as *subject-object*. Its own feelings, thoughts, and purposes awaken feelings, variously distinguished in themselves. Such feelings are emotions, being characterized by this relation to the mind's own acts or affections which they immediately respect.

But other spiritual activities besides those of the proper self address the mind, although perhaps in the present condition of man as invested with a material body only through the bodily organism, and so through the nervous structure. It may, however, be reasonably supposed that the universal energy working throughout the universe, regarded as the revealed activity of the infinite spirit, may immediately interact with the human spirit ; and so emotions be awakened without the intervention of any material medium. But however reaching the human soul the address of a spiritual activity to it may awaken feelings of the class distinguished as emotions. The sensation by which the object that awakens the emotion may be conveyed to the mind may be consciously noticed or pass wholly unnoticed. We often in reading take no note of the sensation of sight produced by the printed characters that bring to us stirring intelligence. The surprise, the exultation, or the grief alone engages our minds ; we overlook the vehicle of the physical sense. But the distinction between the sensation and the emotion is broad and obvious ; the one has its immediate object and source in the sphere of the body ; the other, in the realm of spirit. Emotions are accordingly to be recognized as the passive side of the mind's interaction with other spiritual activities.

§ 57. We have recognized a threefold division of spiritual activities or, as they are called, ideas ; all forms of such activities that are conceivable by us being comprehended under the three grand ideas of the true, the beautiful, and the good. § 27. We have thus the fundamental and exhaustive distribution of the emotions as related to their object or source :— 1, Those awakened by what is true ; 2, Those awakened by what is beautiful ; and 3, Those awakened by what is good.

As pleasure waits on all normal acts and affections of the mind, § 38, we have what may be called *emotional pleasure* and its opposite, *emotional pain*, as we have proper sensational pleasure and pain.

In a similar analogy, as we designated the capacity of sensation the *bodily sense*, so we have in reference to the respective classes of ideas awakening emotions what may be designated the *intellectual sense*, meaning by the term the soul's capacity of emotion from what is true ; the *æsthetic sense*, or the soul's capacity of emotion from what is beautiful or perfect in form ; and the *moral sense*, or the capacity of emotion from what is good in the object addressing it. There arise thus the designations of the three classes of emotions, as the Intellectual, the Æsthetic, and the Moral.

These classes suffer each divers modifications.

§ 58. Intellectual emotions are awakened by objects as true, addressing the soul. The apprehension of truth or the soul's reception of objects as true or revealing truth is natural to man. He is fitted for truth ; and the truth acts upon him. He feels it. The true received or contemplated, that is, the reception of the true by the mind, awakens a peculiar feeling or emotion. So far as simply true, irrespectively of the contents as good or evil in itself, the true is pleasing. We desire to hear news even when it is sad. The false is on the contrary naturally displeasing.

The imperfectly true, knowledge imperfect in any way, naturally disquiets us; we seek the perfectly true, perfect knowledge. That an object is real is a fact that of itself may excite a certain emotion more or less vivid, connected or unconnected with other characteristics or relations which it bears. The apprehension of these characteristics or relations awakens feeling more or less intense. So a stated principle or law, a proposition of any kind, discerned as true, awakens emotion. These emotions are designated as intellectual, in reference to the character of the object of the emotion as the true, that is, as the expression of an intelligence, rather than in reference to the subject or the intelligence that receives the object.

Emotions of this class are variously modified. They vary in intensity—from barely wakeful intelligence to the elation of soul attending discovery of momentous truth. Truths that more immediately concern us touch us most deeply. Discoveries by our own minds have a special interest to us. Novelty intensifies the emotion. Surprise is a modification of the intellectual sense. Quickness of intellect in revealing the true heightens emotion. Here lies the peculiar enchantment of wit.

§ 59. Æsthetic emotions are awakened by objects regarded in respect to their form—as perfect or beautiful, or otherwise. The perfectly beautiful is the perfect in form; and form denotes simply that in an object which fits it to be in interaction with other realities. § 31.

Emotions of this class are variously modified in respect to intensity and quality. They vary with the varying character and relations of the mind addressed and also with the varying nature and relations of the object. The more important distinctions in the æsthetic emotions are founded on the constituents of beauty in the object. These will come appropriately under consideration in subsequent chapters. But two varieties of these emotions may be mentioned here. The three constituents essential in all beauty are the idea revealed, the matter in which this idea is revealed, and the actual revelation of the idea in the matter—summarily designated as idea, matter, form. As the one or the other of these constituents is more prominent to the contemplating mind, the æsthetic emotion awakened is correspondingly modified. Such modifications form a distinct class of æsthetic emotions. A second class of æsthetic modifications and the class most demanding notice here is founded on the relations of these elements to one another in the constitution of a beautiful object. There is a threefold gradation in these internal relations of the object : First, the idea may be in exact equipoise with the matter in which it is revealed. In this case we have the emotion of *proper beauty*. The characteristic of this emotion is that of tranquillity, quietness, the constituents of beauty being in harmony. Secondly, the idea may transcend the matter or preponderate over it. The constituents of the beauty are now in disproportion, inharmonious; the contemplating mind is lifted from its balance, as it were, by the surpassing power and greatness of the idea. We here have the emotion of *sublimity*. The characteristic of this emotion is that of agitation, unrest. The surging ocean is sublime; the placid lake is beautiful. Thirdly, the matter may preponderate over the idea, giving us what we call the *pretty* and the *comic*. The constituents here are in disproportion and the effect of the contemplation is not the rest and quietness of proper beauty. Neither is it the violent agitation of spirit that characterizes the sublime. It is the gentle ripple of soul. In the pretty, the idea is in defect while the contemplation is pleasantly entertained and gratified approximating the experience of proper beauty. In the comic, the unreason is in greater predominance, approaching the character of the sublime, and the effect of the contemplation may be convulsive laughter.

§ 60. Moral emotions are awakened by the good or its opposite in the object. They accordingly respect the end or aim of the activity that awakens the emotion. The moral emotions do not necessarily involve any voluntariness or act of will, and therefore do not of themselves indicate what is known as moral character. The good and the bad alike are susceptible of the emotions which arise from the contemplation of right conduct or a virtuous act ; just as the sage and the dunce may alike experience intellectual emotions and the artist and the boor alike feel in their respective ways and degrees the effects of beauty. The emotion may, however, sometimes be joined with the action of the free-will and so the complex activity take on a properly moral character. But the emotion may be experienced without any conjoined action of the free-will. In other words, moral emotions are so denominated, not because they are in themselves morally right or wrong, but because they are awakened by what is right or wrong. This is a distinction of grave importance in ethical discussions.

The moral emotions suffer divers modifications. They vary with the character and condition of the contemplating mind. The virtuous feel more intensely than the vicious what is noble and excellent in act and character. Their hatred of the evil is likewise deeper and stronger. The sympathies of the two are dissimilar, as well as their relationships generally to virtue and to vice. Their emotions are correspondingly modified. Moral emotions vary with the character and relative prominence of the three constituents entering into every moral action and state ;—the loving intention in the doer or moral subject ; the good effect in the object of the action ; and the performance of the act itself or the carrying of the loving intent into the good to be experienced by the object. The emotion varies as it is engaged more with the loving heart, or with the good achieved, or with the righteousness and unswerving rectitude of the act, involving it may be more or less of heroic fortitude, struggle, and persistence. Moral emotions freely mingle with intellectual and æsthetic emotions, as parts of the same organic and emotional nature. As native endowments of the mind they do not necessarily take on a character of merit or demerit, of desert or blameworthiness, and accordingly, as before observed, are not of themselves tests of proper moral character. Poets corrupt in life have sung deeds of heroic virtue in enrapturing verse. The experience of a moral emotion, by the very constitution of the soul, gives a peculiar pleasure, which the contemplation of the morally perfect of itself awakens. Moral displeasure as naturally in the moral condition of the human soul attends on the contemplation of the evil in act and life. It remains true that no act or condition among men is absolutely simple; it is ever complex both in itself and in its relations. It is possible, therefore, to abstract any one ingredient or any one relation from the rest; and so the emotions awakened by the same act or state may vary greatly in intensity and in kind in the experiences of different minds.

# CHAPTER V.

## THE AFFECTIONS.

§61. *The* AFFECTIONS *are feelings complicated with a certain satisfaction or dissatisfaction in respect to their objects.*

The classes of feelings hitherto described are purely passive affections of the mind. The first class, pleasure and pain, simply attend on the mind's own actions or states and it is only through those actions or states that they can even suggest any exterior objects. The sensations and emotions are the impressions received by the mind from objects interacting with it. In these classes the mind is mere passive subject. In the affections, the active nature of the soul is engaged; a positive reaction appears directed toward the object. It is the expression of its organic nature putting it into sympathy with other members of the same organic whole—the expression of the principle of kind—kindliness—as the natural reaction of the mind when addressed by them. The affections express thus the content or discontent, the satisfaction or dissatisfaction which it must experience more or less in all such addresses. It is by this element that they modify or color the purely passive feeling produced by the object.

§ 62. The fundamental distinction of the affections is indicated in this account of their nature and genesis. It is twofold, into *love* and *hate*. Love is the expression of content, satisfaction, kindly sympathy in the reaction of the mind toward the objects that address it. Hate is the corresponding expression of discontent, dissatisfaction, antipathy in this reaction.

§ 63. Love and hate are properly emotions, inasmuch as they are awakened not by physical, but by spiritual objects. They exist in the realm of spirit alone. Although often interchanged, they differ mainly in this particular feature from *likes* and *dislikes* which are more indefinite in regard to their objects and have a less purely spiritual or at least a lower import.

They appear in each department of emotional experience:—intellectual, æsthetic, moral. § 57.

In themselves they cannot be characterized as morally right or wrong. They become so only as they come under the control of the free-will. The moral affections, like the moral emotions, are denominated not from the subject experiencing them, much less from the subject as acting freely and voluntarily in them, but rather from the object of the affection as being an end and so a good.

§ 64. The affections, further, appear as single transient experiences or as habits. Habitual dispositions thus are recognized in language under the names of *good-nature, complaisance, friendship, patriotism, piety,* etc., or of *ill-nature uncharitableness,* and the like, being variously modified in respect to degree and object.

§ 65. One variety of the affections deserves a special notice—the *resentments.* They are responsive affections—acting back on other feelings as the objects impressing the mind. To this class belong the affections of *gratitude,* as responsive to kindness; *forgiveness* and its opposite, *inexorableness,* responsive to sense of wrong; *self-complacency* and *remorse,* responsive to consciousness of right or wrong in one's self.

# CHAPTER VI.

## THE DESIRES.

§ 66. THE DESIRES *are feelings complicated with the drift of mind as an active nature toward some good.* § 24. They are feelings awakened by some form of good in their objects which engage the telic properties of the mind. They are thus telic or end-seeking feelings. They add to the elements of a proper affection this element of a drift or set of mind toward the object in order to secure and appropriate the good there may be, or may be supposed to be, in it.

This telic drift or set is characteristic of all life. The plant tends toward—seeks—the moist and the rich in the soil around it ; seeks to send upward its branches and downward its roots ; seeks to grow, to mature and perfect itself ; to reach the end proper to its being. The animal, in like manner, seeks the growth and perfection proper to it, and in order to this seeks the conditions favorable to this end. The whole constitution of the human soul is thus telic ; every active element in it pressing to attain the condition and character proper to it. The desires are the respective forms of this telic bent to meet the wants of its nature. There are not only desires which are native to the mind, instinctive, and normal, there are also those which arise out of its ever-changing character and conditions. There are desires which are factitious, which are acquired, springing out of new relations or new developments of character, or the result of habit and association; abnormal desires, moreover, arising out of morbid conditions of the soul or body; and those which are irregular—whether in kind or degree.

The desires lie close to the free voluntary activities of the soul. They easily and naturally pass into actual volitions. In their widest comprehension they may be said ever to precede acts of will, since such acts of will ever respect some object in character or condition as an end or motive, and this end must be a good to which the soul and active nature tend, and which thus becomes an object of desire. But desires exist which do not enlist the free action of the will. In their own proper nature they are spontaneities; they are not morally right or wrong as being praiseworthy or blameworthy; they are moral in the higher sense only when the objects which they respect lie in the more strictly moral realm—in the realm of moral freedom. The desires can be morally wrong only as they are allowed and cherished toward forbidden objects or in forbidden degrees, only as they are in some way or degree directed or controlled by the free-will.

§ 67. The desires distribute themselves at once into the two great classes distinguished from each other as bents toward their objects, or away from them. There are thus the *desires proper* and the *aversions.*

§ 68. Both classes—desires proper and aversions—include subdivisions corresponding with the distinctly recognized tendencies in the activity of the mind. Each of these constitutional tendencies has its respective object. The subdivisions of the desires may accordingly be denominated either from the tendency or from its object.

The first and most fundamental of the desires of the human soul is *self-love*—the desire for the maintenance and perfection of its own being in character and condition. This is an instinctive principle of the soul, proper to all life. It is, subject, of course, to the limitations pertaining to man as a finite being, not only a most worthy principle of action, but also one whose legitimate promptings are ever to be recognized and to be obeyed. It appears not only as a general principle controlling the whole life generally, prompting ever to the highest, most perfect, most enduring life in the most favoring condition, but also manifesting itself in modified forms in each separate tendency or bent of the soul's activity, giving rise to so many specific varieties of desire. They may be embraced in the two generic classes of *appetites* and *rational desires,* as they respect the physical or the rational nature of man.

§ 69. As self-love, which is in itself an instinctive and worthy principle of human life, both generally and in its specific forms, may be perverted or ill-regulated in degree, it becomes unworthy and is known as *selfishness.* The two forms of desire are to be sharply distinguished. Selfishness is ever perverted or ill-regulated self-love.

§ 70. The APPETITES are desires seeking the maintenance and perfection of the bodily life in character and condition. They embrace the two classes of the personal and the social instincts, such as the desires for food and drink—hunger and thirst; for muscular exertion, for rest and sleep; and the manifold propensities and appetencies which seek as their end the best condition of the individual life, as well as those which respect the continuance and perfection of the outward condition of the race. They are in themselves legitimate and worthy. They rise as the wants of the outward life require. They may be perverted and ill-regulated; they thus become corrupting, debasing, and destructive, defeating the very end for which they were kindly intended and wisely fitted.

§ 71. The RATIONAL DESIRES, which seek immediately the maintenance and perfection of the soul itself in character and condition, divide themselves at once into the two classes of *per-*

*sonal* and *social*. Each of these classes suffers divers modifications in reference to the particular form of tendency recognized in the mind. These specific modifications may be denominated indifferently from the tendency or from its object or end. We recognize here the two classes of *personal* and *social* desires.

§ 72. First and most fundamental of the rational desires of the proper personal class, is what may be denominated the desire of *power*. The essential nature of the human soul we have found to be activity. The perfection of its active life is thus the most comprehensive and most fundamental desire of the soul; and this is what is meant by *power*, the term being taken in its largest sense. The desire of power in this large sense, as the desire for largest measure of capability and best condition for exertion—the principle of *ambition*—in the legitimate sphere and form of human action, is not only legitimate in itself and worthy, but ever to be cherished and fostered in rightful way and degree. It may be perverted and ill-regulated, like all other instincts of human nature; and as it is the most fundamental instinct, so it may become the most dangerous of human passions.

The desire of power is modified in manifold ways, and embraces manifold subdivisions. The desire, as personal, extends to all the functions of the soul. It includes the desire of *freedom*—the largest measure of power in the free-will as the highest and most distinctive characteristic of man, within the limitations incident to man's finite nature. The desire of *intellectual culture*, of increase in intellectual force and acquisition, is another modification of this generic desire. A third modification is *the culture of the function of form*, in its active and in its passive character— the culture of sympathetic affection, of æsthetic taste and skill, of all departments of the sensibility and the imagination. Still further may be enumerated here the general desire of *perfection as a rational spirit* in the well-adjusted and symmetrical development of the entire nature as an organic whole, having divers members all to be co-ordinated and brought into sympathetic relationship of ministry.

§ 73. The desire of power brings in the desire for the best opportunity and means for exercising power. This personal desire respecting condition includes divers subordinate desires. Such are the desires for *wealth*, which when abused and becoming inordinate, is perverted to *avarice* when riches are sought as ends and not as means, or *covetousness*, when sought in excess; the desire for *rank* or *station*, as affording opportunity for the exercise of power; the desire of *fame*, also, as opening avenues or affording facilities for power to achieve its ends. These desires often more or less involve social elements; as power is relative, and is greater or less as measured in relation to other persons or to institutions or to circumstances. *Emulation* is a leading form of these relative desires; the desire to excel others in power, in some form or relation, as in intrinsic efficiency or ability; or in actual attainment bringing in the increase of power from self-confidence and relative depression of others ; or, still further, in superior command of means or conditions. Human activity is appointed to manifest itself in a large degree in social conditions, and so inevitably often becomes competitive. Emulation is competitive desire ; as such, it is legitimate, and becomes wrong only as it is abused.

§ 74. The more purely social desires respect as objects the persons constituting the social relationships and the conditions of acting determined by these relationships. Here belong the generic desire of *society*, modified in manifold ways in respect to object, as the desire of companionship, of family, of civil and religious communion, of accidental associations with others. More subordinate social desires are those of esteem, affection, approbation, and the like.

§ 75. The desires are often complicated more or less with expectation of attainment. They become then *hopes*—a most important class of human affections. The opposite desires of this class are *fears*—the expectations of failure to attain the object desired. Hopes and fears vary with the manifold diversity of human desires or tendencies. They vary with their respective objects and also in degree. Rightly directed and controlled, they are legitimate and worthy; only as misdirected or inordinate, do they become blameworthy and hurtful.

# CHAPTER VII.

## THE SENTIMENTS.

§ 76. *The* SENTIMENTS *are feelings complicated with intelligence or will.*

As functions of the same organism the sensibility must ever be conjoined with its co-ordinate functions. The mind, in fact, never entirely represses either one; while one or another may more or less predominate and so give character to a particular mental act or state. In the strongest passion there is ever in exercise something of the intelligent nature, something of the free-will. Otherwise the mind parted from one of its essential functions would cease to be a true rational organism. The degrees in which these associated functions may take part in particular experiences conjointly with the affection of the sensibility vary indefinitely. Sometimes they may be too indistinct to be within our power to discern them; and at other times they may rise to equal prominence with the feeling or even transcend it. In this latter case the mental experience passes under a new denomination; it is then no longer a state of the sensibility, but a cognitive or a purposive act of the mind, only colored by more or less of feeling. It is so with the character of the whole mind. One man is characteristically a man of feeling; another is a man of a cool judgment; a third is a man of resolve and determination. With other persons, the three functions may be in equipoise and form a symmetrical nature.

As these functional expressions vary thus by indistinguishable gradations, one state shading itself into another by imperceptible transition, it is only those general and vague distinctions which language recognizes that can be noted in classification. By a sentiment language denotes an affection of the mind more or less modified in character by the intelligence or the will—or it may be by both, the feeling being recognized as the predominating and characteristic feature.

§ 77. The sentiments naturally distribute themselves into three general classes :—*the Contemplative, the Practical*, and *the Rational*.

§ 78. The Contemplative sentiments are such as unite with the feeling a characterizing exercise of the intelligence.

In this class of sentiments the cognitive element may be the ground or source of the feeling as in *wonder* and *surprise*, the former looking rather to the intelligence side, the latter to the feeling itself; also in *esteem, respect, reverence, vanity* and *self-conceit, confidence, trust*, etc.

The intelligence may appear also simply as

8

associated with the feeling and mingling with it, as in *taste*, as an intelligent sense of beauty.

The cognitive element may also arise from the feeling while the feeling maintains its presence and predominance in the complex experience, as sometimes in the sentiments of *approbation, kind-heartedness*, etc.

The emotions, affections, and desires, generally readily take in this intelligent element and so gain the character of sentiments.

§ 79. The Practical sentiments are feelings that unite with them some determination of the will. They are also known as the *moral sentiments*.

As in the preceding class, the two elements may exist in either of the relations of source, or consequence, or of simple association, the same general sentiment sometimes originating in one way, sometimes in another. The elements also unite in ever varying proportions, as is the case with all the sentiments. They appear, moreover, either as transient affections or as permanent dispositions.

§ 80. The Rational sentiments are feelings that unite with them both of the other functions of man's rational nature.

Language recognizes sentiments that are thus properly rational; but it denominates them vaguely and with little or no discrimination of the relative prominence of the constituents. The several classes, in fact, for the most part fail to be discriminated in language.

§ 81. The several classes of sentiments may be modified in reference to their objects and accordingly be distributed into corresponding species. We have thus:

1. *The personal sentiments*, which respect one's self as their object, as *modesty, humility, vanity, self-conceit;*

2. *The social sentiments*, which respect one's friends, as *friendship, courtesy;*

3. *The patriotic sentiments* which respect one's country, as *patriotism, loyalty;* and

4. *The religious sentiments*, which respect God, as *godliness, devotion.*

# CHAPTER VIII.

## THE PASSIONS.

§ 82. THE PASSIONS are simply *feelings intensified*. They are distinguished from the other classes only in degree. Any feeling of any class becomes a passion by increase of intensity.

The passions admit of no exact gradations. They rise from lowest to highest by imperceptible stages. They are momentary or enduring.

They are found in all the departments of human feeling. They simply represent the intensest forms in each respectively.

Men differ in respect to their susceptibility of passion. We characterize some as being of a passionate nature; or of a passionate disposition, humor, or turn. The native disposition admits of change through culture or neglect. A truly great and noble soul is one that feels deeply, warmly, passionately. The spirit of enterprise, of efficiency, of achievement—the spirit of might —is animated by a soul that feels intensely and passionately.

Passions are evoked originally by objects addressing them. An excitable soul will burst into a flame of passion, as gunpowder from a spark that falls upon it. A word, a hint, a remote suggestion, will kindle it into a rapture, a fury, a storm of passion. The imagination taking up the impression of an exciting object upon the soul feeds the original feeling and nourishes it up into a strong body of passion.

The passions, though strong and sources of strength, are subject to control. The highest virtue lies in right government of them. " Better is he that ruleth his spirit than he that taketh a city."

# CHAPTER IX.

## THE IMAGINATION.

§ 83. THE IMAGINATION *is the faculty of form.*
The imagination is accordingly the active side
of the general function of form, the passive side
of which we have recognized under the name of
the sensibility or the capacity of form. By this
term *form* is designated "that characteristic or attribute of the mind through which it sympathetically communicates or interacts with other beings."
§ 31. It will be understood that in a proper sense
the mind interacts with itself. It is in this re-
flexive interaction that we have found that important class of feelings denominated the emotions to
have their seat and distinguishing characteristics.
§ 56. As abiding form to itself, moreover, the
mind presents its continuous activity to its own
consciousness and so knows itself to be itself ever
the same in conscious personal identity. Thus
this function is seen to be the ground and necessary condition of memory, of habit, of mental
growth. §§ 12–15, 102. The wide-reaching significance of this function in relation to all mental
phenomena can hardly be overestimated. Without it the human mind could have no sense of

exterior reality, no sense of its own being; no self-consciousness, no connected knowledge, no art, no morality; it would be little more than an abiding speck, at most a mere vibrating atom on the surface of being.

§ 84. A diversity of names, with little scientific precision in the use of them, have been applied to this function. From the Greek language we have *phantasy*, contracted in English use to *fancy*. From the Latin we have *imagination*, denoting the imagining power of mind, also in more restricted use, *representation*. The faculty has also been sometimes called the *idealizing* power, its products being *ideals*.

§ 85. It will not be difficult to identify a proper act of the imagination among the phenomena of mind. If an object, as an orange, be presented to the sensibility so as to impress it, and if we suppose the impression to abide for a longer or shorter time, the idea of the object as thus imparted must abide as an object of consciousness. This idea is something that can be contemplated; it is a form—a form of the mind that has continued after the impression of the orange on the sense, and of which the mind may be conscious. It is in the nomenclature of Kant a *schema*, a *habitus* or holding-on of the sense-impression But we have now nothing but what is purely mental; the external object—the orange—has removed; it has done its work in impressing the sense; the effect abides only as a pure mental state. It is, however, a state of an active nature; the mind is active in *the schema*—in holding the idea. It holds it up to the view of consciousness. This act of holding the sense-impression, this *schema*, is an act of the imagination. The orange has become idealized by it, so that it abides in the mind only as an idea.

It is, however, not a mere bodiless idea. It has entered into the life of the mind; it has incorporated itself into the mind's own forms and conditions. It is no longer the primitive idea of the orange, as the orange was in itself or as the Creator formed it. It has become shaped and colored by the mind itself in its own peculiar natural and acquired characteristics. So far from being the same as the primitive idea of the orange as it impressed the sense, it has been subjected to changes not only through the action of the medium through which it reached the sense, the medium of light and vision, but also still more by the mind itself, so that different minds and even the same mind at different times and in different conditions would not hold it in the same way and form. The idea has become an ideal; something that preserves somewhat of the original identity of the idea, but still preserves that somewhat only in certain respects like the original. It has a new form or body given it by the mind itself acting through its function of the imagination. This ideal may be embodied in other matter than that of the mind's own state and affection at the time, and so be made by the same idealizing power to take on still new forms. We have thus the following definitions.

§ 86. AN IDEAL *is the proper product of the imagination as an active function.* It ever consists of three distinguishable elements: the idea imaged; the matter or body in which it is imaged; and the action of the imagination itself in embodying it. The term *ideal*, it will have been seen, differs from *idea* by its referring directly to the work of the imagination in forming it.

§ 87. Ideals are primitive or secondary. A PRIMITIVE IDEAL is the first product of the imagination as it embodies the idea received in the mind's own furniture at the time of receiving the impression.

A SECONDARY IDEAL is an ideal shaped in some new matter or body.

§ 88. Secondary ideals embrace two species: 1. Such as are shaped in proper sensuous matter— *sense ideals;* and 2. Such as are shaped in proper spiritual or mental matter—*spiritual ideas.*

The human mind, then, it may be said in re-capitulation, is a communicating or interacting nature, and in the exercise of this function of communicating with other beings, as also with itself, on receiving an impression in the sensibility as the passive side in the interaction, at once exerts its active function of imagining in holding the impression. This is the first and lowest stage and form of this active function, simply holding, retaining. This is the essence and radical characteristic of memory as retentive. But the idea received in the impression or the sense is immediately embodied in the mind's own life; and then we have the second distinguishable stage or form of an act of the imagination. The idea received and retained in memory is invested with a new form; it exists in the mind modified more or less from its first character, the idea has become an ideal. Then still farther, the imagination as an ever active function and in its proper work of communicating or interacting, proceeds to put forth this ideal into a new body, whether in modes of the physical sense, as for instance in voice, or in proper spiritual investitures or forms of mind. And now the imagination branches out in directions and shapes of unlimited diversity as determined by the numberless occasions and uses of ordinary life or the higher uses of science and art. These diverse products and modifications of the imagination will be separately considered in the following chapters.

# CHAPTER X

§ 89. SENSE-IDEALS are products of *the imagination shaped in sensuous matter.*

We have recognized a twofold structure in the nervous constitution : one for receiving, the other for putting forth ideas, whether feelings, thoughts, or purposes; a twofold system of nerves: one *afferent*, otherwise called *sensory nerves*, bringing to the mind; the other *efferent*, otherwise called *motor nerves*, carrying from the mind. § 46.

The mode of connection between the mind and the material system of the brain and nerves is wholly wrapped in mystery; and we are utterly unable to explain either how the brain carries ideas to the mind or how the mind conveys outward its ideas through the brain. The keenest anatomy cannot discern the point of this connection. No science, indeed, can tell us whether the connection is at a single point or over an extended portion of the organism. It is accordingly entirely inexplicable how it is that one state of the mind, one ideal, should be followed by a motion of the hand, and another by that of the tongue or lips. All that we know is the simple fact, that we think, we imagine, we form ideals, and instantly the nervous organism reports the act and this or that nerve, this or that nervous center, this or that part of the brain responds. We know that excessive mental action, particularly excessive exertion of the imagination, by putting the brain, or some part or other of it, into movement, induces weariness, and, perhaps, disease and ultimately death; and that injury to the body—to the nerves, to the brain—reacts upon the mind and disturbs or even diseases its action. This mental action, at first affecting the brain proper, may ultimately reach the portions of the nervous system not immediately connected with the brain, as the ganglions or nervous centers from which nerves go out into the respiratory, the circulatory, the digestive systems of organs. A mere recollection, for instance, of some tragic scene, of some danger encountered, of some wrong done, sometimes suspends the breath, quickens the pulse, moves a sigh or a sob, disturbs all the alimentary functions. We have well authenticated records of the influence of fear or distress in changing the hair to white or gray in a single night.

§ 90. The affections of the sensuous organism by the sense-ideals vary indefinitely in kind or character, and also in degree.

They vary with the kind or character of the ideal itself. An ideal of a visible object, as of an orange, affects the brain and its nervous retinue

differently from an idea of a sound; an ideal of
a picture differently from that of an action. For
the most part, different parts of the brain, different
nerves, are brought into exercise in the different
cases.

They vary with the condition of the body and
particularly of the nervous organism. A diseased
body may make the imagination even of a generally agreeable object disagreeable or offensive.
The imagination of dainty food nauseates in sea-
sickness. We are credibly informed that a man
who had been wrapped when sick at sea in a
cloak, could not wear the cloak afterward on
land without the return of the nausea with which
it had been associated.

They vary in degree with the energy of the
imaging act, and also with the susceptibility of
the organism. A vivid imagination may quicken
the blood, suffuse the cheek, brighten the eye,
fill with animation the whole frame; while a dull
imagination, even when framing an ideal of the
same object, may not sensibly stir a fiber of the
body. A susceptible organism, too, moves quick
and strong from an ideal that would scarcely stir
a dull and gross sense.

§ 91. That mental activity of whatever kind is
attended by some change in the brain is a truth
beyond question. Mind and body constitute a
single organism and whatever affects one part or
member affects the whole. How they interact
with each other, science is unable to determine

with any exactness or assurance. Perhaps the most unobjectionable theory that can be devised to meet the difficulties in the case is that which assumes that the body is pervaded throughout by an energy or force with which the soul immediately interacts. The human will exerts itself on this energy or force and through it acts out on external nature. I will, thus, to bend my finger ; my volition acts upon this energy residing in the body, awakening it into action and directing also its movement ; and to this movement the finger responds in bending. This energy, thus pervading the body, with which the mind interacts and through which it effects results in the body itself and even in the external world to a certain extent, is of course none other than the universal force or energy that manifests itself in nature ; and as specifically excited in the bodily organism is known as nerve-force or neural energy. This theory is reconcilable with any view that may be taken of the nature of matter. It is also a theory that may conveniently be used in the generalization of nervous phenomena with little liability to error.

§ 92. Sense-ideals, like other mental states, while of course ever within the sphere of consciousness, are not always noticed by us. They may be too weak, too faint, to impress us so that we become distinctly conscious of them. Our mental life is made up to a very large extent of these unconscious workings of our imaginations within our sensuous organisms. Thoughts, feelings, purposes, live on in these ideals that take on their proper sense-form and direct the nerve movements of our nerves of which we take no notice, of which, perhaps, we are unable through the finiteness of our natures to take distinct notice. A strain of music, thus, will run, as we familiarly say, in our brains; we modulate our breath in answer, or our vocal organs respond, or our fingers, our feet, our bodies, move in rhythm. A picture will in the same way stir sympathetic imaginings which will at once, all unnoticed by us and uncontrolled, bring tears to the eye, or color to the cheek, or violent contractions to the muscles. Many of the phenomena of dreams find their solutions in this influence of the sense-ideals on the body as also on the mind.

These general statements of the reciprocal influence of the mind and the bodily organism we will illustrate by some well attested facts. They will be presented under the several classes of Phantoms; cases of Exalted Sensibility; and instances of Suspended Sensibility.

§ 93. 1. PHANTOMS.—*A phantom* is a sensation, produced not by an external object, but by an impression from the mind—from the imagination —or from the sensuous organism.

Here there is a real affection of the organism, but the cause is not from the exterior world but from the mind or the body itself. The impression on the organism is reported back to the mind

just as if the impression were from without;
and, therefore, it appears to the mind precisely
as if an external object had made the impression.

Sir David Brewster, in his letters on Natural
Magic, narrates the case of a lady of high character and intelligence, whose vivid imagination so
affected her nervous organism as to occasion
frequent and very striking illusions. She heard
unreal voices, as that of her husband calling her
by name to come to him, repeatedly, distinctly,
and loudly. One afternoon, on entering the
drawing-room, she saw, as she supposed, her husband standing before the fire and looking fixedly
at her. Supposing he was absorbed in thought,
she sat down within two feet of the figure. After
two or three minutes she asked him why he did
not speak to her. The form then moved off
toward the window at the further end of the
room and disappeared. The appearance was in
bright daylight, and lasted four or five minutes.
At another time, sitting with her husband in the
drawing-room, she called his attention to what
she supposed to be a cat. She pointed out to
him the place where the phantom was; called
the cat to her; when, trying to touch it, she followed it as it seemed to move away from her.
At another time she saw a favorite dog apparently
moving about the room, while she was holding
the real dog in her lap.

A similar case, equally well authenticated, is
that of a lady who, while seated by a table, saw

the figure of a man enter the door opposite, and move slowly toward her, and then distinctly heard him say that he was come from the spirit-world, charged with a message to her, which he then communicated, solemnly enjoining it upon her to do what was required. The form passed slowly by her around the table and vanished by the window on the opposite side of the room.

In these two cases, there had been disease which had affected the nervous sensibility. In each case the senses of sight and of hearing were both concerned.

Such spectral illusions are, in fact, not infrequent in fevers. The writer, in the approach of a febrile attack, at intervals when free from delirium, imagined the phials of the medicine closet in the room to be men and women of the most grotesque and fantastic shapes and movements. They seemed as real as the doorway and the shelves on which the phials stood. His nervous system, in some part, was affected just as such real objects would have affected it in order so to impress the mind.

The cases already instanced were cases of involuntary imagination. The late President Hitchcock, of Amherst College, relates his experience of similar illusions which, in part, and particularly at first, took place without any design or expectation of his, but in part and subsequently were occasioned and induced of express purpose. He was able, by bandaging his eyes and thus

9

entirely excluding the light, to bring before his
mental vision images of various kinds of objects
and scenes as distinctly and as vividly as if realities. Having thus covered his eyes on one occasion for the purpose of experiencing these visions,
he reported what passed before his view succes-
sively to one who took down the reports thus:
" The space around me is filled with huge rocks
moving past me in all modes, full of caverns, but
too dark to be well seen ; they hang over me now
and look splendidly ; some of them appear to be
serpentine. Some of these rocks seem a hundred
feet long. Against the side of a wall I see three
young ladies sitting and laughing ; lighted candles
are before them, and chains, machinery, etc.,
around them. I lie in a vast cavern ; the rocks
are rolling around me like clouds ; they are
within a foot of my face ; some are sandstone and
some granite. I have a glimpse into a large city ;
but a carriage-maker's yard, full of rubbish, almost
entirely obstructs my view." This is but a brief
extract from his account of these phenomena
which occurred during an attack of fever, in
which, however, there was no tendency to mental
derangement.

§ 94. 2. EXALTED SENSIBILITY. The sensibility sometimes exhibits extraordinary tenderness
and life. This occurs most strikingly when both
the bodily organism is unusually excitable and
the imagination is also unusually vigorous and
active. Well authenticated facts explain to us

much that might otherwise seem to be the effect of supernatural agency.

The case of Jane C. Rider, of Springfield, Mass., related by her physicians, is one of many, but one of remarkable interest. At intervals during several months, in a great variety of circumstances, she could, at night, or in a darkened room, and with her eyes closely bandaged, distinguish by her eye all ordinary objects presented to her. She at one time read, with her eyes thus bandaged, audibly and correctly, with some hesitation, however, at the most difficult words, nearly a whole page from a small volume handed her. The distinguished physicians, who observed and narrated the case, correctly ascribe the result to " the combined effect of two causes; first, increased sensibility of the retina, in consequence of which objects were rendered visible in comparative darkness; and, secondly, a high degree of excitement in the brain itself, enabling the mind to perceive even a confused image of the object." We must interpret " the excitement in the brain enabling the mind to perceive a confused image," here spoken of, as not in the body, but in the mind itself, whose imaginative function was in a state of exalted vigor.

The most frequent exemplifications of this state of exalted sensibility occur in cases of fever and of *delirium tremens.* The power of the imagination over the nerves in this last named disease is almost incredibly great. Robust, stout-

hearted men, even men who had seemed hardened
and callous to every impression, reckless and fear-
less of everything, in this disease see visions and
hear sounds that only the pit of despair can
know as realities, and strong frames sink down
rapidly to death under the horrors of an excited
and uncontrolled imagination.

§ 94. 3. SUSPENDED SENSIBILITY. The more
normal and familiar phenomena of this class occur
in ordinary sleep. The characteristic feature of
sleep is the partial suspension of the reciprocal
action of the mind and the body on each other.
This suspension, in healthy sleep at least, is
never entire. As sleep comes on, one sense after
another in quick succession becomes inactive.
The order varies; but the hearing and the touch
are generally the last to sink into repose. Commonly the nerves of sensation and the nerves of
motion cease their functions almost simultaneously. The eyelids droop, the head sinks, the
limbs drop to some external support, while, nearly
at the same time, the taste, the smell, and the sight
first, and then the hearing and the touch, suspend all communication between the soul and
external things. All the vital functions, nevertheless, as those of respiration, circulation, nutrition, secretion, and absorption, go on as in wakefulness. The heart, however, beats slower, and
the breath is less rapid, and in early life absorption and nutrition are more active. The brain

collapses from the diminished flow of blood into it.

Sleep is more or less profound, the suspension of the connection between mind and body is more or less complete in different persons and also in different conditions, internal or external, of the same person.

Facts abundantly show that one sense may be fully awake while others are asleep. A nurse, watching the sick, will wake on hearing the striking of the clock, or on hearing the slightest call of the patient. Erasmus relates of his friend Oporinus, a celebrated professor and printer of Basle, that after a wearisome journey with a bookseller, he undertook in the evening at the inn to read aloud a manuscript about which they had been conversing during the journey. The bookseller discovered after a time that Oporinus was asleep while he was reading. A like experience has repeatedly befallen the writer. Once, after an exhausting journey by night and day, he undertook to read to others a long document of much value and interest with which he had become familiar during his journey. He fell asleep, but continued reading till, after a page or two, the hand which held the manuscript dropped and awakened him. At other times he read from books which were new to him. The sight in these cases remained awake, as also the motor-nerves concerned in reading, while other senses were asleep. Sir William Hamilton relates the case

of a postman who daily traversed, on foot, the
route between Halle and a town some eight miles
distant. Over a part of the route which lay
through a meadow, he generally slept ; but on
coming to a narrow foot-bridge, which was to be
reached by some broken steps, he uniformly
awoke. Soldiers, it has been often observed,
wearied by a long march, sleep while their feet
move on as when they were awake.

§ 96. DREAMING is a familiar phenomenon of
sleep. Ordinarily we include in the notion of
a dream that of a connection between mind and
body, reciprocally acting upon each other. But
a right explanation of this interesting phenomenon involves the truth of the continued activity
of the mind even in what we call profound and
perfect sleep. The mind, as we have seen, is essentially active. To cease its activity, for it, is
to die, since action is its very life. The life of
the body even ceases when all action in it ceases,
when circulation and respiration and secretion and
absorption cease. Certain modes of thought or
feeling may be suspended ; but to conceive of all
thought and feeling and willing as stopping is to
conceive of an extinct soul. There is no evidence
that the mind wholly suspends its action in the
profoundest sleep. That we cannot recall the
thoughts we may have had in sleep does not
prove that we did not think. Let one give himself to musing for a half-day, letting his mind
rove uncontrolled in any direction and toward

any object that may offer; he will, in all probability, be unable at the close to recall one in a
hundred of the objects that have flitted before
his mind. The mind is active when it loses itself, as we say, in sleep—when it falls asleep; it
is active when it recovers itself to wakefulness; it
certainly is sometimes active during sleep, as
what we can recall of our dreams evinces; who
can suppose it ceases action in sound, undream-
ing sleep, more than in those wakeful hours, the
flying thoughts of which wholly escape our recollection? We say loosely we are not conscious of
thinking or feeling during our sleep. If we mean
that the mind was not conscious when acting,
this is to mistake utterly the essential attribute
of mind which is by its very nature conscious of all
its own action. If we mean that we are not now
conscious that we had any feeling or thought
while we slept, then we mean only that we are
unable now to recollect—to bring into our present
consciousness the fact that we thus thought or
felt. Still further, there are curious facts which
make this supposition, that the mind may be
active, and therefore consciously active, even during the profoundest sleep, extremely probable.
There are many well accredited facts showing that the mind not only acts in sleep in
ways that of itself it is utterly unable to recall, but
also sometimes acts with an energy and intensity beyond what it ever knows in wakeful hours.
A mathematician, who had long labored in vain

to solve a mathematical problem, one morning found the solution on his table. He had risen in his sleep and worked out the solution, but of the operation he had no recollection, and the only evidence that could convince him of his dream-work was the paper on his table. Franklin was wont to find in the morning political questions that had tasked his wakeful hours the day before clearly resolved in his mind. Coleridge dreamed out his poem, " Kubla Khan," while asleep in his chair. He wrote out from recollection immediately on waking what appears of the poem in his works, but being interrupted lost the power to recall the rest, which he yet believed he had fully composed in his dream to the extent of three or four times what he had written.

Dr. Carpenter, in his mental physiology, relates an occurrence which proves not only that the mind may be capable of more intense activity in sleep than in wakefulness, but also that a protracted mental operation of the highest character may take place in sleep of which no adequate recollection survives on waking. A man was called to compose a discourse for public delivery on a set occasion. He gave himself to the effort, and the evening before the appointment was to be met, he had composed something, but lay down utterly disgusted with his performance. He fell asleep and dreamed of a novel method of handling his subject. When waking he rose to commit his new thoughts to paper, but found to his astonishment on opening his desk, that they were already written out, the ink being hardly dry.

Of the greatly increased activity of mind sometimes experienced in sleep, we have indeed manifold illustrations. The following may be added to the instances already given : A person, aroused from sleep by some water sprinkled on his face, dreamed of the events of an entire life before coming to full wakefulness. There is an accredited record of an officer awakened by the morning gun, who dreamed of hearing an alarm-call to battle, of rising, equipping himself, going to the field, marshaling his men, engaging in a long and doubtful battle and of driving the enemy from the field, every step as orderly and as complete as if all real, yet dreaming through all this before the reverberations of the gun had died away on his ear. De Quincy says of his mental activity in his dreams that he sometimes seemed to have lived seventy or a hundred years in a single night.

The mind, thus, never in sleep entirely dropping its activity, is more or less in sympathetic connection with the body. A patient in a hospital in France, who had lost a portion of the scalp and of the skull, thereby exposing the movements of the brain, was observed in calm sleep to exhibit a motionless brain, but in a sleep disturbed by dreams to be in proportionate agitation. It would be rash to infer from the apparently motionless brain in calm sleep that the mind itself was also inactive ; but the agitation of the brain at times evinces the fact of the continued interaction of mind and body in sleep. This motion in the brain occasioned by the mental action, may take place interiorly so as not to show itself at all on the surface ; it may extend throughout the entire structure of the brain ; it may extend farther into the nerves that issue from the brain ; it may reach a part or the whole of the entire nervous organism. This may depend on the nature of the mental activity. Dreams often occasion movements of hands and feet ; sometimes of the organs of speech. A dream of fright will occasion sudden convulsive bodily movements, as if to avert or escape danger. Dreams often occasion sighs and groans and outcries of alarm, or smiles and audible laughter. Some persons talk frequently in their sleep. Conversation with them can sometimes be carried on to some considerable length. The writer knew a student in college who acquired the art of leading his room-mate when asleep to translate his Greek lessons for him night after night. An English officer was led in his dreams by his companions, who were aware of his peculiarities, to go through the whole process of a duel, and was awakened only by the report of the pistol which he fired in the supposed combat.

The bodily organism acts upon the mind during sleep, as does the mind upon the body, in modes and degrees variously modified. A bright light brought into the room where one is sleeping, or a noise or a touch, there is reason to believe, often influences the mind and shapes the dream. Dr. Gregory having placed a bottle of hot water at his feet dreamed of going to Mount Etna and of extreme heat. In the same way the disturbance of the vital functions, or any pain in the body, often occasions distressful dreams. A posture of constraint in which the mind becomes conscious of inability to command the muscles, gives rise to incubus or nightmare. The mind, conscious of this inability to move for defense or for escape from the danger which the constrained posture of the body had occasioned, suffers the extreme anguish and horror of one in real danger from which he sees no way of extricating himself. He is in the mental condition of one whose limbs are inextricably entangled in the burning wreck of a railway train, and who sees the flames steadily and irresistibly moving upon him.

§ 97. Besides the normal phenomena of suspended sensibility in sleep, there are the abnormal states of *catalepsy* and *somnambulism*.

In CATALEPSY, the subject seems like one in quiet sleep, with regular pulse and respiration, but beyond the reach of all the ordinary excitants from sleep. Intense flashings of light on the eyes, loud noises, pungent odors, punctures of the skin, shakings of the body, severe blows and bruises, prove of no avail to restore to wakefulness. A variety of this affection is *ecstasy*, occasioned often by religious excitement. In these cases the mind continues active, although the connection with the senses is more or less suspended. Sometimes only a part of the nerves seem to lose their functions, as is shown in the case of persons who have been supposed to have died under these paroxysms and have been laid out for burial, who yet continued conscious of all that passed and on recovery repeated what was said by the attendants. More frequently, however, the memory fails to recall what has passed during the attack. Yet radical and permanent changes of disposition and character, as from dissoluteness and irreligion to soberness and piety, which are known to have attended these experiences, show that, although impossible to be recalled, there must have been clear, strong thoughts, deep feelings, decided purposes.

§ 98. SOMNAMBULISM is a form of partially suspended sensibility, combined with more or less exalted susceptibility in some of the senses, and particularly with a controlling activity of the intellect and will, reaching to the bodily functions. This is indeed the special characteristic feature of somnambulism, distinguishing it from dreaming and from catalepsy; the somnambulist prominently manifests a use of the bodily organs for some set purpose or object. In dreaming, the control of will is relatively dormant; the mind is floated along hither and thither without guidance of its own. In catalepsy the mind may exercise its reason and its will, forming purposes that shall be permanent and govern the future life, but its action does not go out into the bodily movements. In somnambulism this last is the characteristic feature. The somnambulist is "a dreamer who is able to act his dreams." He rises from his bed and walks the street, or climbs to the top of the house, passes quickly along dangerous ways, or delivers an harangue, or recites poetry, or works out mathematical problems, or executes works of art. The affection proceeds from a highly excitable nervous organization, which may be stimulated either by some mental act or by some affection of the bodily system either in ordinary health or in disease, or even by artificial appliances.

Many instances of this phenomenon are on record. They have been noted from the earliest times; they were described by the ancient Greeks. As we should suppose beforehand, they are diversely modified. The mental activity is sometimes most marvelously stimulated so as to transcend all ordinary experience; sometimes it is only of the most usual degree; sometimes one function of the sensibility is suspended while another is exalted to an extraordinary degree, or, it may be, remains only of the usual energy; sometimes the experience during the somnambulistic attack is remembered as in dreams; sometimes it is beyond recollection while in the normal condition, but it may be revived again fresh and vivid when the attack recurs, so that the subject seems to live two lives, remembering in the normal state only what has occurred in that state, and in the somnambulistic state only what has passed in that.

Several cases will be cited to illustrate these general characteristics. The Archbishop of Bordeaux relates that a young ecclesiastic was in the habit of getting up night after night, and, while giving conclusive evidences of being asleep, going to his room, taking pen, ink, and paper, and composing sermons. When the Archbishop placed a piece of pasteboard between his eyes and the paper, he wrote on, not seeming to be incommoded in the least.

Gassendi reports that a somnambulist used to rise and dress himself in his sleep, go down to the cellar and draw wine from a cask, seeming to see in the dark as well as in full daylight. He answered questions that were put to him. In the morning he recollected nothing of what had passed.

Colquhoun relates that a young woman of twenty years of age frequently passed from a state of proper catalepsy into that of somnambulism. She sat up on the bed and spoke with an unusual liveliness and cheerfulness, and in continuation of what she had spoken in her previous fit. She would then sing and laugh, spring out of bed, pass round the room, dexterously shunning anything in her way, then return to her bed and sink into the cataleptic state. All means tried to awaken her were ineffectual, such as burning a taper close before her eyes, pouring brandy and hartshorn into her eyes and mouth, blowing snuff into her nostrils, pricking her with needles, wrenching her fingers, touching the ball of her eye with a feather and even with the finger. When informed of what she had done, she manifested deep mortification, but never could recollect anything that had occurred.

Cloquet reported to the French Academy the case of a lady who, having been thrown into somnambulism by some artificial means, had an ulcerated cancer removed without manifesting the slightest sensibility. She was kept in the somnambulistic state for forty-eight hours, and so completely that when she awoke she had no idea of the operation till she was informed of it. She talked during the attack calmly and freely about the operation when it was proposed to her, notwithstanding she had shrunk with horror from it when awake, quietly prepared herself for it, conversed with the operator during the operation, without any motion of limb or feature, or any change of respiration or of pulse evincing that she was sensible of pain.

In Massachusetts, some years since, a girl of fourteen years of age, of a nervous temperament, but without any extraordinary intelligence, after having fallen asleep in the day time, would rise from her chair and deliver a sermon, which she introduced by the usual religious services, as if to a large audience. These discourses, which far transcended in mental power her wakeful ability, she would deliver day after day or on alternate days, without repetition, however, of thought or language.

Another interesting case of somnambulism is that of a young lady who became a competitor in a school in which prizes had been offered for the best paintings. As she returned in the morning to her work, she repeatedly observed that additions beyond her own skill had been made to the painting. She charged her companions with the interference, and when they denied it she took precautions to prevent further interference with her work. Her own movements were now watched, and she was seen to rise in sound sleep, dress herself, go to her table and work on her painting. The prize was given to her, but she was loth to receive it, as she insisted that the work was not her own.

# CHAPTER XI.

§ 99. SPIRITUAL IDEALS *are products of the imagination shaped in the mind's own furniture.*

It is not improbable that any mental activity may, from its mysterious alliance with the body, draw in with it also some movements of the bodily organization. But it is clear that we may conceive of a purely mental act separated from all sensuous elements. Such a mental act as formed in the mind by the imagination is a spiritual ideal.

§ 100. These ideals are all formed out of the mind's own possessions—out of the stock of thoughts, feelings, and purposes which it has in itself.

They are not made from nothing. Their variety, richness, greatness, depend on the growth and the attainments of the individual mind. A child's ideas are simple, narrow, meager, compared with those of a mature, cultivated mind.

Of this stock of material out of which the imagination forms its ideals it will be important to obtain a fuller and clearer understanding. If one were to be asked in regard to a journey he had

10

made during a preceding year, he would be able
to answer so as to convey some idea of it; as, we
will assume, in what month he set out; how long
he was gone; what places he visited; what objects and scenes most interested him.    All these
ideas of his journey which he thus communicates
in his answer are the products of his imagination,
which, entering into the stock of his recollections,
shapes its ideals out of them.    These ideals thus
formed    go    out,    as    he    communicates    them,
through the sensual organism in sounds, in words,
which the inquirer on receiving them garners into
his stock of ideas or mental possessions.    This
complex act of taking out of the stores of the
mind's ideas such as would meet the demands of
the inquiry and of shaping them in ideals to be
then expressed in words, Sir William Hamilton
with a nice analysis has explained as involving
the exertion of a threefold faculty, (1) the *memory* proper, the retentive or conservative power
by which the mind retains its ideas; (2) the *reproductive* power by which the mind calls forth
what was lying dormant in memory; and (3) the
*representative* power by which the mind holds up
before itself the ideas which it has reproduced
from memory.    Whatever may be thought of the
propriety of recognizing these faculties—retention, reproduction, and representation—as faculties of the intelligence, it is clear that we have
this threefold phenomenon to recognize and explain; first, we have the fact that the mind re-

tains its ideas; secondly, that out of such retained ideas it frequently calls forth this or that for its use; and thirdly, that it shapes such recalled ideas into new forms for communication to others or for its own study. It is obvious, moreover, that the retention and the reproduction into present consciousness of ideas are the two necessary conditions of representing or imagining. We shall therefore in order consider these two conditions of ideals—memory and reproduction—in separate chapters, reserving for a distinct chapter some additional explanation of the imagination itself as an idealizing power.

§ 101. It remains to be observed that these spiritual ideals are not only shaped out of the mind's own stock of ideas, but are also shaped in them.

The recollections of a journey shape themselves very differently at different times. If one has observed the Parthenon of Athens, and should in after years recall and represent his idea of it retained from the impressions made upon his mind at the time of observing, his account of it would be different in some particulars, if given the first year after his return, from that which he would give the tenth. Some details would in this latter instance have slipped out of his ideal; the others would be more or less differently arranged, and the several features would stand out in different degrees of prominence relatively to the others. His account, and consequently his ideal, more-

over, would vary with the design or end for which
he recalled it. To describe the Parthenon to a
child, he would shape his ideal in one way; to a
cultivated artist, his description would set forth
his ideal shaped in quite another way. But in
every case his imagination shapes its product in
the mental furniture of the time. It is outlined
in existing feelings, thoughts, and intuitions. It
is not only outlined in them and bounded out in
and by them, it is also colored by them. His ideal
will be at one time glowing with the feeling which
transports him at the time of describing; at another, it will be dull and dim, as his mind at the
time is heavy and clouded. The same idea of the
Parthenon thus will be embodied in the varying
experiences of the hour and assume a form corresponding to them. The character of the ideal, the
distinctness of its outline, the perfectness, the
completeness, and the richness of the rendering,
will also vary with the vigor of the imagination
at the time and with the design for which it acts.

# CHAPTER XII.

## MEMORY.

§ 102. BY MEMORY, in its stricter sense, is meant simply *the retentive attribute of mind.*

The best view to take of memory is to regard it as the holding on of a feeling, a thought, or a purpose in the continuous life of the soul. § 13. Every impression made upon it abides in its effect; every thinking act continues, never becoming extinct; every choice and purpose likewise remains a part of the mind's ceaseless activity. We may as well suppose that matter or force can be annihilated as that the effect of force can die out utterly; and so we may as well suppose that the mind or a part of it may die out, as that its action, any movement it may experience either from the impressions of other forces or from its own prompting, may utterly cease to be. We easily enough accept the truth that strong feelings, momentous thoughts, decisive purposes of our lives, may live on forever; we cannot with any consistency hesitate to believe that less important acts of our minds also live on. If a great thought has a life that reaches through the entire life of the mind, every lesser thought must have the same perpetuity. The single drop, as well as the great tributary, remains in the swelling river. The great tributary of thought is in fact made up of the little drops of experience, and cannot be without them.

The impossibility of recalling all the transient thoughts of past years, does not disprove this supposition of the continuance of every thought and feeling. This impossibility is to be attributed to the limited power of the human mind to recognize the minute parts of its experience, not to the annihilation of those experiences. The originally clear stream of the Mississippi receives into its volume the whitish, muddy waters of the Missouri, then the greenish, muddy Ohio, and then the reddish, muddy streams of the Arkansas and Red rivers. For a little space each tributary maintains its separate integrity so far that it may be distinguished ; but as the augmented stream rolls on, the waters intermix more and more, till in the lower course of the river the several discolorations seem to our limited vision to be all blended into one mass of turbid color. But each particle, it is conceivable, can by an infinite mind be traced back to its source, and the whole volume of water in the channel is what has come into it from these separate sources. In this case, indeed, some of the original supply is wasted into the air by evaporation, by diversion into little lakes, by use for irrigation or other purposes ; but in the great current of the mind's activity, nothing can be supposed to be thus wasted. All that has entered the stream, the contribution of every minute transient experience, remains to swell and to characterize it.

In the strictest truth memory in the largest and fullest sense is nothing else than the whole soul itself regarded as form. In other words, it is the entire mental nature with all its existing modifications by reason of growth and habit, being the full and complete abiding body of all its exerted activities and received impressions regarded as that which may be contemplated by itself or may impress other minds. In the narrower sense, it is the abiding form of any special act or affection of the mind, whether thought, feeling, or purpose. It cannot be regarded as a special function, certainly, if the term be employed to denote the retentive capacity of the soul ; for all states of the soul are retained alike, feelings and purposes as well as thoughts. Much less can it be regarded as a subordinate function of the intelligence ; it is in no respect a cognitive function in any other sense than it is likewise a special function of the sensibility or of the will. We may be conscious indeed of existing mental states which are mere continued activities or affections that had begun to be in the past. In the same way we feel such states and they are the objects of our volitions. We grieve over a mistake or blunder of yesterday ; we purpose to avoid it in the future. Intelligence or consciousness enters, it is true, into such feelings and purposes; for the whole soul is present in every special act and affection. The consciousness of a mental state which is the result or renewal of a previous experience is also equally attended by feeling and will. If we mean by a state of consciousness or intelligence, of feeling, or of will, simply a mental state that is characterized, either in itself or in our view of it, by a predominance of one or the other of those several functional activities, then it is true of each of these functions alike that their acts or affections are all remembered on the one hand, and on the other hand all these several functions, one as well as another, go forth alike toward these remembered acts or affections. It leads to serious mistake thus to confound memory generally with consciousness of memory—recollecting with consciousness of recollecting. The error is occasioned, perhaps, by the fact that when an appeal is addressed to the memory by ourselves or by another—as when we are asked whether we remember a past experience—in order to an answer we must recall the experience into distinct consciousness, that is, into our intelligence; and thus giving the answer involves a predominant and characteristic exercise of the intelligence—of consciousness. But just so if we are asked whether we continue to feel grief over yesterday's mistake, we must, in order to an affirmative answer, bring up the present grief over the mistake into consciousness. But the grief, because retained and therefore capable of being noticed in consciousness, does not become characteristically a form of the intelligence. It is a state of consciousness only in that broader and looser import of the term in which the term *consciousness* comprehends the entire activity of the soul, including feeling and purpose as well as intelligence;—in which, in other words, it comprehends all that of which we may be conscious, all the experiences of the mind as well as the proper consciousness itself—the intelligent notice —of this.

The great law of mind in relation to its power of retaining—its function of memory—may accordingly be thus stated :—

§ 103. EVERY FEELING, EVERY THOUGHT, EVERY CHOICE, ABIDES IN THE MIND.

The proofs of this principle of memory may be summarily exhibited as follows :

1. The presumption is that every action of the mind continues. It may not continue entirely unmodified ; its form may change ; it may exist as cause or in its effect ; it may be now more or less connected with one mental experience and then with another; it may be variously colored or shaped thus in the progress of experience. But as we must believe that everything that is, continues, unless we have some reason for believing that it has ceased to be, and as there is no such reason for supposing our mental action to

dic out utterly, we must accept the law of the deathlessness of memory as valid.

2. Analogy confirms this view. Matter, we believe, is never annihilated; force is never annihilated; motion, the effect of force, is never annihilated; we conclude that, unless something can be shown to destroy the analogy, mind and its action continue. Matter changes its form; force changes its direction and also its form; one motion passes into other motion, as the motion of gravity or of the mass passes into the motion of cohesion and repulsion, the motion of atoms; but with change of form each continues. The quantity of matter in the universe, the quantity of force, the aggregate of the quantities of motion remain the same. At least created things have no power to destroy their own being or their own essential attributes. We are led thus to believe that mental activity once originated abides in some form, positive or negative, as long as the mind itself exists; that every feeling, thought, and purpose hold on and are retained in the mind's being.

3. Facts from ordinary experience strengthen these arguments from presumption and from analogy. It frequently happens that little circumstances, which we should have supposed were too trivial to be retained in memory, reappear in our thoughts, called forth by some association perhaps strange to us. Objects which we have seen, words which we have heard from

others, or had uttered ourselves, that had all
vanished from our consciousness, somehow come
up into our thoughts afresh. In old age little
circumstances that occurred in childhood are recalled with a freshness and a vividness that seem
surprising. Sometimes all the great experiences
of middle life have faded out from the memory
of the old, while the scenes of childhood are
revived, and are lived over in recollection with
wonderful exactness and fullness. In the same
way, too, that which we have dreamed and
which had so lightly impressed us that we did
not recall it when we waked, returns, months or
years after, it may be, in second dreams that recall even the little details of the first. Still further, we have the great fact that thoughts and
feelings and dispositions are perpetually coursing
through our minds, which could appear there
only as the retained acts of previous life. These
thoughts and feelings may not come up, and for
the most part do not come up, into distinct consciousness one by one. But there is a volume
of thought that is retained from the past, streaming along and shaping and coloring our present
thought. We meet, for example, an old friend
in the street after a long absence ; thoughts, feelings, scenes, objects, pleasures, sorrows, plans,
hopes, actions, that have lain buried for years
out of conscious thought, pour through our
minds. In truth, every thought we have must
be affected more or less by every thought we

have ever had, really, although it may be imperceptibly to our finite vision. The little boat that floats on the broad bosom of the great river near its mouth, is sustained in its part by every drop that has come into the stream from the most distant little spring from the other side of the continent. We are unable to discern any lifting of the water except for a few inches from the boat that presses down into the stream and so displaces the water around it. But every drop at the remotest bank is displaced according to its relations, and every drop on the bottom of the channel feels its part of the pressure.

One of the most decisive proofs of this great law of the perpetuity of our mental experiences is found in the familiar fact of *being turned round*, as it is called. We enter a strange place without having observed a turn we have made in our course. We have been going on a road leading northward, for example, and, without noticing it, we have turned into one leading eastward; this road will seem to us afterward as if leading northward: the sun seems to us to rise in the south. We reason against the impression but the first impression resists evidence and argument. If our intelligence is corrected, often our governing impulses follow the first impression whenever we are off our guard. If we are thus turned round in a strange city, we may move aright through one or two streets while we are guarding ourselves against being

misled by the feeling; but as soon as we sur-
render our movements to the control of our
governing determinations, we turn north when
we should go east. It is marvelous with what
presistence such impressions in regard to the
points of the compass abide in the mind. The
writer has known of an instance when such an
erroneous impression remained fresh and strong
for many years, and, although the street was
traversed several times a day, still remained so
vigorous and strong as to require habitual care
and watchfulness to prevent mistake.

4. Facts of extraordinary experience confirm
in our minds the conviction that what is once
experienced by the mind is ever retained by it.

In insanity it is often observed that thoughts
are recalled which, both before and after the
attack, were beyond all power of recollection.
These retained thoughts, also, reappear with a
marvelous freshness and completeness. The
records of hospitals for the insane are replete
with instances of mental activity stored with
thoughts and feelings and volitions from past
experience that have so outmeasured the seeming capacity of the mind in a sound state as to
be well-nigh incredible. A gentleman in an
insane retreat, says Dr. Rush, astonished every-
body with his displays of oratory; and a lady,
he writes, sang hymns and songs of her own
composition so perfect that he used to hang
upon them with delight whenever he visited her,

and yet she had never shown a talent for poetry
or music in any previous part of her life.

In fever, also, similar facts are frequently oc-
curring.  The Countess de Laval was wont in
sickness to talk in her sleep in a language that the
servants could not understand.  A nurse from her
native province, Brittany, being engaged to attend her, however, recognized the strange speech
as her native tongue.  Yet when awake the
Countess did not understand a word of Breton,
so entirely had it seemingly passed from her recollection.

Coleridge narrates a similar case of an illiterate
young woman of four or five and twenty, who in
a nervous fever was heard to talk in Latin, Greek,
and Hebrew.  The matter excited great interest
and on a protracted and thorough investigation
it was ascertained that at the age of nine years
she had been taken in charity into the house of a
learned pastor where she remained some years
until his death.  This pastor had been accustomed to walk up and down a passage of his
house into which the kitchen-door opened and
to read aloud from his favorite books in these
learned languages.  Sheets full of her utterances
were taken down from her lips; they had no
connection with one another, yet each sentence
was complete and coherent with itself.  It was
discovered thus that these recitations of her
master from languages utterly unknown to her
had been retained so perfectly that even after the

lapse of years, in the excitement of the sensibility in fever, she was able to render them distinctly and perfectly.

The experiences of persons recovered when near being drowned are in evidence here. They frequently say that the events of their whole lives pass in clear, distinct, full review before them. A case narrated by the subject to the author is a sufficient exemplification. He had been entrusted with the keeping of a package of valuable papers by a relative when about taking a long journey. On the return of his friend, he was utterly unable to recall where he had placed the package. The most diligent and careful search as well as every effort of recollection failed to discover the desired package. Years after when bathing, he was seized with cramp and sank. He rose and sank again ; and, as he was just sinking the third time, a companion succeeded in reaching and rescuing him. During the momentary interval between his disappearance the third time and his being seized by his companion, his whole life in its minute incidents passed in review before his mind; and among them the fact of his secreting the package and the place where he had concealed it. He proceeded immediately to the spot, where he found, just as he had placed it, what he had so long sought in vain.

A singular case of catalepsy, cited by Hamilton from a German work by Abel, is also in evidence that men's forgetfulness is not decisive proof against this perpetuity of mental experiences. In this case a young man, some six minutes after falling asleep, would begin to speak distinctly and almost always of the same objects and connected events, so that he carried on from night to night the same history. On awakening he had no remembrance whatever of his dreaming thoughts. Thus it was that by day he was the poor apprentice of a merchant; while by night he was a married man, the father of a family, a senator, and in affluent circumstances. If during his vision any thing was said to him in regard to what occurred to him during the waking state, he would declare that it was all a dream.

While memory proper has for its essential attribute this character of retentiveness, it must be borne in mind that it is the retentiveness of an active nature. It is not the retentiveness of a rock or of steel that may retain the lines which may have been inscribed upon them. It is not the retentiveness of a vessel or cell that retains what has been poured in or packed away in it. It is not the retentiveness of an animal organ that retains the disposition of fibers or of cells which it may in any way have received. It is the retentiveness of an enduring active being, which not only receives impressions according to its own active nature, but uses these impressions afterwards more or less in all its ceaseless action.

Memory is to be conceived of as something

more than a mere capability to recall past experiences. At least an empty capability of recollection does not express the full truth. These past experiences live on in a true sense and are active parts of the present mental being. The man of learning, of achievement, of suffering, is more than a being capable of recalling his past thoughts and deeds and trials. These experiences have entered into his soul and have enlarged and strengthened it; whether any one or more of them are distinctly in his present consciousness or not, he is more and different because of them; his words, his steps, all he does, evinces a fullness of power, a mode and form of movement, a character in short altogether different from a nature that had not had these experiences. The adult man differs from the child in something more than a mere capability of bringing into his consciousness certain things of the past. His consciousness is a capability, a power indeed, but a capability, a power replete with knowledge, with skill, with passion.

§ 104. This law of retentiveness in mind as an active nature imposes three conditions of a good memory. They are founded respectively in the subject-matter of remembrance—in what is to be remembered; in the relation of each thing remembered to other things in the mind; and in the character of mind itself.

§ 105. 1. The first condition of a good memory is that it accept as what it is to retain, so far as

11

possible, only what the mind may need or wish to use.

The mind, as we have seen, is subject to impressions from without, beyond its control. It has consequently feelings, thoughts, and volitions, which it could not altogether prevent. But it has nevertheless a power to a large extent both to regulate the kind of impressions to which it will allow itself to be open, and still more to shape them when received to its own uses. Now, nothing can be more important to all the great ends of memory, which is to retain forever for future use and influence upon the mind every feeling and thought and desire and purpose, than that just the right impressions, the right feelings, the right thoughts, the right volitions, should enter the memory. No feeling or thought or intention which we do not feel willing to have ever confronting us, ever shaping and coloring our destiny, ever present in our soul's very being, and working in us and on us whether we are conscious of it or not, whether we are willing or not, should, if it lie in our power to prevent it, ever be allowed to enter our minds. If any such impression comes upon us, then should it be so controlled and shaped as that ever afterward when it reappears it shall be in a welcome form, and shall when we are unconscious of it be silently influencing our whole mental action favorably. Our observations, our readings, our reflections, our reveries even, should be such as will fill our memories with nothing but what we shall in every moment of our subsequent lives be glad to find there. The scenes, the objects, the associates, the books, all the occasions of our feeling and acting should be carefully regulated with this view and under this momentous consideration, that what they bring into our minds is to remain in us perpetually.

Particularly does this characteristic of a good memory—good for the mind's uses—prescribe that our observations and our thoughts be accurate and true, as we would not have falsehood or error to mar all our coming thought.

It prescribes, also, that our feelings and acts should be in the most perfect form into which our imaginations can shape impressions or suggestions; that every recurring thought and imagination may shed the radiance of beauty on all our inward experience. A feeling of pain, thus, that a stroke of malice has inflicted, may continue to exist in our minds to color more or less their whole future, according as our imagination, reacting on the received impression, invests the pain in a form of forgiveness and of pity, or of bitter resentment. Thus it may be with all impressions which in themselves may be undesirable. They may be put in forms that shall never recur but to gladden and refresh us.

It prescribes, moreover, that all our intentions, our plans, our endeavors, and all other voluntary acts should be just and right, so that none shall

in all the future of our being be present in our
minds to disturb, to annoy, or to bring righteous
retribution of evil of any kind upon us.

§ 106. 2. The second condition of a good memory is that it so link in every fresh experience with
past acts and feelings, as to make it most easily
to be recalled, and to work most serviceably for
all that the mind can properly desire.

The importance of observing this principle in
the culture of the memory will be more fully
seen when the nature and laws of association are
explained. This will be the topic of the next
chapter.

§ 107. 3. The third condition of a good memory is that it enlist a lively energy of the whole
mind in its interest.

What is to be preferably remembered, what is
to be present with us when we may happen specially to need it, what is to influence greatly all
our future thought and feeling, should receive
the most of the mind's vigor and strength.
What we receive listlessly, while it may in a
sense abide with us, can influence us but little,
can be little at our command in the time of need.
What engages our interest deeply and vividly we
retain best for use and service.

§ 108. Under the great principle of memory
that every act and feeling abides forever in the
mind's active nature, in its degree and way shaping and coloring all its movements, we have thus

the three specific rules of memory that have been stated :

1. That, so far as may be, only true thoughts, beautiful imaginings, good intentions and endeavors enter our memories.

2. That all fresh acts and feelings be properly associated with existing thoughts and feelings ; and

3. That what we wish to be most ready and serviceable in our memories engage at the time the mind's utmost interest, attention, and care.

# CHAPTER XIII.

## MENTAL REPRODUCTION.

§ 109. MENTAL REPRODUCTION, or, as it is familiarly named, Recollection, is formally defined as *the re-awakening in the present consciousness of acts or feelings abiding in the mind from some previous experience.*

It is a law of mind, generalized from abundant particular observations, that any act or affection once experienced may in the possibility of things be revived in the consciousness. The ground of the possibility of such re-awakening is found in the fact of the abiding nature of mental activity and affection. § 11. The re-awakening is but the calling out into distinct consciousness of what is still a part of the activity of the mind, abiding from some previous experience.

§ 110. Mental reproduction is either spontaneous or voluntary.

Spontaneous reproduction takes place as perhaps the more characteristic element in what is known under the familiar name of *Reverie.* It is a common characteristic of the mental state in dreaming. § 96.

In reverie the mind surrenders itself with no

conscious control to its own current, so to speak, allowing thought and feeling to flow on according to their own tendency. In this state we discover, as we reproduce it for study into our thought, that one thought is followed by another, one feeling by another, and thought is followed by feeling, as well as feeling by thought. The interesting question arises, what determines this suggestion of one mental state by another. "Therein," says one, "lies the greatest mystery of all philosophy." This mystery psychologists have sought to explain by indicating the general principles or laws of reproduction or suggestion, otherwise called the laws of the *association of ideas*.

That there is some bond of connection, that there is some ground of association, psychologists have admitted or assumed. These thoughts and feelings that pass along through the mind one after another, they agree, do not come haphazard; they succeed one another under some governing law.

It may be remarked here that beyond all reasonable question the succession of thoughts and feelings in dreams and in insanity, is similar to the succession in reverie, and with some modifications is subject to the same laws.

From the earliest times philosophers have presented, one after another, each his own enumeration of the laws of association. Sir William Hamilton has gathered up these proposed principles and reduced them all to the following classes.

Thoughts are associated, he says, in the respective opinions of these philosophers, 1, if connected in time ; 2, if adjoining in space ; 3, if related as cause and effect, as means and ends, or as whole and part ; 4, if similar or in contrast ; 5, if products of the same mental power, or of different powers conversant with the same object ; 6, if the objects of the thoughts are the sign and the signified ; 7, if their objects are directed by the same word or sound. He himself thinks these principles may all be reduced under one law, which he calls the law of Redintegration, (restoration to a whole), and which he thus enounces: "Those thoughts suggest each other which had previously constituted parts of the same entire or total act of cognition."

The law as thus enounced, it must be said, however, is palpably insufficient to meet the demands of the problem. It does not embrace feelings or volitions; no explanation whatever is given of the fact that one feeling draws in another feeling, and one purpose another purpose, nor of the fact that feelings suggest thoughts. Nor does it even cover the familiar fact that a perfectly new thought, which therefore could not have previously constituted a part of any act of cognition, suggests old thoughts or new thoughts. I meet a stranger in the street, whom I have never seen or heard of before; the sight may suggest any one of ten thousand different thoughts or feelings. Moreover, thoughts and feelings are associated with affections of the body ; a shoot of pain in a defective tooth may suggest any feeling or thought experienced months before in a dentist's chair.

The same fatal deficiency in meeting the demands of the problem, characterizes other attempts to gather up into an exhaustive statement the manifold grounds of association or suggestion. It is true that one part of a past thought may suggest another part ; it is true also that some similarity in thoughts is a bond which unites them so that they may suggest one another ; it is true that connection in time or space, or as cause and effect, is a ground of suggestion ; and so of all the other proposed laws ; they are grounds, but all together they do not make up all the grounds of suggestion. The problem to be solved, the mystery to be explained, is somewhat analogous to this. A particle of the green mud from the Ohio is found united in the Great River with a particle of the red mud from the Arkansas ; they come together under the operation of inflexible laws of nature ; can now—this is the problem—can these laws be stated and be traced in their operation to their bringing together these two particles? The analogy would be more exact if we were to suppose all the particles that have ever come into the channel of the Great River to be brought to a stand against some immense perpendicular barrier, and the river under its own laws to be shifting continually the positions of the entire mass of particles and thus bringing the two parti-

cles into ever new yet ever shifting positions and
relations.    That the two particles meet and unite
is undoubtedly due  to  some  fixed  law or  laws  of
nature.   We  have the  great law of  gravity bearing  the  two  down  together  in  the  same  open
channel ;  we have the probability that if  the  two
particles entered the same part of  the current at
the  same  time,  they  might  come  together.    If
they  had  been subject  to  equivalent  forces  of  repulsion  from  the  banks,  of  impulse  from  winds, of
depression  from  floating  objects,  of  rarefaction
from  heat,  and  the  like,  we  have  in  these  conditions  other  reasons  for  their  being  together.
But so manifold  are  the  influences  at  work,  that
human  reason  recoils  from  the  task  of  tracing
them all.

It  is  so  with  the  associations  of  any  two
thoughts  or  feelings  in  the  mind.    The  one
principle that covers  the  whole  matter is  simply
this :  they  are  states  of  the  same  one  mind, as
the  two  particles  supposed  are  parts  of  the  same
rolling  river ;  and  this  mind  has  power,  under
favoring  conditions,  to  call  forth  into  consciousness,  within  certain  limits,  at  least, any part of its
collected  activity  of  thought  and  feeling  and
volitions ;  and  therefore  power  within  such  limits
to  connect  any  present  state  of  consciousness
with  such  recollected  thought  or  feeling  or  volition,  and  so  bring  to  the  surface  of  its  great  volume  of  accumulated  experiences,  that  is, into  distinct  consciousness, a  new  mental  experience.    It

is not presumable that any absolutely universal law of association can be framed other than this, that all associated ideas must belong to the one same mind; and that any one idea may, in the possibility of things, be associated with any other idea of the same mind; just as two particles of white and red mud in the Great River must, to be brought together, be in the same stream, and any two in that stream may, in the possibility of things, be brought together. This is the one fundamental and comprehensive principle of mental association.

This is a principle, it should be remarked, that respects ideas as forms of mental activity. The explanation of the ground and source of association should be sought ever in the mind itself, its actions and affections, not in products or results. Thought, as a product, has no power in itself to awaken another thought; it is the mind as thinking, that brings in another way of thinking.

In co-existence with this general law there may be, and in fact there are, other more specific laws implying the existence of specific causes which may effect the association of ideas. As these more specific laws may be convenient helps to recollection, it may be of service to make a formal and collective statement of the principles of association. Whatever limitations of this power of recollection may exist, it may be remarked, pertain only to the mind as finite; not to the relation between any two thoughts or feelings. The general principle is, that nothing but the weakness of mind as a finite nature hinders the association of any two mental acts or feelings which the mind has ever experienced. The principle implies both that no mental exercise ever becomes annihilated so that on this account it cannot be recalled, and also that every exercise is so connected with every other that the one may possibly suggest the other.

§ 111. LAWS OF MENTAL ASSOCIATION. 1. Any part of the mind's total experience may be associated with any other, and so in favoring conditions suggest it. In briefer terms: in the same mind any idea may suggest any other idea.

This is the comprehensive law. It includes all kinds of mental experience, feelings and volitions as well as thoughts. Any feeling may suggest any other feeling, or any thought, or any volition which has entered into the mind's experience. By suggesting here, it should be borne in mind, is meant bringing forth from unconscious experience into distinct consciousness.

§ 112. 2. Any part of the mind's experience may suggest any co-ordinate part ;—any idea suggests with special power a co-ordinate idea.

A feeling may suggest a co-ordinate feeling. A man in a mood of excited feeling is easily drawn into another feeling. We pass more easily to weeping from laughter than from an utterly unfeeling state.

In the same way thought helps thought. It is

a common practice with intellectual men to prepare themselves for clear, accurate, vigorous
thought on any subject by putting themselves on
the intense study of some other subject into which
the mind can more readily enter.    Lord Brougham
trained himself for a great intellectual effort by a
long and intense study of Demosthenes' Oration
on the Crown.

An active will in any one direction easily slides
into action in any other direction.    It is easier
thus to enlist an active man in a new enterprise
than the dull and idle.

§ 113. 3. A generic part of mental experience
may suggest any subordinate part ; and conversely
the subordinate may suggest the generic or comprehensive.    Ideas that are respectively super-
ordinate and subordinate to each other mutually
suggest each other.

A man in an angry mood easily breaks out
in new passion toward any particular object,
whether newly presented or re-awakened in memory.    Compassion toward a single sufferer in-
clines to pity for all of the class, for general good
will.

To recall the individual of a class to our
thought, we naturally turn to the class and from
that seek to recall the desired object ; or conversely, having the individual in our mind and de-
siring to recall the class, we naturally endeavor to
realize our wish by thinking of the individual.

It is the same with the will.    We form a gen-

eral purpose ; it brings on all subordinate purposes.  We resolve to speak, and the determination leads on to an indefinite number of subordinate purposes controlling our attitude, our gestic-
ulation, our sentences, our respiration, our vocal-
ization, our single words, our articulations.  The
single purpose reacts, too, on the general purpose
and carries it on, keeps it alive, as well as guides
and modifies it.  Nothing better seems to revive
a dormant resolution than to do some particular
thing involved in it, or which may be made part
of it.

§ 114. 4. Parts of the same object of mental activity suggest co-ordinate or subordinate parts.

This is but another and briefer form of stating
the preceding laws ; it designates the action by
its object while they directly respect the mental
action itself.

§ 115. 5. Parts of the same symbols or signs of
objects in the same way suggest other co-ordinate
or subordinate parts.

If the mind has before it either part of the
word, *farewell, fare* or *well,* that part may suggest the other ; or it may suggest any one of the
parts of which it is composed.  The philologist,
for instance, may think of one or another of the
sounds or the written characters which constitute
the word.  The cherubs in Raphael's Sistine
Madonna will suggest the Madonna herself or any
other part of the picture, or any posture, expression, or feature in the cherubs themselves.

§ 116. 6. Mental experiences of more recent occurrence have greater suggestive power: the more recent the idea, the greater is its power to suggest.

This law of association, it will be observed, is of a different source and character from the preceding. It is founded in the attribute of growth that we have found to belong to the human mind. Every new stage of its existence brings in a new stage of growth, a fresh life, a large development. Such at least is the general law. The most recent life consequently has a greater vigor and intensity.

This fact of association we all familiarly recognize. We recall the occurrences of yesterday more readily than those of the last year; and these more readily than those of ten years before. The law, of course, regards experiences of the same character otherwise, such as experiences of the same closeness of connection with the suggesting act or feeling; or experiences of the same interest and importance.

An apparent exception to this law is found in the experience of aged persons, who often recall the events of childhood and youth more readily and more vividly than those of later years. But this fact may be accounted for, in part at least, on the ground that their habitual thoughts at this period of life run in the channels of earlier experiences. These, therefore, from their being revived and lived over again, are really the freshest and

latest in their minds. Farther than this, other
principles of association may come in. External
scenes and objects, individual associations, and
numberless influences from personal attachments
and repulsions, come in to make parts of a mental experience by which other parts are suggested.
But more than all, it is the early shootings of any
growth which are the most permanent and the
most controlling. "As the twig is bent, the tree
is inclined." These germinant activities of the
soul take to themselves, more and larger associations. They recall and are recalled more freely.
"The child is father of the man."

§ 117. 7. The intensity of the mental experience is an important element in association or
suggestion :—the more vivid the idea, the
stronger is its suggestive power.

Intense feeling kindles at once from the faint-
est impression. An angry man bursts into
stronger passion from a provocation of any kind.
Energetic thinking fuses all the particular
thoughts together, so that, as if inseparable, one
cannot return into the mind without drawing in
the others. Our resolutions carry all subordinate purposes just in proportion as they are strong
and energetic, enlisting the whole soul. When
such a governing purpose is earnest and decided,
all purposes that are foreign to it, even if occasion
should suggest them, give way at once. When,
likewise, a specific purpose is thus earnest, all
other specific purposes under the same general

resolution, fall in more easily. Weak souls are ever characterized as inconsistent.

If the demand be pushed farther for the reason why in any particular case this part is suggested rather than that, while sometimes a more subordinate law may be assigned, ultimately we are obliged from the finiteness of our power to fall back upon the first general law given,—the unity of the mind itself carrying in its complex activity all the special activities of feeling, of thought, and of volition, just as we are forced, in attempting to account for the union of the two particles of mud, to fall back on the general fact of their being in the same whirling rolling stream. So many forces come in, of such various intensity, from the world without; from the state of the body and its nervous organism; from the habits, tastes, moods, of the individual mind itself, that it is beyond the power of created intelligence fully to account for all the associations of ideas that it experiences. It must be recollected that these forces come up as well from the vast volume of our unconscious experience as from the mere surface of mental action which our distinct consciousness takes up.

§ 118. The principles of mental suggestion have obviously a sweep far broader than those of the mere " association of ideas." Leaving out of view the determinations of thought and feeling by the direct action of the will and also by external objects, and confining our attention simply to the mere spontaneous flow of mental experience, embracing, however, in our view here the organic connection between the human mind and the body, we have the following general statements which to some extent at least may account for the particular direction or kind of feeling and thought in reverie.

First, we have the fact that the mind's activity is itself automatic. § 22. Then there is the analogous fact of automatism in the bodily energies. Particularly here is to be noticed the reflex action of the nerves or the spontaneous response of one part of the nervous organism to a movement of another part. § 48. There is no reason to doubt that this principle of reflex action, so familiarly recognized now in biological science prevails in purely mental life as well as in nervous phenomena. Farther, in both mind and body, each being a living organism, every part in each is so associated with every other part, that an affection of one part may reach any other. § 49. Still more, there is a correlation between soul and body, so that certain affections of the one occasion affections in the other. § 50. The principle of reflex action shows itself here also in the combined organism. These correlations we recognize in part as natural, as when, in walking, the feet move on of themselves, that is, without a repeated intervention of the will and if they encounter any obstacle in their way, they surmount it without any conscious effort. But besides these, there are in-

numerable correlations that are acquired or established by habit, voluntarily and involuntarily,
which have no supposable special ground in the
essential nature of our mental and bodily consti-
tutions, so that a certain affection of the sense
will bring on a certain affection of the mind—
awaken a certain feeling, or thought, or volition.
There is in short, so to speak, an automatism in
the correlated action of mind and body—in the
whole man—so that, without any intervention of
the will, any bodily state may be associated with
any mental condition. Hamilton's law of redintegration must be greatly broadened to take in all
this organic correlation in mind and body—in the
whole and in the parts. We cannot account for
the facts in mental suggestion without embracing
this automatism in mind, in body, and in their
union as one living organism, each member of
which lives in every other. This principle of so-
called *reflex action*, characterizing all living things
and ever operative in them throughout their entire being, is ever to be recognized in interpreting
mental states.

§ 119. Voluntary reproduction is familiarly denoted by the term *recollection.*

We recognize the fact that reproduction is in
some measure subject to our wills when in our
desire to recall some past experience, to call forth
into distinct consciousness the abiding impress of
such past experience now lying latent in the soul,
we endeavor to direct our thoughts or feelings

toward it. We do this in two different ways: positively, by keeping in our consciousness some experience associated with what we wish to recall; and negatively, by repelling thoughts and feelings that are more foreign to it.

The positive endeavor to recall a past experience will of course best be guided by association. It assumes some feeling, or thought, or volition from which it is to proceed as its necessary ground and starting point. With this experience in the consciousness, recollection properly sets out and then puts itself under the lead of this principle of association. The best rules of recollection may accordingly be thus summarily given :—

§ 120. RULES OF RECOLLECTION. I. Recall feeling by feeling, thought by thought, purpose by purpose.

Early affection for a friend long separated from us may best be revived from a similar state of affection in exercise toward a friend still with us. In like manner a former thought is best revived when thinking rather than feeling or endeavoring is the predominant characteristic of the mind. Free action in the same way revives a dormant purpose or endeavor. Even if the mind in a state of excited feeling desires to recall the train of thought out of which the feeling rose or with which it was associated, for the most part success will be most probable if the existing feeling first recall the old feeling and then that feeling revive its associated thought.

§ 121. II. Recall ideas through the relation of whole and part.

If the feeling or thought or purpose to be recalled be generic or comprehensive, start from a subordinate experience ; if subordinate, start from a generic or comprehensive experience.

To revive a governing disposition of filial dutifulness, a present purpose in doing some particular act of filial duty will be the most hopeful. So a general thought is best recalled by thinking of some particular fact or instance in which that principle is exemplified. As for example, in recalling the general law of material gravitation, I may succeed best by beginning with the law as instanced in a falling weight and thinking of the number of feet of fall in the first second, the number in the second, the number in the third, and so on.

So to recall a subordinate purpose, it is best, if it be practicable, to begin with a generic or governing endeavor. To revive a neglected religious duty, the most hopeful method is to begin with a freshened endeavor to do all religious duty. To recall a specific thought, it is well to begin with the general law that comprises that thought.

§ 122. III. Recall objects through the same relation of whole and part, as associated either with one another or with the mental state which they respect.

§ 123. IV. Words and other symbols are most suggestive of like words and symbols, or of the objects or mental states with which they are associated.

# CHAPTER XIV.

## THE ARTISTIC, PHILOSOPHICAL, AND PRACTICAL IMAGINATION.

§ 124. Ideals, as the proper products of the imagination, may be distinguished into three general classes, corresponding to the three general functions of the mind: feeling, thinking, willing; also to the three generic objects of all mental activity: the beautiful, the true, and the good.

We have thus three functions of the imagination determined in reference to the character of its product or ideal—three forms of the imagination as an active power:—

1. *The Artistic Imagination.*
2. *The Philosophical Imagination.*
3. *The Practical Imagination.*

It must be borne in mind here as everywhere, that these products of the imagination, these ideals, are so distinguished only as they are more prominently characterized respectively either as beautiful, true, or good. Every act of mind, every idea, has necessarily each of these attributes in some degree; but it may have one more prominent than the others, which thus gives character to the act. If an artist frames an ideal of a virtue, as, for instance, of patriotism, or of filial affection, he necessarily regards more or less the principles of truth, of intelligence, and also those of right-doing. But his governing end being a beautiful form, his ideal is characterized as properly artistic, not philosophical nor practical. The philosopher, in the same way, although his governing end is truth, and his labor is to attain or set forth what is true, still must regard the form which his speculations take and the effect in some way or other which they may work. But his prominent ideal being the true, it is easily distinguished by this characteristic; it differs from a mere ideal to be marked by its beauty. A geometrical treatise does not properly take on a poetical form. The practical man, moreover, cannot disregard the form of his product, nor the essential attributes—the truth—of things; but his act is characteristically distinct from the proper work of the artist and of the philosopher.

Still further, the degrees in which the one or the other of these three great attributes of all mental activity, the attributes of form, truth, and practical effect, predominate in ideals, vary indefinitely. The practical philanthropist, who aims to do good as his chief governing aim, may put his act of kindness into such a frame of loveliness that we may hesitate which to admire most, the beauty or the goodness of his act. In truth the imagination which shaped his act may be regarded as having been both artistic and practical;

both graceful and beneficent. It may have been also eminently wise, conformed in all particulars to the truth of things. His act will be characterized as good, or beautiful, or true, according as one or another of these attributes is recognized as predominant in it.

§ 125. THE ARTISTIC IMAGINATION produces ideals characterized by their form, as beautiful or the opposite.

The governing end in the artistic imagination is form. The work may be more or less conformed to truth, may more or less promote truth ; it may proceed from a general benevolent intention and may be productive of good ; but the artist in his own proper specific work, looks to the form of his product. His work will indeed be more or less perfect in form according as he more or less strictly conforms his work to the truth of things, or as he works more or less perfectly in the line of goodness ; yet we have no difficulty in recognizing the work as characteristically a piece of art and not a work of speculation or of morality.

It is the proper province of the science of æsthetics to ascertain and apply the laws of the artistic imagination both in the production and in the interpretation of beauty.

§ 126. THE PHILOSOPHICAL IMAGINATION produces ideals characterized by their essence as true or the opposite.

The philosophical imagination seeks truth as

the governing end of its activity. The artistic imagination produces for the form's sake, although not transgressing the laws of the true; the philosophical imagination, on the other hand, produces for the truth's sake, although not transgressing the laws of the beautiful. The mental act has a twofold aspect. One and single in itself, it yet engages the imagination or the faculty of form and the intelligence as the faculty of the true. If we regard the mental activity on the side of the imagination, we denominate it the philosophical imagination; if we regard it on the side of the intelligence, we call it the intellectual representation.

It is the proper province of the science of logic to expound the laws by which the philosophical imagination or the faculty of the intelligence acting in the representation of truth or knowledge, is to be governed. This science thus determines the valid forms of all thought or knowledge.

§ 127. THE PRACTICAL IMAGINATION produces ideals characterized by their tendency to a result or effect as good or the opposite.

The practical imagination frames ideals of character to which the whole activity of the soul is to be shaped. It devises plans of active exertion and methods of execution. As the life of the artist is characteristically that of one who is ever shaping beautiful forms, idealizing for the purpose of impressing beauty, and as the life of the student and the philosopher is characteristically a life busy with framing new and truer ideas of doctrine, of objects, of events, so the life of the practical man is characteristically the life of one busy in devising schemes of exertion, new pursuits, new enterprises, new methods of operation.

It is the proper province of the science of ethics, in its broadest sense as comprising not only the duties of religion and morality, but also the acts of social life, of polity, civil and domestic economy, and those which pertain to personal well-being, to bodily and mental health and vigor, as well as the fulfillment of man's destiny as an active being,—it is the province of this broad science to unfold the laws by which practice in all these departments is to be regulated and controlled.

## CHAPTER XV.

### FORM—ITS NATURE AND MODIFICATIONS.

§ 128. FORM is the proper object of the sensibility and the imagination ; it is that which these functions of the mind immediately respect. § 31. The sensibility receives form ; the imagination produces form. As has been before stated, any object of mental activity may, through the analytical power of the mind, be regarded at will either in respect to its essence, or its end, or its form. Thus form may be more exactly defined to be *that attribute of an object by virtue of which it may impress and so make itself to be felt.* In like manner the sensibility may be defined to be that attribute of mind by virtue of which the mind may be impressed by the object and so feel the object as a power impressing it.

If an object be perfectly suited to affect favorably the sensibility, in other words, if it be perfect in form, we call it beautiful. If there be in any respect a lack of fitness in it to impress the sensibility favorably, it is imperfect in form—it is imperfectly beautiful. If, instead of affecting the sensibility thus favorably, that is, instead of impressing it so that the affection should legitimately be one of pleasure, it on the contrary legitimately give pain in the contemplation, it is positively ugly. All these gradations of beauty are comprehended in the one general denomination of the beautiful, or the category of form. Each gradation, even the ugly, is proper object to the sensibility. These gradations together make up the entire object of that function.

These statements involve the truth that beauty, form, is real, in the sense that it belongs as a true attribute to something real. Nothing but reality can affect or move the soul. Even although it be a mere fancy, that is, although it be a mere fiction of the imagination the object of which is devoid in itself of all reality, the fiction itself— the fancy—as an exertion of mind, is a fact, is real. The one and sufficient mark and sign of the real, indeed, is precisely this, that it affects or moves the soul.

The theory that for some time gained prevalence in Great Britain, that the experience of beauty is a mere effect of association, being simply the pleasure resulting from certain trains of associated ideas, is founded in entire mistake as to the nature of the experience or, indeed, more radically, in erroneous views of the mental activities and capacities generally, and is now exploded, as is also the implied supposition which identifies the emotion of beauty with simple pleasure. All that can be held as true here is that pleasure as a natural accompaniment is often an available test or sign of beauty as it is equally a test of truth and of goodness. As created in order to experience the true, the beautiful, and the good, the soul finds specific ends of its being realized in such experiences; and the pleasure native to all legitimate exercises of its activity, in so far as it attends upon these experiences, is a valid test of their legitimacy. The satisfaction, thus, that waits on the exercise of the intelligence in regard to a proposition, and of the will in regard to a moral act, is a sign that they have respectively attained the really true and the really good. The satisfaction, in like manner, that attends on the contemplation of the form of an object, is a sign that it is in truth beautiful. Such satisfaction is a sign or proof to a certain extent; while it raises a certain presumption, it is not of itself, however, absolutely conclusive.

§ 129. As is apparent from the definitions that have been given of the different classes of feeling, form, when engaging the passive side of the sensibility, must be supposed to address itself ultimately to that class of susceptibilities which we have denominated the emotions. It is true that form in physical matter can only reach the soul through the physical or bodily senses. But if its effect reach no farther than the bodily sense,

there can be no proper experience of beauty.
It was indeed a theory of Burke that beauty " is
for the greater part some quality in bodies acting
mechanically upon the human mind by the intervention of the senses, and acts by relaxing the
solids of the whole system." The beauty of a
fine picture must reach the soul through the
sense of sight ; and it may be true of it that the
lines and colors are such as to engage agreeably
all the bodily organs concerned in beholding, and
so occasion pleasing sensations. But there is no
proper experience of beauty in this physical sensation. The properly beautiful is not felt until
the soul back of the sense-affection is reached.
Not till then is the ideal of the artist and the
taste and skill with which he has embodied this
ideal in outline and color, really felt in the soul ;
and these constitute the essence of what is beautiful in the picture. Form, or that attribute in
the object by which this ideal and taste and skill
are apprehended, passes through the bodily sense
to fasten at last on the mental or spiritual nature.
The physical affection is simply medium between
the external object and the mind. As will be
seen in the case of perception, the sense-affection
itself or the impression on the nerves and its
effect in the nerves themselves, are all on the
bodily side. The mind itself, while at the same
time it is affected by the bodily state or by the
power which works through the nerve-system of
the body, is yet the proper seat of the experience of

the beautiful or form, just as it is the seat of the
experience of the true. The emotion of beauty,
just as the perception or knowledge of the true,
is in the mind alone. Form, thus, strictly speaking, has no proper seat in the mere physical sense ;
it works through that and so reaches the sensibility in the character of a proper emotion which is
determined immediately not by a material object
but only from a properly spiritual or mental
source.

Still farther, it is apparent that beauty is not
proper object for the affections which are feelings
that are characterized by the fact that they go '
out and fasten on their objects. We may experience to the full the beauty of a painting or of a
landscape without love or hate in the more restricted and proper meanings of those terms.
Beauty lies wholly within the range of the contemplative. Much less can form be regarded as
proper object to the desires. A beautiful picture
may be desired as well as loved ; it may be loved
or desired because it is beautiful ; but the emotion which beauty awakens may be perfect when
it is followed by no such affection or desire. So,
still more, form may awaken an emotion which
shall be pervaded by intelligence or will ; it
may address feeling awakened in conjunction
with the intelligence or choice which the object
regarded in its essence or as an end may address.
The emotion of beauty may exist in connection
with an act of knowledge or of choice ; and this

combination characterizes the experience as a sentiment. But the emotion of beauty has a proper individual character of its own independently of such a combination with a thought or a purpose.

§ 130. Turning now our study upon form itself to determine more fully its nature, we see that, as idea revealed, it must include three essential and co-ordinate constituents. There must be, first, the idea itself which is revealed; secondly, the matter in which it is revealed ; and thirdly, the more essential co-efficient, the revelation itself of the idea in the matter. Thus in a statue, as, say a statue of Apollo, there must be the sculptor's idea of the divinity which he proposes to embody in the marble—there must be his ideal to be expressed in the sculpture. Then there must be the matter—the marble—in which his ideal is to be expressed. But ideal and marble are not enough of themselves for the realization of the statue ;—there must be the artistic or rendering power of the sculptor, characterized and guided by his taste and skill to put the ideal into the marble. So in a picture, there are, first, the ideal of the painter—the person, the landscape, the scene,—which he proposes to depict ; secondly, the outline and color through which he represents this ideal; and then, thirdly, the work of putting the ideal in this outline and color on the canvas. In the same way, in a proper spiritual ideal, as in a poem, the ideal is first shaped in

13

the poet's imagination; there is then the imagery and the words in which he is to incorporate
the ideal; and finally the actual composition—the
making of the poem, which consists in putting the
ideal into language.

§ 131. It is evident there can be no form without each of these constituents. Form accordingly ever embraces these three as essential elements. These constituents, however, may exist
in all supposable gradations of relative perfection
and of preponderance. Form, or the beautiful,
as object, may accordingly be divided into three
general kinds as the one or the other of these
constituents predominates. We have thus *Ideal*
beauty, in which the ideal revealed is the governing characteristic; *Material* beauty, in which the
beauty resides more prominently in the matter;
and *Formal* beauty, in which the rendering or revealing energy is the characteristic.

Under these general classes are embraced manifold subdivisions. We have thus under ideal
beauty, the beauty of action and the beauty of
repose. We have, further, the different kinds
characterized by the relative prominence of the
several mental functions, as intellectual beauty,
comprising the beauty of truthfulness, of fitness,
of unity, of harmony, of contrast, of proportion,
of symmetry, of æsthetic number, and also generic beauty. Under material beauty we have the
subdivisions of inorganic, organic, sentient, and
spiritual according to the material in which the

ideal is rendered. Under formal beauty we have the three kinds of, first, artistic beauty as determined by the special character of the revealing energy; secondly, free and dependent beauty according as the revelation of the idea is for the form itself or for some object ulterior to the mere embodiment, as for instruction or some utility ; and, thirdly, the kinds of beauty characterized by the relations of the revealed idea to the matter in which the idea is revealed, embracing the *sublime*, in which the idea appears outspanning the matter ; the proper *beautiful*, in which the idea revealed and the matter are in harmony ; and the *comic* and *pretty*, in which the matter preponderates over the idea.

We have found the function of form to exist both as proper capacity and as faculty; in other words, as sensibility and imagination. In a corresponding way, form as an object may be considered in two ways, (1), in relation to the sensibility and (2), in relation to the imagination. The sensibility is a recipient, and the form which it is to receive is to be interpreted out of the concrete object which addresses it. The imagination is a producer and its office is to produce or create form. These two aspects of form as object will be considered in distinct chapters on (1), the Reception or Interpretation of Form and (2), the Production of Form.

# CHAPTER XVI.

## FORM RECEIVED.

§ 132. IN the experience of beauty it is often supposed that the object in which it is sought must contain beauty as a distinct intrinsic element or constituent. This element, it is thought, is accordingly to be studied out and separated by careful analysis from the other constituents for distinct contemplation, as a kernel to be uncased and separated from the husk or shell. In an analogous way, pleasure is sometimes sought as if it were a coin or a purse that might be picked up in the way, in utter exclusion of the conditions on which alone pleasure ever waits. The error is a fatal one. Not so is pleasure or beauty to be found. The soul that would be pleased, that would be happy, must act or feel so that the pleasure or happiness, which by the laws of unerring nature ever comes of itself when its conditions are supplied to it, may have its needful source and occasion. The experience of beauty is the experience of an interchange between soul and soul— of the imparting and receiving of idea. The reception of the idea is the experience of beauty; and the satisfaction or pleasure that attends upon the emotions of beauty is but the natural consequent of the reception of the form. The pleasures of taste are the pleasures thàt attend upon the feelings awakened by the reception of idea just as the pleasures of the imagination are the pleasures that wait on the active exercises of the imagination.

Form received is beauty experienced, as form communicated is beauty produced. The pleasure that is felt comes as natural consequent on legitimate feeling and legitimate imagining. To see or feel the beauty of any object is accordingly to see or feel that which constitutes its form, the three constituents of which, as we have seen, are idea revealed, matter in which it is revealed, and the activity or energy revealing— the three not separable in reality, but only in the analysis of thought. Only as we apprehend form as thus constituted—idea revealed in fitting matter—do we experience beauty; and in such apprehension we ever experience the beauty there is for us in the object. In order to experience beauty we are not to seek for it as separable from some idea communicated to us, but solely in our properly receiving idea as communicated.

The subjective conditions on which form or beauty is to be experienced are accordingly easy of determination. We must, in the first place, be in communication with the object so as to be impressed by it; we must be in sympathy, at least in that largest sense of the term which in-

cludes possible communicability with it or capability of being impressed by it. The livelier and
broader the sympathy, the tenderer the sensibility
and the closer and more absorbing the communication with it, the fuller and richer will be the
experience ; in other words, the more engag-
ingly and perfectly will the form or beauty of the
object enter the soul.

But the sensibility into which form or beauty
enters and the imagination from which beauty
proceeds is in organic connection with an intelligent and also with a free or moral nature. Idea
revealed and idea received come thus to be characterized alike by intelligence and free-will. The
contemplation of beauty goes limping and weak
when there are not both light and freedom, as the
production of beauty stumbles or fails when these
attributes are in defect. So in order to the ready
and full and satisfactory reception of beauty there
is necessary a soul that can not only feel but can
feel freely and intelligently. Beauty, form, must
be rational in its full import, both as received and
as imparted.

§ 133. Closely connected with these subjective
conditions for the full reception of form or experience of beauty is the condition of time, to which
all mental experience is subject. The longer the
impression, the deeper. This is the general law :—
the more protracted the contemplation, the fuller
and richer the experience. By an analysis of the
constituents of beauty or form and an acquaint-

ance with its several specific modifications in the relative combination of those constituents, the contemplation of beauty may take the form of a protracted study of each of these modifications separately, but yet a study that does not overlook the natural relation of each to the others. The study of idea itself in its possible modifications received from the intelligence, the sensibility, and the free-will ; the study of the medium in the diversities of its nature ; and the study of the revealing or rendering activity in its various modes of manifestation ; as also the study of the relationships between these constituents, and of the degrees of perfection in which they appear ;— such studies give opportunity for the fuller unfolding of the form or beauty of the object under contemplation. The full recognition of the character of the revelation, bringing into view the general conditions and laws to which revelation of that specific character is subject, becomes here especially helpful to the full reception of form. There are peculiarities in the beauty of nature and the beauty of art. There is ground of æsthetic sympathy between the soul and nature. The individual mind, the poet has taught us, is exquisitely fitted to the external world and the external world is as exquisitely fitted to the mind. They sympathetically interact. Nature speaks to us, reveals her ideas—the ideas of the creating spirit in her. It is a radically erroneous notion that nature has no ideas, but those which we put into her forms. There is a mind, a soul, in all nature, living and acting. Nature has her own voice as well as her own ideas, and has moreover her own design. As we open our eyes and hearts to these revelations in sympathetic and intelligent communings, protracting the impression she makes upon us by intelligent study of the manifold laws and relationships to which she is subject, we receive the fuller impress of her ideas, and experience a larger, richer beauty.

In like manner, in the contemplation of form— of the beautiful—in art, we are to bring in, first, the subjective conditions—an active, impressible, sympathetic, intelligent, and an unreluctant and free spirit or disposition and then regard the objective conditions which attach themselves to the freest communication of form. These are the æsthetic determinations of the object which we contemplate, first, in respect to the medium through which our sensibility is addressed—the medium of light and color as predominant in painting, of sound as in music, of imagery and spiritual form in poetry, with their manifold diversities of modification; then, in respect to the idea itself revealed whether in action or repose, and whether more characteristically of thought, of feeling, or of purpose, with their respective modifications.

It is the province of proper æsthetic science to set forth in their details these very general conditions, both subjective and objective, of the successful contemplation of beauty whether in nature or art. The summary view presented, which is all that is permissible here, is sufficient to show that the reception of form, the experience of beauty, is simply the one side of a twofold activity engaged in the interchange of idea—the imparting and the receiving—mind speaking and mind hearing. The interpretation of beauty is ever but the interpretation of some mind voicing forth its idea in whatever way, and is most successful, as the interpreting spirit apprehends most fully and freely the movements of the addressing mind in their own nature, and the modes—the medium and ways—of its address. All æsthetic pleasure in contemplation hangs on this interpretation. And the beauty there is in the object contemplated is nothing but the form of mind thus communicating itself, or to speak with more technical exactness, idea thus shaped out and imparted. The human mind is made for communion ; and one great source of the pleasure, the joy, the happiness, which it can experience, is to be found in this communion. If it be legitimate and right, if it be free and full, the pleasure will be correspondingly perfect. Thus the pleasure that attends upon the contemplation of the beautiful is the natural sign and test of its purity and perfectness.

# CHAPTER XVII.

## FORM PRODUCED.

§ 134. Form produced is idea communicated or, at least, idea expressed. It may be in address to another mind or to the expressing mind itself for its own contemplation. Form, as we have so often seen, is thus ever in the interchange of mental activity, and is that attribute of such interchanging activity by virtue of which it is recognized as communicating. Form, related to the mind communicating, is the mind's mode of action; related to the mind receiving, it is the mind's mode of affecting mind in the communication; related to the act of communicating, it is the action regarded not in its essence, not in its result, but as simply expressing and impressing. If the form be perfect; if the form of activity in the expressing mind—the idea expressed—in its own character, be perfect; if the form of the affection in the receiving mind be perfect; if the expression itself as to medium and circumstance be perfect, we have perfect beauty; if perfect in all these relations, we have absolutely perfect beauty; if in either one, so far perfect; if imperfect in any one or all respects we have imperfect beauty; if absolutely false in idea, false in affection, false in expression, we have the false in form —the positively and absolutely ugly.

The mode of mental activity in expressing itself we have called *idea*. Idea is a specific mode of mental activity; or is mental activity put forth in some specific way. We have recognized three generic modes of mental activity in the three functions of (1) the Sensibility and the Imagination, otherwise named the function of Form; (2) the Intelligence; and (3) the Will. We say, then, in a general way that all form is of one or the other of these three functions of mental activity. Every idea is an idea of feeling, of thought, or of purpose; and accordingly all form respects these ideas in their diverse gradations of preponderance. It must not be overlooked, however, that without any precise discrimination of either of these modes of mental activity, we may suppose one mind to influence, to impress itself in a general way upon another mind. As mind is by nature sympathetic, mere contact of ever active mind with other equally active minds, may be supposed to influence, impress itself upon this other mind— may communicate itself to it—without any very definable specific determination of the mode or kind of its activity. Still even in this case, there is a certain specification, a limitation, a form of mental activity to be recognized. The expressing mind is at least limited as to object, since all action implies object. There is here, therefore, a proper idea—form or mode of mental activity. But as in our study of mind we find it expedient to specify its several more prominent functions and direct our view more exclusively on these in their respective characteristics, with but cursory glances at its more general attributes which yet must embrace more or less these specified functions, so in the study of form we shall find it expedient to limit our view to the more specific determinations of idea with this precautionary suggestion as to the actual limitations of our field of study.

§ 135. We may set forth the general truth that all form, all idea, is either one of feeling, of thought, or of purpose; as expressed, it is predominantly and characteristically an expression of feeling, of intelligence, or of will. The fundamental principle in all production of form, that is, in all art, is accordingly that it ever aim to be an expression of one or the other of these modes of mental activity. It is evident from this, that to speak of the expression of beauty as of an object is to speak absurdly; for beauty is nothing but this expression of idea—that is, nothing but idea as expressed.

A subordinate principle of all art-production follows this,—that one or the other of these three modes should be made predominant and be only modified by the others, since the rational nature of man, to which all art addresses itself, ever demands unity—at least, the unity that exists in subordination. And still another principle fol-lows, that it must be the artist's own idea which is to be expressed. It may be his idea of a tree or a man, his idea of another's thought, or wish, or act; but it must be *his* idea, whatever it be that the expression respects.

The first general principle which should gov-ern in all communication of idea—in all art—is that the communicating mind—the mind of the artist—have an idea to communicate, which should be predominantly and characteristically an act of imagination, of intelligence, or of will.

A second general principle which is given in the very nature of an interchanging activity be-tween minds, is that there should be a distinct notion in the communicating mind of the specific end or design in communicating. This principle is imposed by the rational character of mind which ever seeks an end in its action. This end, further, in all rational communication to mind must ob-viously be attained either in the sensibility, the intelligence, or the will, as the three comprehen-sive modes of mental activity. These three ends —for the sake of form, for the sake of the true, for the sake of the good—will respectively govern in the modes of expression, each in its own way. If the design of the expression be to impart truth —to produce in another mind the experience of the true—then intelligence will address intelli-gence. The laws of thought will control the ex-

pression while also the conditions of thought
—of receiving knowledge—will be recognized.
Intelligence as addressing intelligence will predominate, making the other associated functions
acting under their respective laws and conditions
—the imagination or sensibility and the free-will
—subservient and helpful. This is the art of
teaching. If the end be to determine the will to
right endeavor, the expressing mind will present
some act to engage the will, and will observe
the laws of free activity in the presentation
on the one hand, and the conditions of free action in the consenting acceptance of what is presented on the other. The ministries of the intelligence and of the feelings will be engaged as
subervient to the end. This is the art of persua-
sion. If the design of the expression be to engage the imagination—the function of form—
the principle of form, both as to presenting and
also as to receiving, must govern, and thought
and purpose will be in ministry and subserviency.
This is æsthetic art—art in its narrower import.
If the design be form simply—pure form—we
have the domain of free art, so called, embracing
the special historical arts of painting and sculpture—the two great plastic arts addressing the
mind through the medium of light and entering
through the sense of sight to affect the imagination by outline or figure, conjoined with color as
in the former art, or without, as in the latter. To
the free arts belongs also the art of music, in

some of its forms, at least, addressing the sense of hearing, and of poetry reaching the sensibility through language as interpreted by the intelligence. But art is sometimes made to subserve some end extrinsic to that of pure form in the imagination ;—it becomes thus partly free, partly dependent. Thus it is with architecture and landscape ; also with music, in some of its forms ministering to truth, or to devotion, or to patriotism ; and likewise with discourse both in prose and in poetry.

Thus from this cursory survey of the proper object of the function of form, whether as capacity in the sensibility or as faculty in the imagination, we find everywhere that the object is the exact correlative of the mental activity engaged. The one is for the other. The laws of the one are conditions for the other. The mind engaged acts ever as intelligence, imagination, or will, it engages ever and only with idea as thought, or form, or purpose. The perfect correspondence establishes the correctness of the analysis and defines with exactness the boundaries of both function and object. Each shines brighter in the light of the other. The science of the function, both as capacity or the proper sensibility, and as faculty or the proper imagination, constitutes one leading part of psychological science which in its unfoldings opens out to view the whole domain of the object of the function—the beautiful in its large comprehension of import—the idea of form.

The science of the object as realized in experience is the science of æsthetics, which in its turn, as it unfolds itself in exact scientific method, reflects back in beautiful correspondence the truths of psychology.

# BOOK III.

## THE INTELLIGENCE.—I. SUBJECTIVE VIEW.

---

### CHAPTER I.

#### ITS NATURE AND MODIFICATIONS.

§ 136. THE INTELLIGENCE IS THE MIND'S FUNCTION OF KNOWING.

It is otherwise denominated the Cognitive Faculty and the Intellect. Its function is simply that of knowing; and all knowing is by this function alone.

§ 137. The intelligence admits divers modifications.

It is modified, first, in respect to its stages as complete or incomplete. In order to any knowledge there must be an object presented to the mind to be known. The mere apprehension of this object by the intelligence may, for uses of convenience in study, properly be viewed as a preparatory stage of knowledge. This incomplete and preparatory stage has been denominated *Presentative Knowledge*.

14

But the intelligence cannot rest satisfied with this mere presentative knowledge. Its essential activity prompts to a further stage, in which the object presented to it in the preceding stage is recognized in a twofold aspect—as subject and as attribute. Thus if any object is given to it, as for instance *the sun*, the intelligence at once proceeds to regard it as having an attribute—brightness ; and its knowledge is complete only when the mind is in that state which is properly expressed in a proposition : *the sun is bright.* *Sun* and *bright* are not two different things in reality ; but it is the native function of the mind at once in every single object presented to it to recognize such object under this dual form—the form of a subject and an attribute which it unites or identifies as one and the same. This form of mental action is technically known as *the judgment*, § 158.

This completed form of knowledge has been denominated *representative knowledge*, as it implies, in addition to the first form or presentative knowledge, a reflex act of the mind on the object presented to it. More properly and more significantly it may be denominated *attributive knowledge*.

In the earlier stages of mental development, presentative knowledge has a greater relative prominence than in maturer life. The child perceives, simply apprehends, relatively more ; but as he advances, his simple apprehensions pass more habitually into reflection or judging, that is, into proper thought.

Further, it is to be observed, that although the mind instinctively passes on from simple apprehension to reflection as its goal, the movement may be instantaneous, or protracted, may even halt or be held in suspense. But whether longer or shorter in its actual presence this presentative knowledge forms a part of the mind's activity at the time, and works there with its due organic force. A perception, such as a sight of some threatening danger, thus may, in what is called reflex action, without waiting for a matured judgment, affect the nerves and through them the action of the heart and limbs and agitate the whole body; or with equal power reach the thought and the determinations of the will. An intuition may work with similar effect, outwardly upon the bodily organism or inwardly upon the mental state. So long as actually present in the mind such presentative knowledge works its appropriate organic work on the whole complex being of body and soul.

§ 138. The intelligence, further, is modified in respect to the diverse character of its object.

We have found that the comprehensive object for the intelligence is *the true*. § 28. But *the true* embraces three distinct elements or constituents— the subject, the attribute, and the uniting element, called the copula. These elements may severally

vary in manifold ways. They so far modify the
act of the intelligence in knowing.

§ 139. The intelligence, once more, is modified
in respect to the sources of its knowledge.

Its objects are presented to it from two different directions, which it is very important to
recognize distinctly. These objects are brought
to it in part from without and presented to it
through the external senses. The presentative
knowledge thus attained is called a *perception or
perceptive knowledge*. These objects are brought
to it in part, moreover, from the mind itself—
from its own phenomena—or from supersensible objects. The presentative knowledge thus
attained is called an *intuition* or *intuitive knowledge*.

§ 140. The intelligence, finally, is modified in
respect to the different functions of the mind
itself.

These functions have already been recognized
as threefold—the sensibility, the intelligence,
and the will. As functions of the same indivisible nature, which in no exercise of any one function ever drops entirely either of its other functions, every act of the intelligence is more or less
modified by the sensibility and the will.

Not only this, but the human mind being both
passive and active in every state, we have ever
two sides to study,—the passive side in which the
mind is simply impressed by its object, as in sensation or emotion, and the active side, in which it

properly knows its object, as in perception or intuition.

We shall, in the further exposition of the intelligence, as the knowing factor, present in separate chapters the generic forms of its divers modifications.

# CHAPTER II.

## PERCEPTION.

§ 141. PERCEPTION *is that function of the intelligence by which it apprehends an object presented through the bodily senses.*

The term *perception* is used to denote the faculty of perceiving; the exercise of this faculty or the act of perceiving; and also the result of this act. The term *percept* has been proposed to denote the result or the product of perception.

§ 142. Perception is the active or knowing side, sensation the passive or feeling side of the same state of mental apprehension.

We have already recognized the truth that the mind is in every experience both passive and active. This law of mind is formally proposed by Sir William Hamilton in its general form, as applied to all mental phenomena; it is specifically recognized by him in its application here in the summary statement: "Cognition and feeling are always co-existent." I perceive an orange at the same time that I have a sensation of it through the eye, the touch, the smell, or the taste.

But while perception and sensation are but opposite sides of the same mental state, which has ever an active and a passive side, they are to be distinguished from each other in several important respects.

1. Sensation is the ground or occasion of the perception. It is, therefore, properly regarded as the logical antecedent of perception, and in this sense as prior to it.

2. Sensation is not only the ground of perception—not only conditions it so that perception cannot be without sensation—but it also determines and shapes perception. Only as perception conforms itself exactly to the sensation is it legitimate or sound.

It will ever·be borne in mind that the cognitive act, the perception, does not always fasten immediately on the actual impression—the feeling, the sensation as first springing from the interaction of the mind with the object. Sometimes, perhaps generally, it is the sensation only as retained by the imagination which is immediately regarded, as already indicated. §§ 85–88. We could not err much in saying that the mind is often feeling, imaging, and perceiving at the same time. The mind is a nature of ceaseless activity. Ever changing from one state to another, as well as a nature having a diversity of functions which may all be in simultaneous action, it is difficult often to mark the transition or to distinguish exactly where one form of mental act or affection ends and another begins. The whole exposition of mental phenomena must be presented and regarded in the light of this unceasing complex activity, bringing in by indistinguishable gradations one mental state out of another, changing from one into another. It will not be necessary in the discussion of the cognitive act to bring out into more formal notice this distinction between the form in the sensibility and that in the imagination.

Generally and loosely speaking, sensation and perception are in the inverse ratio of each other. The stronger the sensation, the weaker the perception; and the stronger the perception, the weaker the sensation.

Sir William Hamilton has exemplified this general law in the comparison of the several special senses. In sight, perfection is at the maximum, sensation at the minimum. We are hardly conscious of any feeling in seeing an ordinary object; we are conscious of a decided knowledge of objects that we see. We look at the orange; the sight itself is without any feeling intense enough to be noticed; the knowledge of its being before us, of its being round and yellow, is perfect beyond that given by all the other senses combined. In hearing, there is far more of feeling than in sight; far less of knowledge. In taste and smell and special touch, feeling greatly predominates and the perception is relatively slight and limited.

If we take again any particular sense and regard it separately from the other senses, we notice that generally if the feeling is strong, per-

ception is weak, and the reverse. If the sensation of sight, for instance, be strong, we are daz-
zled—we feel intensely; but we perceive comparatively little.

This law, however, cannot be adopted as absolute or universal. The sensation may be so
weak as to occasion no perception at all, when
by the law it should be at its maximum. The
strength of the perception often varies directly,
not inversely, as the sensation. If a man touch
me gently with his finger, I hardly feel it perhaps, and hardly perceive the fact that I am
touched, or what touched me, I have but little
knowledge because I have but little feeling. If
he strike me violently with his cane I both feel
and perceive intensely.

This general truth, however, is ever to be
borne in mind that whatever the relation between the sensation and the perception in respect
to their comparative intensity or strength, either
one may become the object of consciousness to
the exclusion of the other. The light may come
streaming in from every visible object upon my
eye and engage my whole mind with the mere
feeling of its cheering impressions, so that I shall
distinguish not a single object and have no conscious perception; or I may so attend to the
knowledge of particular objects as not to be distinctly aware of any sensation.

§ 143. THE SPHERE OF PERCEPTION is the
world of sensible objects—the entire realm of

external phenomena of which we can have any intelligence.

§ 144. Perception is an act of presentative knowledge. It gives the knowledge of the object simply, without distinguishing it into subject and attribute.

I perceive an orange; but in the perception itself I only know it as an object without passing on to think it to be round or yellow.

§ 145. Perception gives accordingly only an immediate knowledge, in the sense that the knowledge which it gives is not mediated through the distinction of subject and attribute. In another relation, it should be observed, perception is said to give a mediate knowledge in so far as the knowledge of the external object is mediated through the sense - perception. Knowledge is thus in one relation immediate, and in another, mediate.

It is true that every object that can be known must have an attribute. It is true that the mind tends to pass beyond the stage of incomplete knowing to the complete knowledge under or through an attribute. But perception is confined to the first stage. It does not discriminate attributes. This discriminative or completed knowledge will be investigated hereafter.

§ 146. It has been a question much discussed among philosophers whether in perception we have an actual and immediate or only an inferential knowledge of the external reality:—when

I perceive *the sun,* have I an immediate knowledge of the sun, or do I make up my knowledge
by divers observations or from divers impressions or by inference from such impressions.
The discussion has been confused through differing uses of language and differing apprehensions
of the point at issue. The conclusions, moreover, have been influenced greatly by more general theories of knowledge. The simple facts,
which will hardly be questioned by any candid
thinker, are :—First, that in perception proper,
the object reaches the mind at last only through
the medium of the nervous organism, whatever
other agencies may have previously intervened.
Secondly, the energy in the nervous organism
thus reaching the mind is recognized as an energy coming from without, so that the mind
must be conscious of an exterior energy impressing it, and accordingly be conscious of an external reality immediately present and interacting
with it. The source from which the energy originally issued, it may be, is a matter for inference.
When we feel the heat of the sun, the energy
immediately impressing us is the nerve-force of
the body, which only represents the force that
had impressed the nerves, and this latter force
may have reached the body through divers
agencies. The sun itself is not immediately
present with the perceiving mind. It may be
that it will be possible to determine the original
source of the energy causing the sensation, to

identify the sun as the source of the heat which we feel, only after divers experiences and by inference. The conclusion is accordingly that in perception we are conscious of an external object, but may not be able to identify the object except by the exercise of the judgment. Perception gives externality of object, but not necessarily the particular external object. § 20.

This great truth that the human mind is thus in immediate conscious communion with the outer world, cannot then reasonably be questioned. The universal consciousness of men attests it. The inability to determine in many cases the actual source of the energy that impresses the mind, to trace back the movement of the energy to its original source, cannot in reason shake our confidence in the general truth. Presumably there are many things which the finite mind of man does not know, perhaps even is not able to know, at least in its immaturity. But it does know some things; and it knows that it knows them. It does know, by immediate perception and beyond all question, that it sometimes receives impressions from an external force upon it; it does accordingly know immediately external realities. It may know but a part. It may be that it knows vastly more of external realities mediately than immediately. But this great fact of immediate perception, however limited and partial,—this fact of immediate consciousness and knowledge of the outer world

—is beyond all dispute. It is a truth of inestimable value to psychological science, to knowledge generally. It sustains a vital relationship to human character and destiny. It is a momentous truth that we are in immediate contact with the outer world, that there is something besides ourselves, without us, about us, above us; something real; something that concerns us; something which has to do with us and with which we have to do.

# CHAPTER III.

§ 147. INTUITION *is that function of the intelligence by which it apprehends a supersensible object presented directly to the mind itself.*

This function has been variously designated as self-consciousness, the faculty of internal perception, the faculty of internal apprehension.

The term *intuition* has been used in psychological phraseology in different senses. It is thus used to denote the power, the object, the mental exertion, and the result;—that is, it is used to denote the intuitive function or power; the intuited object; the intuiting action; and the accomplished act of intuition—its result.

In German science an intuition may be either of sensible or of supersensible objects;—may denote an external or internal perception. In English literature the term *intuition* is often used to signify a necessary or self-evident truth. The preferable use of it as a technical term is that indicated in our definition, to denote the function of the intelligence in apprehending internal or supersensible phenomena, thereby distinguished from perception, which has to do with sensible phenomena. Intuition and perception accordingly constitute the total function of presentative knowledge.

§ 148. The sphere of Intuition, in its narrower sense, comprises all that takes place in the mind itself—all its feelings, thoughts, volitions. We observe or apprehend these mental states; we are conscious of them, we know them. It also, in a broader sense, comprises all supersensible realities presenting themselves to the mind. If there be energies interacting with our minds directly, they must be apprehended by us as having an external reality, and yet not material or object of the bodily sense. It may be that the Divine Spirit thus immediately interacts with our spirits. To this class must belong also the realities of time and space, if they are to be recognized as realities. The consideration of these ideas will come up more conveniently in a subsequent chapter. §§ 190–193. Our immediate apprehensions of these supersensible objects are proper intuitions.

§ 149. An intuition is an act of presentative knowledge. The object—the feeling, the cognition, the volition, the supersensible reality—is simply presented before any resolving of it into the dual of subject and attribute: of course before any attribution in respect to it.

Intuition is, therefore, an incomplete knowledge. It does not distinguish a feeling into something having an attribute. We have in an

intuition only the knowledge of the feeling before distinguishing it as strong or weak, as real
or imaginary, as having this or that property.
Our minds by the tendency of their nature press
on to a complete knowledge.  But it is convenient to recognize this completed knowledge as
attained by two distinguishable stages.  Intuition, like perception, brings us only over the
first stage.  It gives only incomplete and preparatory knowledge.

§ 150. An Intuition gives, accordingly, an immediate knowledge, in the twofold sense, first,
that the knowledge it gives is not mediated to
us through an attribution ; and secondly, that its
object is not presented through the bodily senses.

It follows from this that inasmuch as attribution ever gives a truth, an intuition properly regards an object, not a truth.  If a truth, that is,
if a proposition, be regarded in intuition, it is as
an object simply ; in the intuition proper of a
truth or proposition there is no affirmation by
the mind itself that the proposition is a true one,
or indeed that it has any other attribute, as of
being clear, important, or the like.  Like perception, intuition is simple apprehension without
attribution.

# CHAPTER IV.

## THOUGHT.

§ 151. THOUGHT *is that function of the intelligence by which an object is known by means of an attribute.*

The term *thought*, like *intuition*, is used in the fourfold sense of (1) the faculty; (2) its object; (3) the exersise of the faculty; (4) the result or product of the exercise.

The faculty itself is, moreover, called by different names, as the Discursive Faculty, the Elaborative Faculty, the Comparative Faculty, the Faculty of Relations.

The nature of thought may be thus exemplified. If an orange is presented to my sight or touch, I have a sensation and a perception of it. So far as I am only perceiving, I do not distinguish any attribute apart from the subject or that to which the attribute is supposed to belong; the perception does not reach the distinction expressed in the proposition; *the orange is round.* Perception carries my mind only through the first or preparatory stage of knowing. But when my mind passes on to the second stage or to that of a completed knowledge, it has a

15

*thought* of the orange, which is properly and fully expressed in the proposition, *this thing is round.* I have now (1) a subject of which an attribute is thought—*this thing;* (2) an attribute belonging to this subject—*round;* and (3) that which is expressed by the word *is*, which identifies this subject and this attribute as one and the same. This is a typical form of all primitive thought, to which all thought however complex, however derived, may ever be referred back as the standard and model of all. I think when I distinguish in a perception or intuition, attribute and subject, and then affirm the attribute of the subject, as in the proposition : *the orange is round.*

It will be observed that the thought, *this thing is round*, is before all proper abstraction, before all analysis, before all generalization. A blind person for the first time coming into the warm rays of the sun might have a thought of a thing as warm without knowing anything else about the sun. If his mind were left to its own tendency he could, on perceiving the warmth, proceed to a completed knowledge by thinking a subject as having an attribute. He would have the thought : *this thing—the sun—is warm.* But in this he would not have abstracted anything— any attribute from any other thing or from any other attribute; for by the supposition there had been given him but one thing, one attribute. He had not properly analyzed anything or any attribute; for the thing was one and single and the attribute was one and simple, and neither therefore could be analyzed. He had not generalized; for this thing might have been to him the first and only thing of a supposable class of warm things; it might have been to him the first conscious experience of the attribute of warmth. Abstraction, analysis, generalization, are processes which are applicable properly to complex and to derivative thought and apply to aggregated subjects and attributes. Single and simple thought may take place without any of these processes. In order to obtain a clear and accurate notion of thought in its essential nature it is desirable to clear our view from all those processes which are not of the very essence of thought; from all those processes accordingly which can be applied only to complex or derivative thought.

§ 152. Thought follows and pre-supposes either perception or intuition, the one or the other.

The progress of the mind from the perception to the thought may be more or less rapid. It may be instantaneous, or the mind may linger on the perception to obtain a deeper and fuller impression; and thus it may happen that the progress may be arrested and the perception never ripen into full thought.

It is to be remarked, also, that a previous thought, as well as a perception or intuition, may be the antecedent to a new thought. The finiteness and dependence of the human mind, however, compel us to the belief that perception, perhaps intuition, also, must have preceded the first thought.

§ 153. The three constituent elements of every thought are:—

1. THE SUBJECT, or that of which some attribute is thought;

2. THE ATTRIBUTE, or that which is thought of the subject; and

3. THE COPULA, or that which affirms or denies the attribute of the subject; that is, which identifies them, or differences the one from the other.

These three elements are necessary in all valid thought, whether primitive or derivative. If not expressed they must be implied. Explicitly or implicitly, they exist in all legitimate thought. There is ever to be found in a thought a subject implying an attribute belonging to it, an attribute implying a subject to which it belongs, and the union or identification of the subject and this attribute. In the thought *this thing is round*, the subject, *this thing*—orange—is not really different from the attribute; we do not apprehend *the orange*, and then *roundness;* it is the same as the attribute, and is in fact identified with it in the thought by the copula, *is*.

In interpreting an expression in language of an act of thought, such as this—*the orange is round*—it is often necessary to bear in mind that language is, strictly speaking, the representation immediately of our thoughts of things, not of the things themselves, or even of the things as perceived.

The expression means strictly: the orange as thought by me is round. That is, my concept of the orange is identical in one respect with my concept of roundness. The two terms, known as subject and attribute, that are united or identified in the full body of the judgment, are not things, but thoughts of things. They are correlatives, the one necessarily implying the other; neither can be without the other. They denote distinctions which exist only in thought, not in the reality of things. When we speak of the subject as the unknown basis of attributes, we can mean only that of subject apart from its correlative attribute, we can know nothing; we know nothing except through some attribute, as we can know no attribute except as we know, so far at least, some subject to which it belongs. Knowledge, is in fact, when full and complete, nothing but the recognition of an object as something with an attribute.

The term *substance* is synonymous with *subject*, as is also *substratum*. They are all words from the Latin and alike point to that which is conceived to underlie attributes. *Substance* and *substratum* are used more in metaphysical discourse, while *subject* is a technical word used in logical science, although not confined to this use. An attribute expressed in a proposition, is in logic

termed a *predicate*. The subject and predicate
in a logical proposition are called *terms*, from the
Latin *termini*, limits, being the terminal elements,
while the copula is the middle and connecting
element of the proposition.

Thought is properly called the *discursive* intelligence, inasmuch as, when a perception is presented to it, the mind in thought runs in two
directions—*discurrit*—recognizing the single object presented in the perception under the twofold form of subject and attribute.

The object remains the same ; it is still single.
The change from the singleness in the perception
to the twofoldness in the thought is in the mind
alone.    But the mind retains the original singleness in the object by its identifying the twofold
members of the thought through the copula.

§ 154. The copula, it appears from the fore-
going exposition, is the more vital constituent in
thought.   Its function is purely either (1), that of
identifying some object with some attribute, that
is, of asserting that such object is in whole or in
part the same as the attribute ; or (2), that of
differencing the object from some supposed attribute, that is, of denying that the subject is the
same as the supposed attribute.

As there can be no complete act of thought in
which there are not a subject and an attribute,
identified or differenced, wholly or partially, the
function of thought is appropriately designated
as the function of *the same and the different*.   Its

essential principle, its determining characteristic or law is accordingly the principle of sameness and difference, or, in another like significant phrase, of identity and diversity. This is its one fundamental and comprehensive law :—ALL THOUGHT MUST IDENTIFY OR DIFFERENCE.

§ 155. But of this general law there may be distinguished four different modifications which thus become special laws of thought. The four consist of two pairs, in each of which pairs is one positive and one prohibitory law. They are evolved as follows :

If all legitimate thought identifies or differences subject and attribute, then, clearly, if we think we must do this and do nothing else, we have thus the first pair of laws :—

*First Fundamental Law of Thought, positive ;* THE LAW OF DISJUNCTION ;—*In all thinking we must identify or difference subject and attribute.*

*Second Fundamental Law of Thought, prohibitory ;* THE LAW OF EXCLUSION ;—*In all thinking we must not do anything else than either identify or difference.*

The second pair of laws apply the first pair to specific acts of thought, in determining precisely what is to be identified or differenced.

*Third Fundamental Law of Thought, positive ;* THE LAW OF IDENTITY ;—In all thinking we must identify with the subject only the attribute that belongs to it or difference from the subject only an attribute that does not belong to it—in other words, *we must identify only the same and difference only the different.*

*Fourth Fundamental Law of Thought, prohibitory;* THE LAW OF CONTRADICTION;—In all thinking we must not identify with the subject an attribute that does not belong to it, nor difference from the subject an attribute that belongs to it—in other words, *we must not identify the different, and we must not difference the same.*

The third law in this enumeration has more commonly been placed as the first of the fundamental laws, and the fourth as the second, reversing the order of the pairs. The first and second in this enumeration have been generally combined in one. But logical consistency requires that the two forms—positive and prohibitory—be distinguished in this pair as in the other. A like practical convenience is gained from the separation of the two.

It is evident that there can be no other fundamental law of thought, of this order at least. The enumeration is exhaustive as appears from the application of the laws themselves.

The first pair of laws, it may be observed, prescribe what is requisite in any thinking ; the second, what is requisite in right thinking. The first pair prescribe what must be observed in order to any form of thought; the second, what must be observed in order to any right thought.

§ 156. These four fundamental laws of thought are thus educed directly from the very nature of

thought—from its one essential attribute or characteristic as ever identifying or differencing. They
are valid and authoritative over all thinking,
simply because obviously there can be no true
thinking except as they are observed. Their
validity and authority are founded thus in the
nature of thought, not at all in any consent of
men. They are not assumed; they are not properly *a priori*, for they are evolved from an observed act of thought—from experience; they
are not conditional to thought or experience,
only as they are essential to all thought which
could not be if they were not observed, in the
same way as roundness and brightness are conditional to the existence of a sun; they do not
precede thought—are not prior to it—but necessarily appear in thought.

They are, further, the validating principles of
all thought. If observed we have legitimate
thought—true thought, so far at least as the
essential element in thinking is concerned. The
subject may be erroneously assumed, the attribute may be erroneously viewed; but if as assumed and viewed, subject and attribute are recognized as the same, the thought is so far true
and valid. Here is to be found the only fitting
and decisive ultimate test of thought—in the fact
that these fundamental laws of thought are observed in it.

§ 157. There are commonly reckoned three
generic forms of thought regarded as product:

*the judgment, the concept, the reasoning.* But it is more correct to regard the judgment as the one primitive form of thought. The judgment is tri-membral, being constituted of the two terms or concepts—the subject and the attribute—and the copula. These three members emerge with and in the judgment, as organic parts of the one body. They are congenital with it and with one another. The reasoning is a derivative move-ment of thought from a judgment.

§ 158. THE JUDGMENT may be defined as *that act of the intelligence in which an object is recog-nized under the form of a subject and attribute.*

It is of two generic forms: (1) *affirmative*, in which the attribute is identified with the subject, or recognized as the same in whole or in part with it, as, *the sun is bright;* and (2) *negative*, in which the attribute is denied of the subject or differenced from it, as, *the sun is not dark.* The relation between the subject and the attri-bute in an act of thought is variously indicated in language.

When expressed in language the logical judg-ment is called a *proposition;* and in grammatical science it is known as the *sentence.* The *attribute* is in logical and grammatical technicality known as the *predicate.*

§ 159. THE CONCEPT is either one of the two terminal members of the judgment—the subject or the attribute.

Its name is from the Latin, *con-ceptum*, importing, that from its very nature it is to be *taken with* the other term of the judgment of which it is a member.

As a member the concept ever implies a judgment, as a limb implies the body of which it is a member. It arises or comes to be in the mind simultaneously with the judgment, as members come to be simultaneously with the body. The single object, apprehended by the mind in perception or intuition, is in the act of thinking resolved into the dual of subject and attribute which are identified or differenced in the judgment. § 151.

There are accordingly the two classes of concepts : *subject-concepts* and *attribute-concepts.* It is often of importance to accurate thinking that the characteristics of these two classes be carefully discriminated.

If we unite the subjects of several judgments having the same predicate, we have *generic* or *class-concepts*, which are expressed in grammatical *class-nouns.* This process of thought in deriving this kind of concepts is *Generalization.*

If we unite the predicates of several judgments having the same subject, we have *composite concepts*, expressed in grammatical *abstracts.* This is the logical process of *Determination.*

We may think of an attribute as a subject. We may take thus the attribute *round* and think of it as having this or that attribute. We express it in that case in the form of a noun—

*roundness ;* as we say, *the roundness is perfect, the roundness is imperfect ; it is that of a circle or that of a sphere ;* and the like. Then we may unite several subjects of this kind when parts of judgments having the same predicate, and we have a class of attributes. A class of attributes is called in distinction from a class of original subjects, a *category*, from a Greek word signifying *predicated.* A CATEGORY *is a class of attributes.*

§ 160. THE REASONING is *a derivative from one judgment to another.*

The derivation may consist in a change of the form or in a change of the matter of the primitive judgment.

The derivation may be by a single step as in *immediate reasonings ;* or by two or more steps as in *mediate reasonings.*

It is the province of logic to unfold the laws of thought and the different forms of valid thought, distinguishing the different kinds, with their several characteristics. There are, however, two subordinate movements of thought so important to science that an exceptional mention of them may properly be made here. They are the two forms of Mediate Reasonings, that is, reasonings in which the conclusion is reached from a given proposition or premise through another proposition, and more exactly through one of the terms of a proposition. They are distinguished from each other respectively as the *deductive* movement when from the whole to the part, or as the *inductive* movement when from one part to another part of the same whole. These are the two and, of this order obviously, the only two relationships in thought as respects quantity. They are co-ordinate movements. The deductive movement has received most of the consideration of logical writers; systems of formal logic being for the most part simply treatises on deductive logic. Inductive thought has been overlooked or neglected, and has been much misunderstood, its true relation to the other movement of thought as respects quantity—the deductive movement— being ignored or misconstrued. The term *induction* has recently been very vaguely used in its application to what is supposed to be the characteristic modern method of science, in distinction from the ancient method. In this use it often signifies simply this :—that the method is one of observation, one of individual fact, combined perhaps with generalization. But induction properly is simply a movement of thought from one part to another part of the same whole as deduction is from the whole to some part. Generalization, which is often confounded with logical determination, is wholly foreign from induction and may be conjoined with it or not. Induction has its own laws and legitimate forms, and admits the fullness and preciseness of exposition that deduction has received. It is the vital movement of thought in the study of nature. Modern science can regulate its processes and validate its results only by recognition of these laws and forms.

# CHAPTER V.

## THE CATEGORIES OF PURE THOUGHT.

§ 161. By a Category is understood, as before stated, § 159, a class of attributes, as distinguished from a class of things or of subjects. In the study of the nature of thought it is very desirable to ascertain the attributes that are proper to thought and are presented to our minds in every instance of thought. To inspect any such instance of thought, that is, to bring before our intuition the attributes that are presented when we think, and that may be discerned in every thought, to note the attributes thus presented, to group them into classes, is one of the leading necessities in a complete psychology.

To collect these attributes into classes and thus frame a system of the categories of thought, has been from the earliest days of philosophy a zealous labor of the ablest thinkers. We have as the results of these labors the Hindoo system of categories, the system of Aristotle, and also divers modern systems, among which ranks most conspicuous that of Kant. These systems are certainly but approximations to an ideal per-

fection and have been, each in its turn, subjected
to severe criticism. They have been condemned
and reprobated especially, as was to be expected
they would be, by men who had not carefully
ascertained what a category as a class of attributes means. A system of categories of thought
is simply a systematic collection of the general
attributes pertaining to thought. In forming it
we are to proceed just as we would in forming a
system of the attributes belonging to external
bodies. In this latter case we take some particular body—an orange—and note the attributes
presented to our perception and gather these
into classes, as in Hamilton's enumeration, of
*extension, incompressibility, mobility, situation, at-
traction, repulsion, inertia.* Just in an analogous
way we take a thought in its simplest form and
note what attributes are presented to our intuition. The enumeration which we subjoin may
not be complete; it might be presumptuous to
claim such perfection of investigation in this
stage of psychological science. But we may in
our measure do a satisfactory work for ourselves
if we proceed as far as our ability will allow,
carefully and in scientific method.

§ 162. Reverting to our type-form of a primitive thought—*the orange is round*—we recall its
origin in a perception in which an object, single
and simple, was apprehended by the mind, being
presented to it through the external sense. The
perception was an incomplete stage of intelli-

gence. The mind pressed on to a completed
stage. The transition might be immediate, so
that the thought should be simultaneous with
the perception. It might, however, be prolonged
more or less, or, indeed, possibly be broken off
so as to be followed by no proper thought. The
completed stage of intelligence gave us its discursive form in the judgment, the primitive form
of thought ; the essential characteristic of which,
distinguishing it from the perception, was found
to be that the single object in the perception
was now discriminated into the twofold form
of subject and attribute which, however, the
mind still kept as one and identical—the subject
not being a different reality from the attributes,
but the same as they. The copula, being the
identifying element, is thus essential to all
thought and must characterize every valid derivative of thought. As the mind thus in reflection
turns in thought upon what was given as one
object in the perception, it may recognize a
second attribute or a third, in fact an indefinite
number of attributes—intrinsic, as *yellow, juicy,
decaying*, or extrinsic as *present, selected from a
number*, and the like ; essential or accidental.
Such are attributes pertaining to the object presented to the mind in the perception and originating in that. But there is another more important class of attributes which originate in the
thought itself and pertain to thought as such, and
therefore may be recognized in any judgment

whatever. These we now proceed to enumerate and unfold.

§ 163. CATEGORY OF IDENTITY. In the first place, in reflecting on the judgment, *the orange is round*, we recognize the truth that as the copula, which identifies the subject and the attribute, is of the very essence of this judgment, and of every judgment, and consequently of all thought or completed knowledge, everything of which we can think must admit this identification. There is given in this, as in every judgment, this attribute of *identity*, pertaining to whatever may be thought by the human mind, as every such object must, in order to be thought, present a subject that can be identified with an attribute or be differenced from it.

We have thus what is called the category of *identity*—the most fundamental of all the categories of pure thought. It will be remarked in regard to it, first, that it is an intuition. It is not a perception ; it does not belong to the sensation ; it does not belong to the external object— the orange. It is presented to us by the act of the intelligence in its completed form of a judgment. It is an intuition.

Next, it is a necessary attribute, in the sense that it is impossible to think at all without having this attribute present in the thought, although seldom perhaps brought out into distinct consciousness. It is as necessary to thought as form and color to the orange, or to any visible

16

object.   It is in truth the essential characteristic of thought.

Further, it is universal, for no thought is ever
experienced without it.

Still further, it is presented to the mind in a
way precisely analogous to that in which the
form and the color of the orange are presented.
It is in the thought, and the mind takes notice
of it ; as the form is in the orange and the mind
takes notice of it.   We call this notion of the
attribute in the one case an intuition, in the
other a perception, simply to distinguish the
different sources from which they come.   The
intuition comes from the thought within; the
perception from the orange without.   There is
no mystery about the one more than about the
other.   The one is the attribute of an inner experience, the other of an outer object, both being
founded in the nature of objects—the nature of
mind and body.   It is not to be assumed as if
it had no ground.   Thought itself is such that
it has this attribute ; as the orange is such that
it has this round form.   It misleads in regard to
its nature to speak of identity as a native cognition of the mind, for it is no more so than figure
in a visible object is a native cognition; or to
speak of it as an original principle, independent in
its rise in the mind of actual experience ; or as
a regulative law in any other sense than that
every essential attribute of an object is a regulative law of that object.   Identity is a regulative

law of thought, simply because it is an essential attribute of thought—of thought as an actual experience, as a mental phenomenon.

The opposite of identity is *difference*. The mind separates a subject from a supposed attribute as well as unites; it denies as well as affirms. These are the two alternative forms of thought—identifying and differencing; affirming and denying. We have accordingly the two kinds of judgments, *affirmative* and *negative*, as already named.

Identity is *total* or *partial*. It is total when the subject and the attribute which are identified in the judgment are in all respects one and the same, as *I=I*, or *the self is the self*. It is partial when the subject is only in part, in some respects but not in all, the same as the attribute. Most actual judgments are partially identical. In the judgment, *the orange is round*, the subject *orange* is identified only in respect to its form as *round*—is identified with but one of its manifold attributes.

Partial identity is denoted by the terms *likeness, similarity, resemblance*. These terms denote attributes, and as such ever imply subjects and are properly applicable only to subjects, whether original subjects or attributes treated as subjects. We say : *an orange is like a peach in its form ;* we do not say, *round is peach-like ;* while we might say *the roundness is peach-like.* Similarity and resemblance as the etymology indicates, is but partial sameness or partial identity—sameness in some respects, not in all.

We have thus divers modifications of this attribute of identity. Besides those that have been mentioned there are manifold other intrinsic modifications; and of the extrinsic modifications, or those which are relative to the objects of thought or to other mental phenomena, there is obviously an indefinite number. All these modifications including also all analogous modifications of the category of difference, are grouped together under the one class and known by the name of the category of identity.

§ 164. 2. CATEGORY OF QUANTITY. It is obvious from an inspection of our typical judgment, *the orange is round*, that there is presented to us in a way perfectly analogous to that in which the attribute of *round* was presented to our perception and precisely as the attribute of identity was presented to our intuition, a second attribute of the judgment, which is designated under the name of *Quantity*. There is the one subject and there is the one attribute; these are different in a certain respect; at least so far as this, that one is subject of which something is thought and the other is attribute which is thought of the subject. They are thus two, and yet they are one; they are identical in a certain respect; they are in fact identified in the very nature of the judgment. Two things—the two terms—are united. This property of being known as more than one in such a way that the several parts may be united in one whole, is the essential property of quantity.

Such is the rise of the category of Quantity. It originates in a judgment as the completed stage of the intelligence by which an object given as single in the perception is recognized in the judgment as being in the twofold form of subject and attribute, which terms, constituting the matter of the judgment, are identified in it. Perception gives no quantity ; this is a property of thought. All thought is thus necessarily quantitative. We may discern this attribute in every thought, every judgment, as we discern the attribute of *round* in the *orange*. It belongs to thought as thought ; it characterizes all thought. It pertains, however, it should be observed, to the matter of thought—to the terms.

It is not an original, independent principle, existing by itself in the mind, or arising in the mind by any law of its nature, otherwise than as a simple attribute of thought. It is originally presented to us as an attribute of thought in the inspection or intuition of the thought itself, precisely as the attribute of *round* is presented to us in the perception of the orange.

On this simple notion of quantity as one of the essential attributes of thought, to be recognized in any completed form of thought, rest all the modifications of quantity as diversely applied in the manifold processes of thought.

But one form or derivation or application of this attribute should be specifically mentioned— it is the relation of whole and parts. The two terms of a judgment are parts which are in the identification of the judgment brought into one whole. The relation of whole and parts has thus its origin in the judgment. This relation becomes more pronounced in the process of logical amplification. Thus, if we have two propositions affirming two attributes of the same subject, as *the sun is round, the sun is bright*, we have by uniting them, *the sun is round and bright*, a whole of attributes, *the sun* containing the two attributes of *round* and *bright* as parts of it. Whenever we think of an object as being a whole, having parts, or as a part of a whole, we think such an object under the category of Quantity.

§ 165. 3. CATEGORY OF MODALITY. A third attribute of thought is presented to us as we turn our view on the more essential element of thought—the copula—which identifies the two terms or parts of the matter—the subject and the attribute ; it is the attribute of *Modality.* The copula, or the proper thinking element in the judgment, is in this respect distinguished from the matter or the terms of the judgment. While it is our own, and is presented to our intuition by the mind itself, the matter of the judgment may be originally from a source foreign or extrinsic to the mind, and in every individual instance of

thought is but a *datum*—something presented to
.the thought.

Now, as thought cannot deny itself, it must
ever accept its own action.   To thought itself
the identifying element necessitates its own affir-
mations or negations.   The matter as foreign to
thought, is in reference to our thinking, accidental, contingent.   To question whether the subject and the attribute are identified in valid
thought is absurdity itself.   The skeptic who
questions this destroys the very foundation of all
thought, of all opinion, of all belief, of all knowledge ; and has no right to think, much less to
question the thoughts of others.

Thus we have given in the very nature of a
judgment the distinction of the necessary in
thought from the contingent.   But knowledge
characterized in this respect as necessary or contingent, is thereby brought under the general
category of *modality ;* just as an orange characterized as round comes under the general attribute of form.

The leading forms in which this attribute appears are such as *possible* and *impossible; probable*
and *improbable; necessary* and *contingent.*

As in the case of the other two categories, this
one of modality is applied to objects external to
the mind.   Just so far as such objects approxi-
mate the nature of thought in this respect, they
are regarded as necessary or the opposite.   We
speak thus of the necessities in nature as we

speak of the necessities in truth or knowledge. But this language is not to be taken in its strict and literal import.  Nature reveals no necessities to us.  We know nature only through the testimony of our senses ; and as Reid profoundly and truly says: " Our senses testify only what is, and not what must necessarily be."  This truth is re-affirmed by Sir William Hamilton, who says : " All necessity is in fact subjective to us."

Modality, it is to be remarked, in its different modifications of necessity and contingency, is not an independent, self-existing thing ; it is an attribute, and properly and originally an attribute of thought.  It originates in that ; it is a necessary property of all thought, as all thought, all true knowledge, ever admits of being regarded as necessary or otherwise.

These categories or generic classes of attributes are categories of pure thought.  That is, they are attributes which pertain to thought itself irrespective of its content.  They partake of the very essence of thought and must therefore exist in every legitimate form of thought.  Identity, Quantity, and Modality, which last named category is more commonly recognized under the name of Necessity, constitute the most fundamental class of those ideas which have very erroneously been considered as "native cognitions," "first principles," "self-evident and primitive notions," "*a priori* cognitions," in the sense that they exist in the mind prior to all experience and are even conditional to any experience—any feeling, thought, or purpose. They have been represented as if held, like arrows in a quiver, at the back of all intelligence, and as if thrust forward by some inconceivable force inherent or extrinsic when the suitable occasion arises, or when the fitting object appears, and fastened on the object. These ideas, the ideas of identity, quantity, and modality or necessity, are known to exist; it is known that they do not belong to the object in itself ; the inference has been that they exist in the mind previous to the presentation· of the object, although not manifesting their existence until the object is presented. When that appears, the suitable idea, it is supposed, leaps forth from its hidden repository and invests the object so that in the knowledge of the object it necessarily appears in the garb of that idea. The preposterousness of the whole assumption is fairly imaged in the waggish direction, how to make a cannon :—"take a hollow and pour melted iron about it." The difficulty is to find the " hollow;" —to discover where it is kept ; in what state it exists ; how we are to get hold of it; in what possible mode or form or relation these " native cognitions " exist in the mind. The very essence of the human mind is activity ; its life is first manifested in some action, and can have no conceivable receptacle of ideas till they have been originated in positive exertion of mental energy. Still further, what determines the idea to leap forth and fasten itself upon its object ; how does it know that the object presented is a suitable one to receive the idea? The assumption cannot be viewed from any point without exposing its utter preposterousness. The simple truth in the case is that these ideas are the attributes of the intelligence in the form of thought, to be attained on mere inspection of any act of thought. Sir William Hamilton tells the whole truth respecting them when he says they are "the laws of thought." A law of thought can here mean nothing but an essential attribute of thought.

# CHAPTER VI.

§ 166. The intelligence is modified in a two-fold way in its relations to the sensibility, (1) as receiving truth, and (2) as expressing truth. The intelligence is thus both a capacity of knowledge and also a faculty of knowledge just as the sensibility is passive as recipient of form, and also active as productive of form. In its function as a capacity, the action of the intelligence is denominated *Apprehension ;* in its function as a faculty, it is denominated *Representation.*

§ 167. INTELLECTUAL APPREHENSION is accordingly defined as *the function of the mind in receiving the true.*

It includes Perception and Intuition. These are the different kinds of apprehension distinguished in reference to the two sources of knowledge, external and internal.

It is distinguished also in respect to the grounds on which the true is accepted as such. It is *simple* when the true is apprehended as it comes in its own light or as through the natural

channels of communication as through the senses
or on testimony.      It is *comprehensive* when the
true is apprehended in relation to the grounds on
which its acceptance is to rest, and is accepted
by reason of these grounds, that is, as necessarily
involved in other admitted truths.   Simple apprehension thus is intellectual *faith* in its exacter
sense, as that form of knowledge in which the
intelligence accepts the true as true on the simple ground of the truth's own nature or the
trustworthiness of its natural channels.    The
human intelligence depends on the true as the
object necessary for its action, as its natural correlate.   In faith it gives to this sense of organic
relationship and dependence its proper sway, and
accepts the true as simply accredited by this
organic relationship between it and the true.
This is the meaning of faith as distinguished
from demonstrated knowledge.    The term is,
however, familiarly used to distinguish a lower
or weaker intelligence from a higher and more
intense form of intelligence.

Intellectual apprehension is related on its
passive side to the sensibility.   It is, in truth, as
intimated, the intelligence side of the single mental state which, when regarded on the side of the
sensibility, is named under the forms of that
function.   Perception, thus, is but the intelligence side of sensation.

This mental act or state is modified indefinitely in respect to the relative degrees in which

the sensibility and the intelligence appear in it. The one or the other may greatly predominate in different cases. Yet even when the sensibility is predominant, we may direct our attention rather to the intellectual side, and so make it the really predominant element to our view, and then we speak of the act as apprehension and not as impression or affection or other term denoting properly a form of the sensibility.

§ 168. INTELLECTUAL REPRESENTATION is defined as *the function of the mind in presenting the true.*

It is distinguished as *Demonstration,* in the larger sense, when the grounds of the truth are presented with the truth itself.

It is related to the active side of the sensibility, the imagination proper. It differs from Philosophical Imagination only in this, that it points to the intelligence side of the act or state, while the latter term points to the imagination side.

The two functions vary indefinitely in their relative degrees of predominance in different cases.

# CHAPTER VII.

## CURIOSITY AND ATTENTION.

§ 169. The Intelligence is modified in respect to the will in a twofold way: (1) as determined in its activity only by the instincts of mind as an essentially active nature, in *curiosity;* and (2) as positively determined by the will proper, in *attention.*

§ 170. By CURIOSITY is meant, *the instinctive desire of knowledge in the human mind.*

The mind, so far as active, seeks for truth or knowledge. Such is its natural drift or tendency. This feature particularly characterizes it in its infancy. All objects of knowledge are almost equally attractive to it, for its selecting power is then feeble, and habit, taste, or disposition is undeveloped. In its progress, this instinct, unless overborne in indolence or indulgence, acquires ever additional strength. If rightly directed and cultivated it ultimately makes the intellectual giant in knowledge. With advancing development, it turns more and more to specific fields of truth and acquires distinction in particular branches of knowledge. More properly and characteristically instinctive and spontaneous, it yet comes under the regulation and control of the will, although its nature is not essentially changed by this control.

§ 171. By ATTENTION is meant *the voluntary determination of the intelligence to objects of knowledge.*

Curiosity passes into attention in the natural growth of mind as instinct passes into power of will : and the mind acquires in its growth more and more entire and absolute control over its own acts and states. The desire of knowledge— curiosity—at the same time strengthens in itself, and also " spends itself in will." Attention is susceptible of indefinite development. It is very weak in beginning study. The tyro in knowledge finds it hard to keep his thought steadily on any subject of study. The power of attention grows as he advances. In its higher degrees it marks the intellectual genius ; for nothing more charac- terizes the man of genius than the power of fixed attention.

Attention is conscious or unconscious. At first it is often necessary that the mind with de- liberate, conscious intention, bend itself to its work, exclude distracting objects, and fasten its regard on the single subject of its study. Re- peated effort in this conscious attention passes into habit ; and the mind holds on in its atten- tive study, conscious of no particular energy of the will.

Attention, as applied to external objects, is known as *Observation ;* as applied to matters of our own consciousness, it is designated *Reflection.*

---

## CHAPTER VIII.

### THE TRUE—ITS NATURE AND MODIFICATIONS.

§ 172. The True is, as already shown, § 28, the proper object of the Intelligence ;—it is that which this function of the mind immediately and exclusively respects.

The term—both in the adjective form, *true*— and also in the noun form—*truth*—is used in divers ' senses, or more properly speaking, in divers modifications of its primary meaning. In its most exact and proper uses it is applied to a completed thought or knowledge which, as we have seen, appears first in the logical judgment. A perfect judgment or thought means a true thought, and truth signifies a right or perfect judgment or thought. Corresponding to this subjective use, is the objective employment of the term to denote that which is judged or thought—the object of a perfect judgment or thought. Truth, thus, is the object upon which the knowing faculty acts; it is that which a cog-

17

nitive or knowing act respects.  A "true thing"
is that which may be perfectly known; in other
words, that which has properties congruously
united in one whole and which can accordingly
be thought or known.  A true man thus is one
who has the properties that should characterize a
man in right relationship to one another.  The
term is applied to the object of a judgment or
thought as one whole, constituted of right elements or parts rightly disposed.  A true judgment or thought thus is one in which the subject
is a true concept, that is, a true representative in
thought of the object, in which also the attribute
is one that truly belongs to the subject, and one,
moreover, in which the copula identifies or differences the subject and the attribute.  A true
proposition is such a judgment correctly expressed.  The veriest heart and core of the true
is to be found in the copula or identifying element of the judgment, signifying that the concept which appears in the subject is the same, in
whole or in part, as that in the predicate.  It is
this view of its exactest and most primitive and
germinant import which best discloses to us its
meaning and force in its divers applications and
uses.  A true copy, or generally a true representative thus, is that which, in its content of the
particulars to be copied or represented, is identical with the original; a true concept is one that
is identical in its content with the object or the
attribute which it respects; a true proposition is

one that in its proper expression identifies the subject with its attribute.

As object of the intelligence, *the true* accordingly denotes that which admits of being perfectly thought or known; in other words, that which may be known as subject identified with attribute. Thought and truth thus are exact correlatives—one subjective, the other objective. Used as concrete words they signify the same thing viewed in these two lights respectively: A thought is that which is known—a knowledge—through attributes; a truth is that which may be known—is knowable—through attributes. A perfect truth—a perfect thought—is a perfect cognition, using this term in its twofold import as both objective and subjective, through attributes; in other words, it is a cognition constituted of a true concept as subject and a true concept as attribute properly identified or differenced in the copula. An imperfect truth or thought is one in which there is imperfection in one or other or all of these particular constituents. The false is the opposite of the true, and like that, it may be perfectly false or imperfectly false. These are the three several possible particular forms under the general category of the true—the true, the imperfectly true, and the false. Each of these particular forms, even the positively false, is proper object of the intelligence; and together they make up the entire body of object for this function.  The intelligence can in its legitimate action respect nothing else.

§ 173. It follows from this exposition of the true and of thought that there must be, in every object which contains the true and can be thought, that which will admit of being attributed.  In other words, every such object must admit of being regarded as a subject having attributes.  This is the first, most fundamental and comprehensive category of the true as object of thought.  It corresponds to the first category of pure thought—identity.  This latter is purely subjective, pertaining to the thinking faculty; the former is purely objective, pertaining to the matter of the thinking act, that is, to the two terms, subject and attribute, as identified or differenced in the thinking act.

This fundamental category of the true might appropriately be designated by the name *attributableness*, so that, as we can say under the category of pure thought, all cognition is comprehended under identification, we can likewise say, all that is true is comprehended under what is attributable, that is, under what admits of the relation of subject and attribute.

§ 174. If we return now to our type-form of a primitive thought—of a judgment—*the orange is round*, we observe that the attribute *round* is contained within the subject, *the orange*.  But there are attributes which lie without the subject.  We may attribute to the orange that it is *in the hand;* that it is *now* before me; that it is *one of a number,* and the like. Some attributes accordingly are intrinsic; others, extrinsic to a subject. Obviously there can be no other attributes conceivable. They are the comprehensive forms of the true as modified in respect to attribute. All attributes are accordingly distinguished into two classes, one *Intrinsic,* the other *Extrinsic* to the subject.

INTRINSIC ATTRIBUTES are *those which lie wholly within the subject* and may be thought when that alone is presented to the mind; as *round, yellow, sweet, juicy.*

EXTRINSIC ATTRIBUTES are *those which lie without the subject* and are thought only when something besides the subject is presented to the mind; as *in the hand, present, one of a class.*

This division of attributes, it will be seen, is in exact correspondence with the obvious indications of the second category of pure thought named, that of Quantity, or more particularly that of Whole and Part. Intrinsic attributes belong to the object regarded as a whole by itself irrespectively of all other objects. Extrinsic attributes belong to the object as a part in relation to the whole or to the other parts. It will often be very helpful in study to bear in mind this important ground of distinction between the two most generic divisions of attributes. Intrinsic attributes ever respect the object as a whole in relation to its parts; Extrinsic attributes respect the object as a part.   This relationship of a part is thus twofold—to the whole and to other parts.

§ 175.  INTRINSIC ATTRIBUTES are also denominated *Properties*.   They consist of two species : *Actions* and *Qualities*.

Inasmuch as an object can be known to us only as it acts in some way upon us, only as active or as impressing, all attributes, even intrinsic attributes, strictly speaking, have this property of action in a certain sense attaching to it.   But in the analyzing power of thought, this characteristic may be dropped from view and so an attribute be regarded simply in its own special nature without positive relation to other objects. If, however, retaining a tinge from its primitive source, while yet not thought as actually affecting or impressing other objects, it admits of the designation as a property of action.   If dropping this tinge of origin entirely, the property becomes one of mere quality.

We may define properties of action as those properties which express the active character of the subject to which they belong without, however, necessary intimation of the object to which they relate, as *nutritious, gravitating*.   Properties of quality drop this suggestion of action and of object, as *round, heavy*.

Attributes of quality are generally and normally expressed by grammatical adjectives ; those of action are properly expressed by grammatical verbs combining the copula, and by participles which by themselves do not combine the copula with the attribute.

Intrinsic Attributes or Properties, moreover, are distinguished into the two species of *Essential* and *Accidental;* the former being necessary to the being of the subject, the latter not thus necessary. *Round, yellow,* or at least some attributes of figure and of color, are essential to the orange ; *specked, decaying,* are not thus essential.

§ 176. Extrinsic Attributes, also denominated attributes of Relation, are distributed into the two species of attributes of *Relation Proper* and attributes of *Condition.*

*Larger than the others, nearer,* are attributes of relation proper ; *present, now,* are attributes of condition.

To avoid the cumbrousness of the expression—*attributableness*—we may with propriety now designate this first class of attributes of the true as the category of *properties and relations.*

§ 177. CATEGORY OF SUBSTANCE AND CAUSE.— In the same way as we recognize in every instance of thought the category of attributableness embracing the two grand classes of attributes— properties and relations,—we also recognize, by turning our view to the subject or first term of the judgment, the general attribute that belongs to every object of thought, of its being a subject. The judgment, *the orange is round,* presents to our intuition this attribute of its having a subject to which something is attributed.

Inasmuch now as any subject in thought may have an attribute either in the form of quality or of action, subjects are in this relation distinguished into two distinct classes: (1) *Substances* which imply that as subjects they take attributes of quality; and (2) *Causes*, which imply attributes of action.

This general category of substance and cause accordingly embraces the two subordinate categories, that of substance and that of cause. By some writers these categories, with perhaps more propriety but with a little more clumsiness, have been named *substantiality* and *causality*.

They have manifold modifications all embraced under the general category.

If we assume merely the fact of a judgment, no matter how it came to be, whether occasioned by the presence of some external object affecting our sensual organism, or by some inner condition of our bodies, or even by a direct touch of the creative spirit moving on our spiritual nature directly and through no sensuous medium, —if we assume simply the experience of a judgment, this category of substance and cause necessarily appears. As certainly as there is a subject in every judgment, just as certainly is there this characteristic belonging to every object of thought, that it admits of being thought as a subject and either as substance or cause.

It is to be observed that the terms *substance*
and *cause* suffer a modification of meaning as applied to realities external to thought somewhat
differing from that which they bear in their fullest import as applied to the relations of thought
itself. In the world of reality, in nature as commonly spoken of, there is not, so far as we can
perceive, any such necessity as attaches directly
to every legitimate movement of thought. As
we have noticed, every such movement of
thought must give necessary results so far as the
thinking is concerned, since otherwise thought
would contradict itself, would be no more
thought ; while on the other hand, all relationships in the world of reality we must, until at
last we learn from other sources than simple observation, regard as not having necessarily in
themselves this character of necessity; that is,
we must in our thought regard them as contingent. In other words, as they are presented to
our senses, they nowhere exhibit to us this characteristic of necessity.

In respect to *substance* philosophic thought has
introduced the term *substratum* to mark its use
in the strict sense required by thought, as denoting what there is in a thing distinct from its attributes and as that in which the attributes inhere,
or that which binds them together into one and
constitutes them into a thing. But to suppose
the reality of such a *substratum* distinct from attributes is now generally recognized as preposter-

ous. The true view has been given in our exposition of the nature of thought. The relation of
substance and attribute is the initiative product
of thought in the exercise of its proper function
of identifying. This relation thus created by
thought itself, it is seen at once, must partake of
the necessities of thought. But there is in the
real world no such substance—no *substratum*—
as there is no logical subject. None has ever
been presented through the sense to thought;
and it is forbidden to thought to add any new
attribute to its object; it **can** only identify or
difference what is given to it; and in order to
this it must itself first resolve this object
given it—this *datum*—into subject and attribute.
There are in nature substances regarded as
things which can be thought under the form of
identification of subject and attribute, into which
the single object is resolved in the analysis of
thought; but subject and attribute never appear
as subsisting separately in nature, or as separate
constituents in any existing combination held
together by some bond of necessity. No such
bond is discernible by our senses. In like manner it may be shown that there is no such character of necessity, in the strictest sense, attaching
to things as active in the external world—to the
sequences or successions of nature. No such
feature is presented to the sense; and thought
cannot be allowed to impart to a reality a character which is in no way revealed to the sense.

The sense apprehends power in the external world, but power in action only, that is, change; its keenest vision can discern no real necessity connecting the action of the power with some definite result—connecting the beginning of the change with some determinate end. It is simple onflow, simple succession or sequence, simple power moving on, simple reality in perpetual change, that is revealed to us. Aside from this onflow of active being, no bond holding together the sequences is discernible. Our thought enters this onflow and separates it into parts crosswise and lengthwise—across the stream and along the stream, in wider or narrower belts; and taking up such a portion as suits its purpose, and regarding it as one, separates the upstream section from the lower one, and pronounces the upper to be the cause of the latter, recognizing a continuity that is absolutely necessary in its apprehension of the whole as one. It has resolved that which in nature is one whole into a dual of parts—a beginning part and a resulting part. Here arises the necessity which is recognized between cause and effect—a necessity which exists between the parts of the same whole—a necessity, strictly speaking, attaching to thought, not to object.

The general observation is pertinent here that the furtive transference of the qualities of proper thought to its object is a fruitful source of confusion and error in philosophical discussion. The doctrine of the Realists, thus, who supposed that *genus* and *species* must be real things because we think in the use of general terms, and that there must be a *general man* because we think of man as a genus in distinction from a man as an individual, originated in this transference. *Substance* and *cause* are terms of thought. As such they have properties that cannot legitimately be attributed to real things.

The teaching of Hamilton, it may be added, that there is " an absolute tautology between the effect and its causes," or that " causes and effects are tautological," is partial and misleading, as it leaves out the purely thought character of the causal judgment or principle of causality and can receive no interpretation except as touching merely things as observed and exterior to thought. That of Kant, on the other hand, which makes the notion of cause to " be based completely *a priori* in the understanding," is equally defective. Both cause and effect are comprised in the notion of causation or change which in the simple apprehension is single and in reality indivisible; and it is change in nature, in the real world, mental or physical, which is necessarily pre-supposed as the condition of our having the notion of cause. Reflective thought, from its very nature, without having any quiver already at its back filled with arrowy categories, of itself and by reason of its own inherent energy, seizing this apprehension—the change as observed

—recognizes in it at once a beginning and an ending, resolves the apprehended single into a dual,
one term of which is cause and the other is effect.
The two correlates are thus the pure offspring of
thought; they are the two complementary parts
of one thought-whole; and accordingly they
participate in the character of necessity that
attaches to all legitimate thought.

Such is the genesis of this notion of causality,
the offspring of thought from observed fact;
conditioned on experience, but not given in
experience; generated from thought, but not
pre-existing before actual thinking.

The true, as object, accordingly possesses in
its essential nature the characteristic of becoming
attributable when it comes into our thought, and
as such admits the generic classification indicated by the fundamental division of intrinsic
attributes or properties into qualities and actions,
viz.: into (1) the true of substance and (2) the
true of cause.

§ 178. The true, as object, is, however, but a
part of what may be object to our experience.
Side by side with it as exact co-ordinates and
complementaries, are, as has been stated, the
beautiful and the good addressing respectively
the sensibility and the will, the three together
constituting a totality of object to mental experience. The three have been very properly
styled *the three fundamental ideas,* as every
modification of mental experience must be an

affection from an object addressing us as true, or
beautiful, or good.  As the mind is conscious of
all its affections, it may know the true, the beautiful, and the good in their respective natures and
effects.  They all partake of the nature of reality,
inasmuch as they all address us from without the
thought and make each its own impress.  They
are accordingly all expressions or addresses of
power, of activity.   They are rightly called
*causes* by Aristotle, being respectively the *mate-*
*rial, formal,* and *final* in his enumeration of
causes.  The true respecting each as to its nature,
its modifications, its effects, is object to the intelligence.

We know thus the true ; we know or may
know the fact that we know ; we know or may
know also what it is to know.  It is no pleo-
nasm to say that *we know that we know.*  Our
very knowing, our knowledge, as well as our feeling, or our willing, is object to our consciousness.
We recognize this when we speak of characteristics that mark our knowledge ; as when we say,
*we know imperfectly ; we know by observation ;*
*we know mathematical truths.*  We must of course
know that we have the knowledge which we thus
characterize.  Logical science is the science of
knowledge, specifically determined in its scope
and method from the product or result of knowing, rather than from the faculty—the intelligence
—on the one hand, and from the object—the true
—on. the other.  Its province is the exposition of

the nature, laws, and forms of knowledge or thought as a product or result.

We know also the beautiful; we know that we feel; and to a good degree how we feel; we know that different objects affect us differently. The beautiful—form—is object to our intelligence as a true; as that which may be known. Æsthetic science is the science of the beautiful, determined in its scope and method from the experience or product rather than from the capacity or faculty, that is, the sensibility and the imagination, the two-sided function of form. Its province is the exposition of the nature, laws, and forms of beauty in nature and art.

So, too, we know the good; that it offers itself to us to be chosen; that it is sometimes, in fact, taken as object in our actual choice. We know that we choose, what we choose, how we choose; the good as a true is object to our intelligence; it may be known. Ethical science is the science of free choice, determined from the product rather than from the faculty or the object. Its province is the exposition of the nature, laws, and forms of duty or right choice.

§ 179. That our experience of the true as well as of the beautiful and the good, is a *true* experience,—that in other words this experience is a legitimate response to the object and is its proper effect on the mind, is a truth that will be questioned by none but the most unreasonable skeptic or agnostic. No disproof is possible; the most

that the skeptic can do is to question the suffi-
ciency of the positive proofs of the truth. These
proofs are, first, that the tendency or propensity
native to the mind toward the experience of
these ideas as objects presented to it—toward
the experience of truth, of beauty, and of right,
is presumptive proof that the capacity or faculty
and the object are one for the other, and that the
meeting or interaction between them is normal
and valid. Another proof is to be found in that
peculiar pleasure and satisfaction which follows
the right exercise of our respective functions on
their several objects. We know the exercises to be
genuine, normal, legitimate, by this test or sign.
It is evidence far from being absolutely conclusive : it is presumptive, however, and may be decisive. A further proof which will serve as confirmation of these presumptive tests or proofs, is
to be found in the universal accord between particular truths, attained it may be in many different ways and by many different minds, in different circumstances and relations. So universal is
the acceptance of this fact—that all truth is in
harmony, each part with every other—that if any
supposed truth is found to be in conflict with
another it is concluded at once that there must
be error somewhere. The true can never be in
conflict with the true. This universal experience
is the exact counterpart to the fourth fundamental law of thought in our enumeration—the
law of contradiction. The experiences of the

true by men, the acceptances of what is true by them, are, as a general law, in accord ; the supposable exceptions are few and, in fact, to a large extent at least, only apparent ; they do not materially detract from the absoluteness of the general law. Such accord is not supposable unless these experiences were a true response to their objects. Skepticism here is so irrational that it seems well-nigh needless to notice it.

§ 180. Still further, the true as object comes to us in two distinguishable ways; in one way, freely and spontaneously as it were, addressing us rather as recipients; in another way, as fruit of our endeavor or search—as result of our solicitation and inquiry. It will be serviceable in our study of the true as object to regard it under these two aspects or relations, separately and in different chapters;—first, the true as received ; and, secondly, the true as produced.

# CHAPTER IX.

## THE TRUE RECEIVED.

§ 181. It is certain that many of the truths which we hold, constituting a large share of our stock of knowledge, have come into our minds without our search or solicitation. Objects have presented themselves as things to be known to our minds, and they have been accepted. We have recognized a native element in the mind which we have called *curiosity*, a pure spontaneous propensity or craving for knowledge, combining easily on occasion with a certain voluntariness and so becoming what has been distinguished as *attention*. §§ 169–171. In this state of craving receptivity the true has been presented and been accepted. Such acceptance is properly denominated *faith*. The best definition of faith, accordingly, because the simplest and most comprehensive as well as most consonant with its etymology and use in language, is *acceptance by the mind of the true on its own address or presentation*. It is the free meeting of the knowing faculty with its object—the true. Faith is a form of knowledge because it respects the true; and the true, as we have seen, involves the identification of subject with attribute which is knowledge. But in faith the true is received or known in its own unassisted light. In faith, thus, the true is received on the testimony of the natural bearers of it to the mind, as they have access to it in the constituted interaction between mind and its objects. We believe our senses; we believe our consciousness; we believe what others tell us; we believe the indications of the natural world; we accept what they report to us on their bare testimony.

§ 182. As contradistinguished from knowledge generally, faith thus means acceptance of the true on the unaccredited presentation of itself to the mind. The terms—faith and knowledge —are loosely used, often interchangeably. But faith properly points to a primitive, underived knowledge that is unattested except as coming through natural organs of knowledge, unconfirmed, undemonstrated. Knowledge necessarily begins in faith, in simple acceptance of what is given it. This is absolutely true of the first act of knowledge; it is substantially true of the first acquisitions subsequently made in specific departments of truth. Faith is at the very foundation of knowledge. It is the characteristic spirit of the great promoters of human knowledge. Their maxim has been: "Believe that you may know." Believe the senses; believe what others say; believe the legitimate processes of knowledge. The spirit of doubt is hostile to truth.

But this faith, requisite to the highest attainments in truth, is by no means with men an absolute faith. It is the faith which is exercised with imperfect organs, by imperfect powers. It admits, rather calls for, confirmation. It loves light; it seeks to be examined in light. All truth is harmonious. Each specific faith and knowledge is a member of an organic whole, and lives and strengthens with the life and vigor of the whole body of knowledge. If particular faiths cannot be harmonized with the great body of truth, if they conflict with other better established faiths, they are thereby so far proved to be illegitimate and empty.

§ 183. The true as object of knowledge is divisible into two grand departments as it addresses the knowing faculty directly or indirectly, that is, immediately from within the mind itself or mediately through the bodily sense. It is thus *internal* or *supersensible* and *external* or *sensible*.

## I. INTERNAL OR SUPERSENSIBLE TRUTH.

§ 184. Internal truth is revealed directly to consciousness without the intervention of the bodily sense. It is the so-called intuitive truth —the truth of intuitions or internal perceptions. It is exactly commensurate, in fact it is exactly identical, with the body of revelations made to the mind by itself and other supersensible realities. The mind, regarded as a receptivity of the true which is revealed in its own acts and affections, is simply self-sense. The sphere of intuition, as before stated, is exactly defined as the sphere of internal phenomena. It gives only presentative knowledge.

§ 185. The true as object of conscious or internal knowledge has been sometimes distinguished into that which respects the phenomena of mind, and that which respects the mind itself—the self. This distinction may be allowed in the legitimate analysis made by reflective thought for certain convenient purposes of study. But a most pernicious fallacy has sometimes crept into philosophical speculation by confounding this legitimate thought-analysis with a real separation in the concrete object ;—the self has been regarded as if it could have a separate subsistence from its phenomena—from its acts and affections—from its essential attributes. The error we have elsewhere indicated, but the grand truth cannot be too distinctly before the view, that the real self is none other than its active nature revealed specifically in its exercises and affections—in its phenomena—in its attributes. The self is in every act of knowing, of imagining, of choosing. It is the grossest of absurdities to suppose an attribute really separable from the substance to which it belongs. We may for purposes of distinct investigation abstract in our thought any one attribute from the complement of attributes in an object ; but the complement of attributes makes

up or constitutes the concrete object, and is
identical with it; and no one attribute can be
completely viewed except as co-ordinated with
the rest, and never but as a part of the substance
which ever is, so far and to that extent, the same
as the particular attribute.

The whole field of mental experience is here
presented as the true to be known—the self, the
mind, the spirit, the soul—in its diversified acts
and affections, in innumerable modifications, like
the hues of light blending in indefinable tints
and shades, and only in a vague way distinguishable in its feeling, knowing, willing experiences
according as one or another makes itself more
prominent, really or apparently, to our abstrac-
tive contemplation; as growing, expanding,
strengthening, maturing; as turned in upon itself
in its restless activity or out upon the world
around it, suffering impression alike from within
and from without;—a field, shut up in a certain
sense within very narrow inclosures, a speck or
spark in the boundlessness of space and time,
yet unfathomable in its depths of truth for the
explorer, inexhaustible in the riches of its content.

§ 186. The true we have found to be that
which can be thought or known under an attribute. The mere self-sense, the mere intuition of
the self in any of its manifestations, does not give
truth in its completed, its true, mature, and perfect form. We perceive or intuit a feeling or a

thought of whatever kind, and we press on to
think it—to recognize and affirm some attribute
belonging to it. These attributes are of course
as various as the modifications of the mind itself.
But there is one attribute which is discoverable
and recognizable in every case of an intuition of
a mental act or affection. It is the attribute of
reality—of existence. We do not in every case
of an intuition actually assert this attribute; we
may not be distinctly conscious of it, just as we
are sometimes not conscious of one or another
attribute undoubtedly belonging to an object we
may be perceiving. It may yet be there and it
may be possible for us ever to recognize it. A
thought, a thinking act, which we actually experience and which we perceive or intuit is real, if
anything is real. It is not imaginary; for we
are conscious that we do not impose it upon ourselves. We recognize it to be real as we recognize
the solid earth on which we tread, to be real.
There is no attribute that we are more sure to
recognize, if we try. We cannot help, indeed, asserting this act of thought to be real if our thought
is turned that way. We assert the thought
to be real as naturally and as surely as we assert
it to be legitimate, or painful, or suggestive, or
as having any other attribute belonging to it.
This attribute of reality, existence, pertains to
every object of an intuition, every feeling,
thought, purpose. It is the universal attribute of
intuitive objects, which of itself, even if abstracted

from every other specific attribute characterizing a mental act or affection, enables us to think it; which, in other words, makes such an act or affection a veritable true to us. Every intuition is real; it is a real mind putting forth a real exertion.

§ 187. It is of the first importance to all philosophical speculation to hold this attribute of reality or existence entirely distinct from the logical copula or the merely assertive element in a thought. This certainly very gross error, and, because related to our most fundamental studies of mind, this very pernicious error, is to be detected in the speculations of some great thinkers. It has led them into grievous mistakes and confusions. As is common in all discourse about abstract and spiritual objects, terms used in denoting them have been borrowed from the language proper to more sensible or outward things. The *is* of the logical copula is a borrowed use of the *is* used of external objects denoting being or existence—external reality. As expressing the copula in a judgment, it expresses simply the reality or existence of the judgment. It is obvious fallacy to apply it when thus used to the terms of the judgment. When I say "the centaur is a human quadruped," I by no means intend to affirm the reality or existence of the centaur. I simply put forth the *judgment* as real, as existent, in affirming the centaur to be a human quadruped. The external reality of the centaur or of any human quadruped, is in no way affirmed or implied. In other words, the copula element, the affirmation of the judgment, never of itself necessarily involves the reality of either the subject or the attribute. We may correctly say even, "the centaur is imaginary—is unreal—non-existent," a proposition which is utterly absurd or contradictory, if the copula of the judgment properly implies the existence or reality of the terms of the judgment. Every judgment is real because a real act; but the object which the judgment respects may be imaginary; it is often not real either as respects subject or attribute.

We conclude, then, that reality or existence is an attribute that is to be discerned like any other attribute in order to be recognized as true. It is so actually discerned in the intuition of a mental act or affection. It is not an *a priori* idea—a native cognition, antecedent and conditional to all actual knowledge and mental experience. This is the merest assumption; rather, it is utterly a mistake. The attribute of reality cannot be apart from the object to which it belongs. We cannot have the idea until we discern it in some real object. The real object must first be presented to our mind, or at least to some mind, to reveal the attribute. There is no occasion, no need for presupposing it as an idea laid up beforehand in some mysterious way to be used when some real object comes along in the way of our observation. Its genesis is obvious; it rises in the mind like every other attribute, with the object, as the object reveals itself to us through the attribute and by it. We observe the attribute in the object and then give it its name. We observe the attribute of reality in an object presented to us; and then we name it :—we call it *real.*

§ 188. It is a fitting place here to give a more explicit emphasis to the fundamental statement in the philosophy of the mind, that the human mind never knows, never has notions, ideas, principles, any specific forms of knowledge by whatever name they may be called; never perceives, never intuits, never has perceptions or intuitions; never has any knowledge, any truth; except on the condition that the proper object of knowledge—the true—is presented to it and is accepted as such. The human mind begins its proper life by acting, and accordingly on an object which must of necessity be presented to it without any determination or selection of its own. It is, until this first putting forth of its active nature, if the expression may be allowed, an entirely void activity; it has had no object, has put forth no act; it cannot have any idea, any truth. Notwithstanding this seemingly unquestionable and salient fact of mind, there has manifested itself in philosophical speculation a disposition to suppose there must be some principles, truths, ideas, intuitions in the mind that belong to it as its inborn possession; at least, that are held by it before or without any presentation of object. How can we, it is asked, have any notion of the universal, the necessary, the perfect, the absolute, the infinite, otherwise than as our very birth-right inheritance, as the needful capital in order to any acquisition.

We have shown in the case of one and another of these supposed native cognitions, from time to time as our method encountered them, how they have had their genesis; that they have arisen, like all other cognitions, whether laws, principles, or ideas of whatever character, on presentation of some appropriate object and are simply the results of actual observation and subsequent reflection. A number of these first truths, supposed to be antecedent and conditional to knowledge and to all mental experience, we have found to be simply attributes of thought—of a thinking act —learned by actual inspection. The familiar notion of existence or reality, one of these supposed *a priori* ideas, we have just examined in respect to its origin. There remain still others, some of which we have just named—the universal, the perfect, the absolute, the infinite. In the next chapter, the genesis of these, at least in part, as the universal and the others so far as importing merely negations, will be exhibited, as not at all the antecedent conditions of knowledge, but as simply the consequents or results of the normal action of the knowing faculty on the presentation of its object—the true. They are all attainments not pre-endowments. But we have advanced the proposition that all internal perceptions, all intuitions, all intuitive truth, come to be on the exertion of the faculty of knowing on the acts and affections of the mind itself, or on the immediate revelations to it of other supersensible realities, the sphere of intuition being exactly commensurate with this sphere of internal and supersensible phenomena, and it seems to be appropriate if not necessary here to substantiate this proposition, if possible, by a general demonstration from the very nature of the case, that there can be none of those supposed intuitions or ideas antecedent to experience or outside of it.

If these *a priori* ideas exist and are really contents or forms of mental activity they must be either truths, that is, judgments that can be expressed in propositions, or objects that must be either concretes, or thought-objects, that is, subjects or attributes. There are no other cognitions supposable. But there can be no judgment, certainly, until there is something presented to be judged; the very term *concrete* implies an object external to the cognitive faculty to be known only on presentation to it in actual experience; and a subject cannot be without attribute nor attribute without subject, and neither subject nor attribute can be, except as they arise from the resolving, by the mind of some object presented to it in the legitimate and ordinary exercise of its function of thought. In a word, a cognition in the human mind can exist in it only in the exercise of the knowing faculty on its object being presented to it. We conclude, then, that there are no internal ideas or notions that are not positive intuitions ; that are not the normal products of the exertions of the knowing faculty on its appropriate object—the true—as revealed in acts or affections of the soul, in feeling, thinking, or willing. The simplicity of this teaching commends its truth and its importance to sound philosophy, since the fundamental is ever the simple. The doctrine of *a priori* cognitions is a gratuitous assumption ; having no ground but that of its serving as a support for weak theory, and wholly needless in the interest of truth, since the genesis of every such so-styled cognition can be traced in the ordinary method of knowledge. The ideas of existence or the real, of the true, the beautiful, the good, are given, as we have seen, in the presentation of the objects to which they belong as attributes. The idea of identity, whether as full sameness or partial likeness, and the ideas of quantity and of modality, we have found to be but attributes discernible in any instance of thought. The idea of the perfect, of the supreme, and the like are obviously but modifications of some one or other of these categories of thought. The ideas of the infinite, the absolute, the unconditioned, are, all of them, of the negative class of attributes, being in their proper import respectively the non-finite, the non-related, the non-conditioned. By the law of disjunction the propositions: *A is finite or is not infinite; is relative or is not relative; is conditioned or is not conditioned*, are necessarily true. It does not follow, however, from this that the propositions: *A is finite or infinite, is relative or irrelative, is conditioned or unconditioned*, are true, any more than that from the proposition: *A stone is vertebrate or is not vertebrate*, it follows that *a stone is a vertebrate or an invertebrate*.

The idea of the universal, as will be seen in the next chapter, arises in the way of the established principles of thought as a modification of the category of quantity—of extensive quantity; it is the simple correlate of part. As applied to experience, the term *universal* denotes the aggregate of what has been attained or is attainable by human thought. The notion of the universal, of necessity must start from the single or individual. As observation or reflection extends, the number is increased, and the universality becomes larger and extends till the limit is reached. A law or a principle is universal when it extends to all that is known or can be known—when it applies to all objects known or possible to be known. The idea of a universality beyond all this aggregate of cognizable things and attributes, existing as an independent principle ready to step forth on occasion and embrace newly presented objects, is not only gratuitous and needless, but is actually preposterous, violating the fixed principles of sound thinking. As elsewhere shown the notion of a whole, whether a universal, as in extensive quantity, or a total, as in comprehensive quantity, in contradistinction from its correlate—a part—in logical exactness excludes the attribute of boundedness or limitation. A part is from its very nature, bounded ; a whole, as whole, cannot be.

We have thus disposed of the most prominent of these so-called *a priori* ideas or native cognitions which have played so large and so fallacious a part in philosophical speculation. So far as held to exist in the human mind before all experience, they cannot be proper intuitions, since these always imply objects actually presented and respect only what is actually discerned in such presented objects as actually belonging to them. As activities, intuitions imply objects ; and these objects are simply and solely the mind's own acts or affections in actual experience.

§ 189. The category of reality, which is attained by observation of some concrete being, as of self in some specific act or affection, or, it may be, of some external object introduced to the mind through the bodily sense, embraces manifold categories or classes of attributes, constituted on different grounds or principles. One grand class, standing by itself, is that which comprises *the true, the beautiful*, and *the good*. These we have recognized as exactly corresponding with the respective mental functions, essence, form, and end, according to the Aristotelian enumeration of causes, and with the faculties of intelligence, imagination, and will. There are no other attributes of this order; that is, none others that are determined by this principle of division.

Everything that is real, accordingly, is true, is beautiful, and is good; that is, has an essence, has form, has an end. We may abstract either attribute for exclusive inspection or study; a real object may present itself more prominently or more characteristically in one attribute than in another; but they all must necessarily exist more or less in every real thing.

Conversely, all beauty, all truth, and all goodness, so far as they enter into our experience, come under the category of reality; they are each ever and necessarily real. As already stated, even the fictions of art are, with their unreal subjects, yet themselves as fictions, real, being the actual products of a real imagination.

This category embraces, of course, all the specific manifestations of mind in feeling, thought, and purpose. They all partake of the reality of the mind itself. The essential attributes of an object being, so far as they go, identical with the object to which they belong, are real like that; the reality in the concrete must ever be regarded as extending to both subject and attribute whenever thought has so resolved it into these two logical correlates.

## SUPERSENSIBLE REALITY.

§ 190. Whether this category of reality can fairly be held to embrace the essential attributes of time and space so that we should regard them as properly real things, has been one of the most profound and perplexing questions of philosophy. That the *idea* exists, or, in other words, that we actually have the idea in our minds of time and also the idea of space, whatever may be true of the objects themselves, is assumed by all—is controverted by none. Of the nature and genesis of those ideas, three leading theories have been proposed. One is that of Kant—that these terms denote mere *a priori* forms or modes of our sense which are wholly subjective, that is, are in our minds, and do not at all pertain to the objects of our knowledge. A second theory is, that they are *a priori*, that is, they exist in the mind before any object that is viewed in relation to time or space, and are to be regarded as "native cognitions." The groundlessness as well as the need-lessness to any true science of mind of each of these theories alike have already, it would seem, been abundantly shown. They are mere assumptions, taken up only to support certain theories, or because, perhaps, no other account seemed within reach of the human mind. A third view

19

of space and time regards them as real and as presented to the mind in a way analogous to that of all external objects that are known, through presentation to the mind by some attribute.

§ 191. Time is thus known or may be known on the occasion of any action, whether of the mind itself or of external reality, observed by it. Every action reveals as a necessary concomitant the attribute of *duration*. This attribute is not of the essence of the action itself. No analysis or inspection of that can detect it. From the action—from the mind acting or from the external body moving—may be abstracted every attribute that enters into the action itself and constitutes it, leaving an absolute zero so far as the essence of the action is concerned, while yet the abstraction may bring away no such attribute as duration. Nevertheless this attribute came into the mind as inseparably attached to the action. The simple fact is, that the action is set in this necessary relationship of time as duration, as the sun is set in the sky. If after an experience of the sun we abstract every essential attribute of the sun—color, figure, gravity—and thus think away the entire sun itself, there will still remain the sky in which the sun is set in real relationship. Just so, as just observed, we may abstract every intrinsic and constituent attribute of an action or of a motion, that is, of an active or moving object, as it has come into our experience, and still there will remain the relative attribute of duration. For every action must be regarded as having extrinsic as well as intrinsic attributes, which, although not essential as entering into its essence, are equally indispensable as conditions of its existence, since any part is conditioned on the existence of other parts. Here comes into play the quantitative relationship of part—of part to the whole. The part is necessarily in its whole. Our minds, all its activities, are parts of a whole of reality ; and every manifestation of mind, every action, by the necessities of thought itself, brings in this whole of reality, not in its full comprehension indeed, yet truly, just as the sun necessarily brings with itself into an apprehension the sky in which it is set, although not in its absolute wholeness or just as a severed limb implies the body of which it was an organic part. Time as the whole of duration, is revealed to us thus through this attribute of condition on the occasion of any specific action. It is revealed to us as real. It certainly is not an original product of the imagination, for imagination cannot create out of nothing ; and it creates only forms out of its own materials already acquired. It is not a product of thought, for such a work is entirely beyond the function of thought, which creates only thoughts of what is given to it, adding nothing. It is real, because it is given to the mind from without its own proper action, truly impressing it and determining a new state or mode of the mind's activity. We have an exact analogy in geological science.  The mastodon is revealed to us not as a whole, for the animal is long since extinct.  It is revealed to us as a real existence, through a part—a particular bone.  This part, by logical necessity, compels us to infer the existence of the whole animal of which it must have been a part.  The mastodon is revealed to us thus as a real, through the part which logically implies the whole.  Just so, every action or motion experienced by the mind reveals itself as continuing, as a duration ; and this continuing or duration is given to us as a part which implies its corresponding whole—the whole of time.

The idea of time accordingly has in a certain sense the character of necessity ;—a necessity lying not in essence but in relation.  When we experience an action or a motion, time as the condition necessarily appears, as the mastodon appears to the thought of the naturalist on the perception of a bone.  The supposition of such experience involves the presence of time under the necessities of thought by which the part implies the whole to which it belongs.  Every action or motion has the relative attribute of duration ; and duration is a particular property of time, and so implies it.

The idea of time is universal as well as necessary, as all men have experience of some action or motion.  It is, moreover, self-evident in the sense that, given the experience, time reveals itself in its attribute of continuous duration.  It is a proper object of intuition, not of perception proper; for it is supersensible in its nature. Time touches no bodily sense. The sense decays, the body passes away, while time endures.

Duration is the more interior and essential attribute of time; but this duration itself has the attribute of continuous succession. But time as a real entity has another important attribute. Experience brings to us no beginning to time. Particular actions begin; but they each appear to us as succeeding parts to a pre-existing movement; we can discover no absolute beginning of motion. Every particular motion has a preceding; and, so far as our experience goes and up to the present moment, each has had its succeeding motion. The duration of any particular action or motion is thus a part of a larger duration necessarily implying a whole of which it is a part. Time is the whole of these parts, of these particular durations. Conceived thus as a whole, time does not come under the category of bound or limit, or outer relation. It is as absurd to apply this attribute to time as a whole, as to apply the category of *vertebrateness* to *stones*, or of *gravity* to *spirit;* for the very idea of a whole precludes all consideration of outward relation as pertinent to it, and of course all consideration of bound or limit or dependence. It is as preposterous to inquire whether time as a whole is finite or infinite, as to inquire whether a stone is a vertebrate or an invertebrate or whether spirit is heavy or light. It is logically legitimate under the law of disjunction to affirm that *time is finite or it is not finite ;* but a sound logic distinguishes this widely from the disjunctive proposition *time is finite or infinite.* Only in the looseness of popular speech can we speak of time conceived as a whole as infinite; and in popular discourse the language is perhaps allowable. But speculation which starts with the assumption of time as a whole and then treats it under the category of limitation, is at once involved in the mist of bewildering and misleading fallacy. Duration may be logically considered as a part of time and may therefore be logically considered under the category of bound or limitation. The question is logically proper: is this or that duration finite or infinite. But wholeness excludes all notion of limit or outer relationship. If we have thought of an object as a whole, as, suppose, of an orange having as parts its rind and pulp, we may proceed to think of it as a part, as, for instance, of a larger number, and then it may be conceived of as finite or limited. But so long as it is thought only as a whole, it is not thought at all as thus finite; so far as the thought regards it as a whole the attribute of limitedness is excluded, for the simple reason that all outer relationship is excluded from the notion of a whole.

§ 192. The genesis of the idea of space is in perfect analogy to the genesis of the idea of time. The experience of any physical body brings into

our minds, besides its special essential attributes
or its proper qualities, the attribute of position—
of a *here and there;* of place. This attribute of
position comes by a natural association into this
experience of a physical body, universally. It is
the natural setting of such a body, but is not of
its essence. It is an attribute of condition, of relation in the larger sense. Abstract from our
notion of a physical body all its essential attributes, still the notion of its attribute as being
*here or there*—of having position—remains. It is
of the constitution of things that this association
of body with position should exist in our experience. It is not ours to determine why, or how, or
wherefore. We have to deal only with the fact.
The fact is that position is given to us ever and in-
variably with our experience of a physical body.
We do not say that in the guarded language of
philosophical discussion, this association must be
pronounced to be one of necessity in nature, for
nature does not testify such necessity to our
thought. But the experience of the association
is universal; so universal that common speech
without much liability to error speaks of it as
necessary. But position is a part of a containing
whole—a whole of space. In our experience of
physical body, accordingly, space as whole reveals
itself to us through its part of position or of a
*here and there.* The fallacy in the Berkeleian reasoning, that we can have no knowledge of space as
a real, because it cannot be a legitimate intellect-

ual notion nor yet is it perceived by any of our
senses, is easily exposed. The notion of space is
not attributable in its ultimate ground to the exclusive action of either intellect or perceptive
sense, but to both combined. There is sense-
perception first, as of some object; there is then
the intellectual inference from this, as a part to
the existence of space as a whole, through the
relative attribute of condition—position or place
—as we perceive the bone of the mastodon and
then infer the whole animal of which it is a part.
The notion of space as a necessary idea comes in
precisely as the notion of the existence of the
mastodon becomes necessary on the condition of
the existence of the bone. The existence of the
part implies by the necessities of thought the existence of the whole. But the part, the bone,
must first be given to us in experience, before we
can conclude to the existence of the whole of the
mastodon. And this is a matter of contingency;
we cannot beforehand assume the existence of
the bone before it is presented to us. So position, the here or there, is matter of experience;
it is so far contingent. But position is given to
us as a part; and as the part necessarily brings
into our thought the whole, position, or particularly extension, necessarily involves its whole—
of unlimited extension or space. Given the
fact of position, as part and so limited, the fact
of space as whole and so not limited, is an infer-

ence that partakes of the necessitous nature of perfect thought.

Position as part of space has as its essential attribute that of continuous extension. This extension is in three directions. In other words, real things conceived as particular substances and physical bodies are of three dimensions: length, breadth, and thickness. A mathematical point has no dimensions of any kind; it is without di_ mensions. But a point produced—extended—it is loosely said, forms a line which has one single dimension. A line produced forms a surface which has two dimensions. A surface produced forms a solid, which has three dimensions, and here we find the limit in real being.

Space conceived as a whole cannot be considered under the category of limit or outer relation. Position, as part, is limited, as one part is bounded by other parts of the same whole. It is logically legitimate to inquire of the extent of a position or place as more or less limited; not of space while it is conceived as a whole. Space is not finite, is not limited ; only in the looseness of popular speech can we say it is infinite.

## SYNOPSIS OF FUNDAMENTAL CATEGORIES.

§ 193. It may be serviceable to present here a formulated statement of those most fundamental categories or classes of attributes which are revealed to our view on inspection of any accom-

plished thought or instance of knowledge. In
order to such thought or knowledge there must
be a thinking subject and a thought object.
The fundamental categories of pure thought,
that is, those which are given on inspection of
the thinking element by itself, we have found to
be Identity, Quantity, and Modality or Necessity,
§§ 161–165. But in order that an object may be
thought it must be real and must actually impress the mind. §§ 187,188. Hence the two necessary attributes in anything that can be thought,
the categories of Reality and Activity. But in
any actual thought of any object the union of
the thinking subject and thought object reveals
two other fundamental attributes. The object
or thing thought becomes necessarily either Substance with properties, or Cause with effects.
§ 177. We have thus these three fundamental
classes of categories necessarily appearing in any
actual thought of an object :—

First Class : THE CATEGORIES OF PURE
THOUGHT—*Identity, Quantity, Modality.*

Second Class : THE CATEGORIES OF PURE
THING—*Reality, Activity.*

Third Class : THE CATEGORIES OF THOUGHT-
THING, *Substance, Cause.*

The so-called three comprehensive ideas—the
true, the beautiful, the good—constitute as we
have seen, § 189, a class of categories of an entirely different order. They might be appropriately designated the *Three Psychological Catego-*

*ries*, as they are given in the nature of the mind or soul itself as tri-functional and so involving this threefoldness of attribute in every object which it can apprehend, that is, in its exact correlative and complementary.

## II. SENSIBLE REALITY—MATTER.

§ 194. The Real as external object to the mind and as brought to it only through the medium of the bodily sense, is collectively known as *matter*. By this term is denoted the collective whole ; the parts of matter are *bodies*, including under this term all material or sensible magnitudes from the greatest to the least, from suns to atoms and even the infinitesimal particles of the supposed primitive ether.

The real in the world of matter, as in the world of spirit or mind, is given to us as a concrete which our reflective thought resolves into subject and attribute, by identifying which it effects its product—knowledge or truth. We know here as everywhere in the form of subject and attribute.

The genesis of the idea of matter generally is analogous to the genesis of the ideas of time and space, only that it is reached through the medium of the bodily sense ; it is primitively apprehended in perception, not in intuition. A part of matter—some sensible body—is presented to us ; we apprehend it as a part, implying other

parts, that is, other bodies, the aggregate of
which constitutes a whole, which we call the
world of matter—the material universe. Each
body that we come to know is *real;* for it comes
to us from without and impresses our sense.
This is the fundamental attribute of matter—
reality. Even idealists can, and for the most
part in fact do, admit this ; they only claim that
what we call material substance is after all properly spiritual in its essence ; it is none the less
real.

The particular body or portion of matter that
we experience comes to us as a part—as limited ;
but we discern no limit to the number of these
parts. The whole which is thus brought to us
through the part is given to us without discernible limits ; and there is no indication given in the
nature or relations of these parts of matter or any
ground given in reason for supposing that this
aggregate is limited, that is, becomes a part of
some larger whole. Imagination is as inadequate
to picture the boundaries of matter as it is those
of time and space, or to impute any shape, character, reality even, to what can lie outside of
these boundaries. Beyond them is neither fullness nor void, neither motion nor substance, not
indeed anything, nor nothing; for there is no beyond them. The notion is contradictory to the
deepest convictions of the mind. It is a conviction, attained indeed in experience, but not less
trustworthy, that matter is one of the so-called

infinities; or, more correctly, one of those objects which the human mind apprehends as
wholes and accordingly as not limited—not subject to bounds.

Matter makes itself known to us through the
bodily sense—through some impression it makes
upon that. Matter thus is a source of energy, of
force, of power; it impresses our sense. This,
then, is an attribute of matter which the fact of
our knowledge of it presupposes.

A very troublesome question to philosophers
has arisen just here: What is the nature of this
source of energy? Some eminent thinkers have
maintained that matter is energy—consisting " of
mere mathematical centers of force "—nothing in
fact but force. Others have conceived of matter
as a real substance, but as nothing more than
a mere passive receptacle of force. Matter, they
think, is entered by force; it retains such force,
till some fresh force determines it to let it go; at
most it is but a mere inert receptacle and medium
of. force. A third class of thinkers have conceived
it as a real substance endowed with force as one
of its essential abiding attributes, not as the preceding class conceive, a mere casual visitor. Its
other properties, besides passivity, are inert-
ness, retentiveness, mobility, space-filling.

There is still another doctrine of matter which,
to say the least, is plausible. It is that matter
is *potentialized force;* that is, force changed from
an active state to a simple potency. The univer-

sal force or energy in nature is here conceived as existing in two different modes or states, active and inactive. As inactive it becomes a mere potency—a mere capability of operating. If we suppose the universe of force to become diversified into specific exertions of energy, a weaker energy may readily be conceived to encounter a stronger, and so, without losing its identity, to continue inactive for the time that it is thus overborne. It is now a potency, inoperative, but still subsisting. When the overbearing force is removed or new accessions of force are gained, the potency may resume its active state. The theory has the merit of being conceivable ; of being in harmony with our existing knowledge of things and forces and especially of matter, as inert, passive, receptive, retentive, mobile, space-filling ; of being simple beyond most or all other theories ; and of removing perplexities and shedding light on obscure problems in philosophy. We readily understand in the light it gives us why matter should possess just the attributes here enumerated. We more easily conceive also how mind and matter can interact, since they are not positively different natures, but only states or conditions of the same.

The question is relegated to metaphysical speculation. But beyond all doubt what we have here to observe is that the true is presented to our minds in a form of what we call matter, whatever may ultimately be established as the true doctrine of its nature.

§ 195. Material bodies can make themselves known to us only through the medium of the bodily sense. The true in them is subject to divers modifications in its way to the mind. In fact the true as existing in the outward object is attained only as the result of a process of interpreting. The sun in the heavens thus, as object to the intelligence, as true, is not exactly the sun in our thought. In the first place the actual sun and the thought-sun differ in the very important respect that the one is object, the other is subjective; the real sun is not absolutely and exactly the known sun. How much is involved in this simple point of difference, it is difficult to say. Even when we have what we rightly esteem to be a right thought of the sun, there is a heaven-wide difference between the real sun and the thought-sun. A true thought of the sun is only a recognition of the attributes—the properties and relations—of the sun. But farther, the precise character of these attributes suffers modifications in reaching the mind. The attribute of brightness, for example, is modified by the state of the atmosphere through which the light is transmitted ᛫ a murky atmosphere presents a different light from one that is clear. The light, further, impresses the sense of sight differently according to the ever varying condition of the organ of that sense—the eye—with its connected bodily organism ;—a diseased organ, an otherwise occupied organ, receives a different impression from one in a different condition. Still farther, this impression itself is modified as it is transmitted to the central seat of sensation to reach the mind. And in the mind itself at last the impression is interpreted very differently in different mental conditions; in respect, for instance, of intensity and of relation to other attributes. The other attributes, as of figure and of gravity, are subject to like modifications in these several ways of their transmission to the mind. Besides all those modifications which attend a perfectly healthy transmission as we have noticed, a morbid condition of body or mind brings in manifold illusions and hallucinations in all our experiences of external objects. The attainment of the true is accordingly the result only of a long continued process of more or less unconscious interpretation. The particular character of this process in which the mind interprets out the impressions made on the bodily sense by external objects varies greatly in different cases in respect of difficulty, length, mode, and certainty of result. But the experiences being repeated over and over by the same mind and by the minds of others, by the multitudes of human minds, we cannot question the truthfulness of the results when there is general accord. If no discrepancy worthy of consideration is discovered in the testimony of the senses between one experience and another by the same mind, or between the experiences of different minds, and if no ground of rejection of the testimony is furnished in reason, the result must be accepted as a true interpretation. If it be not a demonstrative knowledge, it may be a certainty. So the race of men have concluded. The testimony of the senses is accepted as trustworthy. Men believe in the reality of external objects; they have a belief of what these objects are. The true respecting these objects they believe themselves to possess by legitimate and unimpeachable means. There is besides a natural presumption in favor of the belief; the laws of probabilities favor it. Moreover there is no valid argument against it.

20

# CHAPTER X.

## THE TRUE PRODUCED.

§ 196. The true first comes into our experience and so gives us a knowledge, a cognition, on presentation of some object. But a mere knowledge or cognition may, without the aid of any additional presentations of object, of itself alone become a source of further cognition. Besides the proper presentative knowledge which may be attained from the simple inspection of a thought or cognition revealing its own attributes and giving us thus the categories of pure thought, the mind may attain still other knowledge through the application to what it has already attained of the different processes of legitimate thinking. Especially after attaining a plurality of cognitions respecting different objects or even respecting the same object, it may without further presentations of object go on to attain an indefinitely large amount of other knowledge. There is a proper sense thus in which the mind may be said to produce knowledge. Acting in accordance with the fixed laws of knowledge or thinking, the mind may bring into light new cognitions not given by any presented object, strictly speaking, yet legitimatcly attainable by thought. The true, as thus produced, we now proceed to investigate, particularly as to the various forms which it may assume in our thought and the specific processes by which it is attained.

§ 197. We are prepared by previous considerations, to accept the principle that the mind has no truth until an object is presented to it. There are no *a priori* cognitions in the sense that there are such before the mind's activity is called forth by some object presented to it. To search for any such truth is accordingly preposterous, and must be fruitless. Knowledge is the product of the mind's activity; and this activity can be exerted only on condition that some object—the true in some form—has been brought or presented to it. Provisionally until light is obtained or for some purpose of convenience in acquiring, or storing, or communicating knowledge, hypotheses or theories which are hypotheses corroborated in some way or degree, are legitimate. But they are not to be esteemed as true cognitions; certainly are not to be accepted as *a priori* cognitions that are not to be challenged. The assumption of some general formula which is to be accepted because a mere formal truism, as the famous formula of Fichte, "$A=A$," out of which to educe real knowledge, can never avail to any solid acquisition or evolution of truth and is pretty certain in the use and application of it to draw in some fatal paralogism. No more can the putting forward of some comprehensive definitions, advanced arbitrarily and without assigned ground or substantiating reason, as we find in Spinoza's system, satisfy the legitimate demands of sound knowledge. Such definitions are sagaciously, perhaps unconsciously of ill-intent, contrived to embrace all that can be required in the way of proof in the development that follows. The fatal paralogism as before is sure to come in somewhere ; and here as there the paralogistic introduction of the real into what was, as assumed, only empty form, vitiates the whole procedure. Neither can any validating ground of truth, or legitimate source of truth ever be found in any mere assumption. The only legitimate procedure for finding either ultimate source or ground of truth is to take some instance of a knowledge accepted as such, which shall have also the character of a first or primitive knowledge and be a fair representative of such a knowledge and from it effect both the production of truth and its validation. We do this when we take either any simple intuition or a simple perception—it may be one of the most familiar character—respecting which we can make no mistake ; as " I feel a pain," or " I see the sun." Each of these assertions is in the form of a truth—subject identified with attribute—the self identified with one form of its essential activity as feeling or seeing. A subject and an attribute, that is, two concepts, and also a copula, which properly combined form a judgment, are in either case attained. Now from this we may proceed to evolve or attain other knowledge. We have attained a valid test of knowledge in the essential character of the judgment which is the primitive and legitimate form of all truth. That is so far true everywhere which bears this essential character of a truth. We read by inspection of such a judgment, further, as in fact we have done, the categories of pure thought, and obtain in the study of them and their manifold relations, a body of truth of indefinite expansion in the realms of pure thought, as, for instance, with the addition at least of the notions of space and time as the necessary conditions of all applications of the science in experience, the entire science of pure mathematics under the category of quantity. Then again we have the concepts—subject and attribute—and first as pure thought and afterwards as having real content—real feeling, real seeing. We find them to yield similar indefinite realms of abstract and concrete truth —truth of pure thought and truth of reality.

Proceeding in this way we find our path clear and our attainments in knowledge sure. We have no need of invoking the aid of *a priori* truths, of native cognitions, of first principles, of rational intuitions, of axioms, of fundamental definitions—of assumptions of any name or any form. We carry with us one validating test—the ascertained character of a genuine knowledge. What ever stands this test—whatever possesses the essential character of a knowledge—is true knowledge. No skepticism can assail it to its harm.

§ 198. The several processes by which the mind may proceed legitimately to attain new truth from that which has already been gained are at once given us in logical science. They are of a twofold order, as determined by the twofold form of thought, a judgment and a concept.

First, the essential element of a truth or judgment—the logical copula—may, when once legitimately attained, be modified in various ways so as to present new forms of knowledge. Such changes are logically known as *Reasonings.* The identification may, under certain limitations which it is the province of logic to set forth, thus be turned so as that it shall directly respect the attribute and identify the subject with that ; in other words, the terms may be made to change places, as in the logical process of *Conversion.* So the breadth of the identification may be legitimately lessened as in *Quantitative Restriction ;* or the necessary truth be changed to an actual or a contingent as in *Modal Restriction.* From the very nature of thought, further, we are authorized to derive new judgments from a disjunctive proposition as in logical Disjunction. Within certain prescribed limits also, we may transfer the quality or modality of a judgment to the terms, or from the terms to the judgment, as in logical *Transference.* These are all instances of what are called, *Immediate Reasonings,* in which one judgment is changed to another without necessary introduction of any other thought.

§ 199. Under the class of *Mediate Reasonings* otherwise styled *Syllogisms*, in which one judgment or truth is derived from another, through the mediation of some third truth or judgment, are comprised two species :—(1) the so-called *Categorical Syllogisms*, embracing those two most important instrumentalities of thought in attaining new truth from that already attained, *Deduction and Induction*, which mediate the derivation through the matter or the terms of the judgment ; and (2) the *Conditional Syllogism*, which effects the derivation of the new truth through the given judgment itself and embraces two species, distinguished in respect to the two kinds of logical Quantity, the so-called *Hypothetical* and *Disjunctive Syllogisms*.

§ 200. It has been already stated that there are two, and but two, relationships of quantity of this order—that of the part to the whole and that of the part to other parts. The process of Deduction moves in the first relationship—moves between the part and the whole. The principle of this movement which legitimates it and validates its product is simply this : that whatever is contained either numerically, that is, in the *form* of a subject of a proposition, or comprehensively, that is, in the attribute or predicate of a proposition, must be contained in the whole or any larger part. The science of Deductive Logic has been, ..

since the days of Aristotle, who has left us the substance of its teachings, developed into a very considerable body of principles and forms, and has constituted a prominent department of instruction in the higher institutions of learning. Its formidable system of formulas has been severely assailed by Sir William Hamilton who has exposed its fallaciousness and its unfitness for practical uses. The study of the principles of deductive thought, however, accompanied by suitable exercises in the application of them is of indispensable service to thorough intellectual training.

The principle of induction is found in the necessary relation of one part to every other part of the same whole; all the parts must contain in common those elements or attributes by which they are constituted into a whole. The principle is as legitimate and clear as that in deduction. It embraces, too, numerous diversified applications, for which definite laws may be prescribed, and valid forms of procedure may be indicated. It is, perhaps, the most serviceable instrumentality of thought in the advancement of knowledge. To it natural science is confessedly indebted for its great achievements. Yet the science of induction has been but slightly elaborated. Indeed, the nature of induction is little understood even by those who boast of its achievements. It is, in fact, even by them grossly misunderstood. Its validating principle or ground has been preposterously, although very generally, set forth as to be found in the alleged "uniformity of nature." Induction is thus made to rest on induction, since it is only by induction that nature is known to be uniform.

Induction suffers divers modifications like the deductive movement; and accordingly a true science of induction must present a large and rich development of laws and forms, the knowledge of which with fitting exercises, must naturally be supposed to furnish not only an invaluable means of mental discipline but also an equally invaluable stock of instrumentality for the effective advancement of knowledge.

§ 201. Secondly, each of the concepts in an attained judgment or truth, each of the so-called *terms*—the subject and the predicate—may also, like the judgment itself, become the fruitful source of new thought, with or without the concomitant accession of other truth. The concept itself, it will be remembered, comes to be simultaneously with the judgment, just as the members of the living body come to be necessarily and only with the body itself. There can be no genuine concept, accordingly, until there is a judgment. In simple truth, a concept, in the legitimate use of the word, is none other than either the subject or the predicate of a judgment; and cannot exist before the judgment, any more than a member can exist before the living body to which it belongs. A single and it may be a simple object may be presented to the mind and be apprehended by it in perception or intuition; but it does not become a concept until the object is thought, in other words, is resolved into subject and attribute which are then identified in the judgment. The truth of a concept must accordingly be validated through the body of the judgment and as a constituted member of it. *Brightness*, thus, can never be accepted as a true concept of *the Sun*, except as it is recognized in the full body of the thought—*the Sun is bright*. As before explained the identification set forth by the copula respects concepts, not things. The true interpretation of the proposition is: my concept of *the Sun* is the same in respect of one attribute as my concept of *round*.

Proceeding in this recognition of the relation of the concept to the judgment, the fundamental principle of which is the identity asserted between subject and attribute, we may out of any validated concept, and especially out of two or more validated concepts, educe an indefinite amount of new truth, which being produced under the fixed law of thought must be genuine, legitimate truth—necessary truth—necessary, that is, if the original judgment be true and the principles of thought be observed in the process. These principles of thought, particularly under the category of quantity, allow of a twofold change in each of the terms of a judgment—in the subject-concept and in the attribute-concept; a change by enlargement called *Amplification*, and a change by contraction or reduction called *Resolution*.

§ 202. We may thus amplify any attained truth in the form of subject-concept by combining two or more together in what is known as *generalization*. The one validating condition to be observed in this process is that the concepts so combined be recognized as having each been identified in a judgment with some common attribute, which in such use is called *the base* of the new concept. Single objects are thus, to the great enlargement of truth, gathered into varieties; varieties into species; species into genera; and one concept under a single name is legitimately made to embrace an indefinite number of subordinate classes and individuals; as "man" comprises races, families, individuals, having in common the attribute characteristic of the class,—that is, the attribute which is the base of the generalization. This movement of thought is of inestimable value in the advancement of knowledge. It is a movement inconsiderately confounded with induction, from which all accurate thinkers will widely distinguish it. The movement is a simple one in its nature and is clearly validated under the more specific principle of a common base, as stated, and the more comprehensive principle of identity in the judgment.

The amplification of the attribute-concept is analogous in process and in validity as well as in importance of result. Like induction as com-

pared with deduction, this process, as compared
with the corresponding process in amplifying the
subject-concept—generalization—as just expounded, has been overlooked and underestimated.
The minds of learners have been less trained in it ;
and the conscious use of it in the advancement of
knowledge accordingly has been less common.
But we may enlarge an attribute-concept by combining into one, two or more attributes having a
common subject, which will here be the base of
amplification, as the common attribute was the
base in the amplification of a subject-concept, and
in this way greatly enlarge the bounds of our valid
knowledge. Under the common subject, *John*,
thus, to exemplify by a very familiar instance, we
may combine *bodily*, *white*, *Caucasian*, or *bright*,
*studious*, *persevering*, and attain comprehensive
concepts, for which we may devise convenient
names or words in language. Such concepts are
comprehensive concepts, and differ widely from
generic concepts ; the former being combinations
of attribute-concepts, the latter only of proper
subject-concepts.

§ 203. The other process indicated, by which
new truth is produced from concepts, is Resolution or Analysis. As applied to subject-concepts
this process is called *Division* and is the opposite
of Generalization. As applied to attribute-concepts, the process is called *Partition*, and is the
opposite of the process just noticed of attribute-
amplification. They are both of them most use-

ful and effective principles in the advancement of truth. They are validated by being recognized as proceeding under the more proximate principle of logical quantity and the more comprehensive principle of logical identity. The resolution of the concept must proceed in recognition of the base, which of course will ever be the opposite term in the original judgment that gave rise to the concept, and must pass downward from whole to part or larger part to contained part, either numerically as in the case of a subject-concept or comprehensively as in the case of an attribute-concept.

§ 204. It will be observed on carefully inspecting these processes and comparing them, that as the subject-concept is enlarged, the corresponding attribute-concept is reduced ; and conversely as it is reduced, the attribute is enlarged. And conversely as the attribute is enlarged, the subject is reduced, and as the attribute is reduced, the subject is enlarged. For example, if to Socrates, Plato, etc., we add Cimon, Pericles, etc., so as to form the composite subject or generic concept *Athenian,* we at the same time reduce the attributes that characterize Socrates, or Plato, such as sage, moral, etc., which cannot be thought as belonging to all Athenians as Cimon. So reducing *Athenians* to *sage Athenians,* we in reducing the number of subjects enlarge the characteristics or attributes, having added the attribute *sage* to the attribute *Athenian.*

This is a method of producing new truth or new forms of knowledge that may be most convenient and most serviceable. It is at once seen that it is a legitimate method, and its results must be accepted as true, provided at least the original concept is true and the procedure regular under the simple and clear principles of thought.

§ 205. By these few processes and in these legitimate modes of thinking we may thus build up an indefinitely large and imposing structure of knowledge. Such knowledge, likewise, is sound, genuine knowledge, for it is the knowing faculty's own building. It is, however, but knowledge—thought—after all. The great question suggests itself: is the world around us, is the universe, is nature, conformed to this thinking of ours, so that in its strictest sense what is true to us is true of nature—of the universe? This question calls for a fair and full consideration.

It is to be allowed at the outset that the forms of the true in nature, using this term—nature—to denote the entire real object of our thought or knowledge, are not the same as those which we may or actually do construct in our thought. The chemist can effect combinations in his laboratory of which actual instances cannot be found in the world without. The heavenly bodies do not move exactly in that perfectly elliptic orbit which Sir Isaac Newton's fundamental principles of motion prescribe. Bodies do not exist around us gathered together in just such groups

as our logical classifications effect for some purposes of convenience to our study; there is no
actual general man, or general tree. Notwithstanding all this, the combinations of elements in
the natural world, the movements of the planets,
and the modes of existence in the material world
generally, never contradict the principles of
thought; and the variations noticed are simply
such as the varying purposes or occasions might
have produced while following strictly the same
principles of thought. We have our peculiar
aims in attaining certain results in particular
forms of thought; and nature has her aims peculiar to her, and so has her peculiar forms of
products. It may be well to bear in mind in pur-
suing the investigation that if there be in nature
that which is really contradictory to our legitimate
thinking, it is really unthinkable to us and does
not concern us in any imaginable way. It is to
us a very zero—a nothing. The agnosticism or
the skepticism that denies or questions the reality in nature of truth to us, denies its own right
to be or to be regarded with the slightest respect
by men who think and who believe in thought.

It is to be considered, moreover, that we start
in our investigation with a well settled determination of what truth is—what true knowledge is.
We know that we know what we know by the
incontestable demonstration that this knowledge
has the accepted and undoubted character and
essence of a true knowledge.

§ 206. We may begin our investigation with a search into the nature within, by a search into our internal, intuitional experience and thought. *We feel*—we have a feeling. The feeling is a fact, at least, we may assume it here as a fact; and we intuit the fact; that is, we are conscious of the feeling. This acceptance of the fact of feeling by our conscious selves, is not a knowledge in the highest and exactest sense, perhaps it is not a demonstrative, a necessary knowledge; it is a belief, a trust, a faith; but it is a certainty. It is a certainty of the highest order. If we are not conscious when we feel that we feel, we cannot be conscious of anything, and agnosticism, skepticism, sound knowledge, are alike annihilated and vanish away together. But this faith in our consciousness of feeling is beyond question, as it is to us the foundation of all knowledge. This consciousness is at once the ground, the prompting cause, and the object of our thought, when we think that we feel; the ground of our assertion in thought that this attribute of feeling belongs to our feeling self. We have then one veritable thought—one sound knowledge—one genuine truth. *We feel;* that is a fact in nature; *we know that we feel*, that is a truth of thought. Nature and our thought are in perfect accord, as object and subject; Nature in our feeling soul is so far exactly conformed to our thinking, so that we can put the statement in words, *we feel*, identifying subject and attribute and so having a true thought of a real fact in nature. We go further. We become in a like way conscious of a purpose, a determination, and think that we thus get a new genuine truth, as tested by the essential nature of a truth ; we know that we purpose or determine. We become conscious, moreover, that we know that we feel and purpose ; this, too, is a truth as tested by the veriest criterion of truth— its essence. We have now three attributes— feeling, willing, conscious or knowing—all pertaining to one subject—one conscious self—and identified with that subject. We combine these attributes under the law of attribute-amplification and find they fall into a true unity—which in fact we designate in a single word—self. The real fact in the realm of nature is so far found to be exactly conformed to our thinking. One process of thought is found to give us the true in nature. The true of nature is found to be the true to us. There is no contradiction or sign of variance.

But we extend our investigations. Feelings, purposes, thoughts, repeat themselves. As having each its own essential property, we combine them into three several classes respectively according to these several attributes. Nature nowhere shows any signs of reluctance. She most freely yields to the needs of our thinking. Nature is thus in these classifications conformed to our thoughts ; she never contradicts in her individual objects our legitimate classifications.

§ 207. Pushing our investigation still farther

21

into our experience of the outer world, we find precisely the same thing substantially with variation only in form. We combine with the largest freedom everywhere into comprehensive concepts and into generic concepts or classes; and never a hint does nature give of opposition or conflict. Nature is conformed everywhere to legitimate thought. We direct our thought on whatever point; it is all the same. Whatever exists of truth in nature knowable to us is conformed to the demands of the true from within our own thought. We combine or synthesize, we separate or analyze, and nature never resists. So well assured are we that there can be no variance, that if there appear, as there may perhaps sometimes appear to our first understanding, a seeming discrepancy, we ascribe it at once to our own weakness and liability to error or mistake. The same result is reached if we investigate the correspondence between nature and our reasoning. We have already indicated the logical unsoundness of the common notion that induction rests on the uniformity of nature, since it makes induction rest on itself, for we can know that nature is uniform only by induction. If it should be thought that this notion belongs to the class of *a priori* or native cognitions, we have, it would seem, sufficiently shown all these to be untenable as ultimate grounds of knowledge. That " nature is uniform " has in fact just the measure of scientific value, that the similar assumption " na-

ture abhors a vacuum," once was imagined to
have. It has a certain truth of meaning, and it especially serves a use ; it is a cloak to our igno-
rance, and protects our studies from inconvenient
molestation. But nature allows as freely our in-
ductions as our deductions, as our generalizations
and our comprehensions of attributes. Nature is
conformed everywhere to true thought. That is
a grand truth which we find by experience, one
which we can legitimately find by experience and
sound thought applied to that experience. Induction like all true thought rests on its own determi-
nable principles. It is to be tested only by its
own ascertained nature—its essential laws and
legitimate forms.

If it be suggested that there are seeming dis-
cords and variances in nature ; and that therefore legitimate thought may reach conclusions
that are at war with facts, it is replied that there
are what are called " sports " and " monstrosities,"
departures from what are conceived to be true
type-forms. So there are freaks in our thinking
pursuits ; we sport these at times and attain monstrosities of product. Even in the purest of all
forms of thought—pure mathematics. By skill-
ful legerdemain the expert mathematician de-
monstrates beyond the possibility of any discoverable error any given quantity to be equal to any
other given quantity. But the certainty of
mathematical principles and the trustworthiness
of their results when legitimately applied in cal-

culation, do not therefore totter and fall.
There are satisfactory explanations of the seeming falsities in the results. So with a higher knowledge and a sharper eye we might satisfy ourselves that nature has a satisfactory explanation for her "sports" and monsters in creation and is never thrown off her balance of exact truthfulness.

Still further, induction itself brings to us strong corroboration of this grand truth that nature is ever true to herself and true to thought. Our conscious selves are a part of nature. The fact of our sympathetic interaction with nature, attested by our consciousness, involves that. Induction accordingly may move freely and securely everywhere among the other parts of the body of creation and find the true and nothing but the true ; for, as parts of the same one whole, what is true of us as one part, is true of all the other parts, so far as parts of the same whole.

That there is truth in nature and that the true in nature is true to us ; that, in other words, nature is exactly conformed to thought, so that our legitimate thinking in regard to nature must ever bring in legitimate and every way trustworthy results, appears then beyond all question. It is a fair presumption beforehand. The instincts of our nature involve it. The experience of our thinking ever corroborates it. The very principles of inductive thought lead to it. No one can advance a particle of valid proof to the contrary. Nature is true. "Order is heaven's first law." The creation is the product of true thought ; the universe in every minutest portion of its infinite stir moves ever along the straight lines of thought.

# BOOK IV.

## THE WILL.—I. SUBJECTIVE VIEW.

---

### CHAPTER I.

#### ITS NATURE AND MODIFICATIONS.

§ 208. THE WILL *is the mind's function of willing.*

This function is otherwise known as the Voluntary Power, the Orectic Faculty, the Conative Power, the Moral Power, the Power of Choice, the Free-Will, the Faculty of Freedom, etc.,

Its product is diversely named; as a volition, a choice, a purpose; also, a decision, a determination, a resolve, a resolution, etc., Of these designations, the three first named are the more technical. The first, *volition*, expresses more exactly the proper essence of an act of the will. *Choice*, from its etymology and its current use, points to the appetency, the relish, the liking, the selecting, which attends volition, as its prompting occasion or the grosser movement of mind in which the volition is embodied. *Purpose* looks rather to the result of an act of willing; it indicates the end implied in all rational volition as a telic activity, § 24.  The other terms are of interest as giving the testimony of language, which to a certain extent at least, is a trustworthy record of the human consciousness, that the will, as a determining, deciding, resolving function, belongs to an active nature.

§ 209. The will is diversely characterized.  It has its own permanent and essential attributes and suffers certain noticeable modifications in this its own essential character.  It is modified also in relation to the objects of its action.  It is still farther modified in relation to the other mental functions.

Our method will be to present the doctrine of the will, as we have that of the other functions, in the twofold view—Subjective and Objective. In our subjective view will be given an exposition of the essential characters of volition as the proper function of the will ; the growth and intrinsic relationships of the will ; and its extrinsic relationships to the other mental functions as in Conscience and in the comprehensive virtues of Faith, Hope, and Love.  The objective view will respect the Good as the one object of the will in the twofold aspect of the Good Presented—Motives—and the Good Produced—Duties.

# CHAPTER II.

## VOLITION.

§ 210. We may readily identify in familiar experience an act of will—a volition—clearly distinguishing it from other mental phenomena. An orange presented to our view, produces a certain sensation;—we have a feeling. The sensation brings in a cognition; we perceive the orange and proceed to distinguish and think it as having this or that attribute;—we have a knowledge. But we often go farther; we reach out the hand and take the orange. We recognize now, besides the sensation and the thought or knowledge, a certain free determination of our mind; we determine to extend the hand, to take the orange. In this determining act we find a proper act of willing, a volition. It is proper here to repeat the observation that most of the terms used to denote mental functions are, without much liability to error, employed to denote the faculty, the exercise of the faculty, and the result of the acting. The term *function* is a synonym of *faculty;* but points rather to the exercise than to the power implied.

§ 211. Inspecting closely this act of willing or

of volition, we discover a characteristic which enters into its inmost essence; it is *directive*. In determining to take the orange there is on the part of the mind a directing of the nervous energy subject to its commands toward the orange. This element is discernible in every conceivable act of will. There is a directing of some power or energy toward some end or object—the ordering of some energy to effect some result. This is clearly signified in some of the terms employed to designate an act of will—as, *determination, purpose.*

This directive character in an act of volition involves selection. As directive, volition is necessarily *selective*. In the universe around it and within the sphere of the mind itself, a vast diversity of objects present themselves for the action of the mind toward them or upon them immediately or remotely; and as all mental action in man must be more or less specific, there must be in any act of will a selection from among this multitude of objects. And when the object has been determined in such selection, there is, still further a selection from among the diverse possible forms of acting in reference to it on the part of the will. In all cases of volition there are these objective and subjective alternatives—alternatives in respect of object and alternatives of action by the will toward it.

It is this selective character in volition which makes the term *choice* a fitting one to designate it, especially as choice often expresses itself or is presupposed in the volition. But selection—choice—does not necessarily involve willing ; for these terms express sometimes mere comparative judgments or comparative preferences in taste in respect to way or degree of pleasing. We may select or choose between an orange and a peach as to some comparable elements, without determining any action in respect to them further than a mere judgment or preference,—without determining to take the one or the other. There may be simple judging without volition. But if I proceed to take the orange, I take another step not necessarily contained in this act of mere judging ; I exert a positive act of will. This indeed presupposes selection or choice ; but the two are clearly distinguishable as pertaining to different mental functions. As well in the subjective as in the objective alternatives ever attending volition, there may be selection or choice presupposed in the act of willing while yet distinguishable from it. I may indeed supposably, on a given occasion, forbear all action of will ; the simple forbearance of all volition may imply what may be called a selection—a selection between willing and not willing. Selection here is obviously not volition. But in positive volition I may either *will* or *nill.* This is always a subjective alternative. But even here, although selection —choice—is presupposed in either case, in willing as well as in nilling, the essence of the volition lies in something distinguishable from the selection. I will or nill something. Even nilling implies something inviting or repelling the action of the will, toward which accordingly the instinctive activity of the will tends by its native drift or trend and the willing act respects properly this instinct to act by allowing or resisting it. I may have this alternative before me of selecting between willing and not deciding at all either to will or not to will. So still further, it may be that two or more forms of desire or appetency are presented, in which case the selective or choosing element in still another form comes into the act of willing. I am offered the alternative of a peach or an orange and I select the one or the other. But here, as before, the mere choosing or selecting is not all that constitutes the act nor is it the essential and characteristic element in it as an act of will. Some one of these forces of desire or appetency, the higher or the lower, this or that, is in a proper volition positively determined. The desire is allowed at least, perhaps fostered and strengthened and given room and sway. It is here in this determining by positive allowance and enforcement of the desire or appetency or by its repression that we find the heart of the volition or willing act. It is here consequently in the allowance or disallowance of the appetency that the proper moral character of the act is seated, not in the appetency itself. In this directive function as the more essential element of an act

of will there is often involved besides the selective
element mentioned, also a proper *evoking* constituent—the power to call forth—to excite—as well
also as to repress the energy working in specific
acts.   It is possibly true that the will cannot increase or diminish the aggregate of energy at any
one moment of the mind's history.   But we are
certainly conscious of being able to summon
forth what energy we have and to infuse more or
less of it into this or that particular exertion.
We can be more or less attentive ; we can engage
our imaginations, our recollections, more or less
earnestly ; we can determine with more or less
decisiveness of will.   It is an important fact
concerning the free-will that it can  evoke in
higher or lower degree the energies of our natures.
The sovereignty of the will reaches to this control over the degree as well as the direction of the
energy to be called forth in any specific case of
its action.

Further, this directive action, constituting the
essence of a proper volition or act of will, necessarily respects some active nature.   We cannot
conceive of a directive activity exerted on what
is absolutely inactive.   We speak, with allowable
correctness in the compression of familiar speech,
of " choosing pleasure," of " choosing honor," and
the like, when we mean something more than
mere intellectual selection and intend voluntary
preference or actual determination of will.   But
we do not, strictly speaking, will the pleasure or

the honor ; for the will has no power to call them into being. They attend only on the conditions which are prescribed in the very creation of man and which the will is utterly unable to set aside or supplant. The native desire for pleasure or for any specific form of pleasure or honor, the will may allow or disallow. Desire belongs to an active nature, and over it the will has a legitimate control. It may repress or, it may be, entirely suppress this desire or appetency, and then all choice in the case is exterminated in its very roots. Or the will may act upon those activities or affections of the soul upon the exertion or allowance of which the pleasure is made to attend. The will accordingly as a sovereign directive power, may prevent choice by suppressing desire or may give it life and effectiveness by activities or affections as required instrumentalities and conditions. But its action is ever directed on active natures.

This action may respect the mind's own energies and susceptibilities. The will evokes and directs thoughts, imaginations, subordinate purposes. It evokes susceptibilities, directs them toward their objects, and holds them under impression. It acts, too, on the soul itself in its native instincts, propensities, appetencies, summoning them forth, maintaining their ascendency in the mind and giving them control ; or on the other hand repressing them and crowding them out by other feelings or thoughts which it evokes and sustains.

This directive action, also, may respect the energy which resides in the body so far as subject
to such control. It arouses the nervous energy
in the body and directs the divers motor forces
of the nerve-system. It also has a certain indirect control over the affections of the soul
through the sensory nerves, directing to a certain
extent what feelings shall be touched by them
and to what degree they shall be allowed.

The soul itself and the body with which it is
united in a living organism are, perhaps, the only
natures with which the will can interact in immediate communication. We certainly know too
little as yet of our relations to other spiritual
beings to determine with absolute assurance
whether our wills can immediately touch them.
But mediately we do beyond doubt act upon
other beings. We manifest ourselves to our
fellow men under the direction of our wills so
as to determine their actions and feelings. We
stir their pity; we summon forth their beneficence; we command their service. Their characters and their condition furnish to us true and
proper ends to our endeavors. We correctly say
that we purpose this or that in their experience.
We purpose their success rather than their de-
feat, working out our purpose in active endeavor
to secure it; our love goes out in positive exertions of will toward them. In our behavior
toward them we not infrequently recognize a
truly moral character which implies the action of

our free-will. Still more ; we often purpose this or that in their immediate experience, as when we intentionally provoke them by an insulting word or an angry blow ; and this effect in them is that which alone comes distinctly into our consciousness. The purpose and the will seem to fasten immediately on their personality ; in the insult or the blow we seem to will directly their hurt or pain. The will is an end-seeking activity ; and these are seemingly its ends—the feeling of hurt or pain in those whom we attack. But a strict analysis, here as before, shows that the action of the will respects as its immediate end, the disposition or the appetency of the soul that craves the supposed effect in the condition of others, or the ministry of its executive activities to effect what is desired. There may be no distinct consciousness of any such complicated action as this, of first allowing the desire and then evoking the executive ministry ; it may seem to us as if we immediately willed the pleasure or the success of others. But our mental activity often evades our notice. When we purpose, for instance, the raising of the finger, the will cannot immediately reach that ; it can only allow the desire and then direct the energy or the active nature that resides in the nerves. The finger rises, not in obedience to the command of the will, but by the action of this nervous energy which we have evoked and set to work. We yet seem to will directly the rising of the finger, all unconscious of the intervening instrumentality.

Once more, volition, as the exertion of a true telic activity, ever regards an end ; and as we accept the truth that man is the creature of perfect wisdom and love, the legitimate action of the human will must ever be for a good end. The proper end in all exertions of the will is embraced accordingly under this category—the good. Pre-eminently and characteristically the will, as the sovereign regulator of the soul, which is itself, as rational, an end-seeking nature, is *the function of ends.* Its action is essentially telic— end-seeking in a sense higher and larger than the action of any other mental function. It is the end in respect to the will which thus acquires the right to be denominated *the good.*

The function of the will, it should be observed further, is limited to this directive work, understood as involving the selective and evoking elements named. In loose popular discourse it is often made to play a much broader part. Creation is thus said to be the product of the Almighty's will. Great achievements are ascribed to mere will-power, when something more is meant than a work of mere directive or evoking energy. There may be great sagacity and wisdom, large judgment, strong feeling, enthusiastic zeal concerned ; but as will, in directing the tendencies, the feelings, the imaginations, the thoughts, is a characteristic feature, the whole joint product or effect is ascribed to that. But

it should ever be remembered that the sole function of the will is to will—to direct and evoke
the various activities of the soul or of the bodily
organism.  It has no power to feel, to imagine, or
to think or judge.  The mind does all its work
of willing in directing and evoking through its
function of will, just as it does all of its work in
knowing through or by its function of the intelligence.  The grand truth, however, is that the
mind never acts but as a whole, as one single
organic nature.  It moves ever as a feeling,
knowing, free activity.  One function may predominate and give character to a specific act, but
cannot appear except in organic union with the
other two.  Analytic thought may of course separate for convenient study any one functional
feature from a joint tri-functional manifestation
of the rational nature.  It may deal with mere
abstraction; the real is ever a concrete.

The summary doctrine of the will thus is that
it is essentially a directive function involving a
selecting and also an evoking element; that the
will ever acts on some active nature; that its
action is immediately on that nature; and that
as directive it ever looks to an end, which end is
known as the good, the term being used in its
large philosophical import.

§ 212.  If now we take an instance of a peculiar
kind of volition, as when, for instance, we suppose the orange, which we have determined to
take, not to be our own, but another's, who re-

22

fuses us his permission to take it, and if we still determine to take it by stealth or by violence, we discover in our act another class of elements. We discover, first, that such a volition involves *freedom.*

It is implied in this that the determination to take was not forced upon us by any insuperable necessity; that it could be withheld as truly as be put forth. We never think of saying, however pressed, in self-vindication, that literally we could not help taking it;—that we were necessitated to take it. We are conscious that in every such act we could take or forbear taking. Accordingly we acknowledge our responsibility for the act. To deny this element of freedom is to belie the testimony of our own consciousness; it is to contradict the universal testimony of intelligent and unbiased men; it is to falsify the universal language of man, which in all its dialects comprises terms significant of this freedom.

§ 213. Another of the higher elements involved in proper volition is distinct *personality.*

This element is indeed dimly given in feeling and in knowing. The phenomenon of feeling gives the distinction of an object impressing and a subject impressed; as does that of knowing give the distinction of object known and subject knowing. But this elementary and germinant distinction of personality rises into perfect outline and fullness in the free-will and with an emphasis not allowable before. The feeling and knowing subject in willing recognizes and pronounces itself a true *ego*, a person distinct from other persons and things.

But this free personality which has its seat in the will and constitutes the leading and characteristic element of that mental power, itself involves several distinguishable attributes of highest interest and importance.

§ 214. First, free personality involves *mental sovereignty*.

The free-will rules over the whole soul, holding the sensibility and the intelligence in strict subjection to itself and under its own control.

This mental sovereignty residing in the personal free-will of man is by no means absolute. The very finiteness of his being, which we have so fully recognized, forbids this idea. The domain of the will is limited both outwardly and inwardly. It meets even within its own proper limited domain with checks and obstacles which it often finds itself unable to overbear or remove. Its universal experience leaves recorded in the consciousness the clear, salient characters of the dependence and finiteness of the human will.

This sovereignty of the human will is limited, also, in relation to the mind itself of which it is the chief function. Its power does not reach so far as to reconstruct the mind or change its essential attributes. It cannot make the sensibility feel, the imagination create or put forth form, the intelligence know or apprehend or represent, otherwise than according to their own nature and laws. It cannot utterly destroy, if it may impair, the essential activity of the soul. It cannot prevent its feeling or its knowing. It cannot abrogate utterly its own freedom or its own activity, however much it may weaken, corrupt, or hamper its proper function and character.

But while thus dependent and limited in its sovereignty, the personal free-will is a true sovereign. It rules the sensibility while it cannot prevent feeling when an object is presented to the sensibility, and cannot remove the mind from the reach of all objects that can impress it, inasmuch as it cannot remove itself from the universe of being,—cannot altogether prevent feeling, it can yet direct feeling in various ways. It can arrest any feeling, any appetency or desire, when going out toward any one object, and turn it toward another object. The angry man expels his wrath by evoking a feeling of fear or of love; by closing his eye on the provocation to anger and opening it on what excites compassion or gratitude or reverence.

The free-will rules also the imagination or the faculty of form. It selects the ideal, the matter in which it shall be embodied, and prompts and directs the embodying act.

It rules in like manner the intelligence, evoking it and directing and sustaining or arresting its activity.

The personal free-will is thus sovereign in a true sense over the sensibility and the intelligence. It is equally sovereign, as will be shown farther on, over its own subordinate movements. It pervades the entire mental nature by its selecting and directive power. As the mind feels only through its function of feeling, and knows only through its function of knowing, and as feeling and knowing pervade the entire activity of the mind, so the mind wills only through the function of willing and willing pervades its entire activity.

§ 215. Secondly, the free personality involves the attribute of *originativeness.*

In a sense, perhaps, in which it cannot be said of the sensibility and the intelligence, the will is a true originator. As part of a finite being, it is dependent on something external to itself for the object toward which its activity is to be directed and with which, if it act at all, it must interact. Free choice is in this sense determined by its object as presented to it. There can be no choice where there is nothing to be chosen, as a man, however strong, cannot lift a weight unless there be a weight to be lifted. In a sense analogous to that in which we say the weight determines the lifting, we may say, perhaps, that the object chosen determines the choice. But there is a true sense in which the free-will may be said to originate action. As the man determines whether he will lift, or not, the weight presented to him, so the free-will ever determines its action in this or that direction to be or not to be. Freedom supposes ever this subjective alternative. If there be but one object presented there is the simple alternative of choice and refusal. If two or more objects are presented only one of which can be taken, the alternative is complicated; the choice or refusal is combined with the act of electing or selecting the one or the other of the objects. Of the choice or refusal, whichever it be, and whether simple or elective, the free-will is justly called the originator and true producer.

The free-will of man accordingly is so constituted by its creator as to be able directly or indirectly to enter the realm of mere nature as it flows on in its necessary flow and to originate new sequences different from what would be otherwise. It does not originate new matter; but it does originate new dispositions of matter. It does not originate new measures of force ; but it does originate new directions of force, so that the sequences of nature are more or less changed from their undisturbed order. It does not originate, in the sense of exerting, new choices or purposes in other free beings ; but it does present to them new objects, new motives, new inspirations which may induce new purposes and character in them while still remaining in unchecked freedom.

§ 216. Thirdly, the free personality involves the attribute of *morality*.

By morality is expressed the relation of a being to right and duty. By virtue of its freedom, however, as necessarily intelligent and feeling, the mind of man has rights which it exacts and duties which it owes. The personal free-will is the seat and center of this relation of man to right and duty, and is the source out of which it naturally and necessarily springs.

§ 217. Fourthly, the free personality involves the attribute of *responsibility*.

The finiteness of man's being and his depend-ence already in themselves foreshadow a power above him, by which he is limited and hemmed in, and on which he depends. But in his free activity this relation to a higher power shines out clearly and in definite outlines. As the exactor of rights and the subject of duties, he recognizes a law from without and from above which has allowed those exacted rights and has prescribed those owed duties. He recognizes a law written in his creation on the very center of his being, his inmost personality, that at once imposes duties and gives rights. He recognizes also a power to sustain and to enforce this law, to which he expects all other beings from whom he has rights to be answerable, to which accordingly he feels they must expect him to be answerable, so far as he is bound in duty to them. The free per-sonality thus makes man moral, as subject to a law which enforces duty and sustains rights.

It is important to remark that this characteristic of free personality, involves at once the distinction of the personal moral self from other personal moral beings.   It involves, also, the recognition of a personal free being who is the source of the law of duty and equally its administrator.   The responsibility of a free person must be not to a thing, not to an attribute, but to a free person.   This free person we call God, who writes the law of duty on the human soul by making it what it is and who rules to sustain that law.   The free personality is thus shown to be the seat and center and source of *religion*, the heart and life of the relation of man to God.

# CHAPTER III.

§ 218. IN the mind as an essentially active nature we have found the will to be the ruling and directive activity. It rules the other functions of feeling and knowing, and also, as we shall now see, in all subordinate volitions, it rules itself.

It is to be remarked now of this ruling energy of the human mind—the will—that, on the one hand it is capable of indefinite increase, and that on the other hand, it is limited and dependent.

In infancy the will is feeble, bordering on impotency. By exercise it becomes mighty through the principle of habit and growth. It is developed out of the instinctive nature of the mind. The transition from action which is merely instinctive and as such necessitated by the appointment of the creator in creating it, is beyond the notice of our limited observation. We can as well observe the development of the bud from its germ. But by the very law of all mental life its action once prompted continues on, and although in a sense changed in its direction or opposed by subsequent volitions, yet it never can

be truly said to lose its record in the mind's history. Each volition not only strengthens the
willing mind itself, as legitimate exercise strengthens all living power, but each repetition of the
volition in the same direction or toward the
same object confirms the tendency to will in that
direction. The will thus may acquire in time
what in popular phrase we term indomitable
determination; it is proof against all motive that
finite power can bring to it. Weakness of will,
in other words, imbecility of purpose, vacillation,
irresoluteness, is the result of varying volitions,
one moving in one direction, another in another.
Strength of will, on the other hand, under the
great law of growth, comes directly and surely by
multiplying volitions in the same direction, that
is, toward the same or similar objects, and by
shunning volitions looking in opposite directions.

§ 219. The will, however, as a single function
in a complex organism, is so far dependent on
the other functions of the mind—the sensibility
and the intelligence.

The objects of volition as motives, without
which the will cannot act, come to it in part at
least, if not wholly, through these other functions.
And further than this, its strength is also dependent on them. A feeble sense, a feeble understanding, is attended by a feeble volition. In
the intensest feeling and the clearest knowledge,
is ever found the most energetic will.

§ 220. The will, as has been already stated,

rules itself, in a certain sense, as well as the feeling and other functions of the mind.

It does this by putting forth volitions which draw along, whether more positively by its own free prompting and sustaining, or more negatively by allowing and suffering other following volitions. Such originating volitions are called *governing*, or *ruling*, or *predominant* volitions. The volitions which they respectively draw along after them, are called, in reference to the former, *subordinate* volitions. We determine, thus, to take a journey: This determination of will is, in reference to the particular acts by which it is carried into execution, a governing or predominant volition. Every particular act of will put forth to carry out this original determination, as getting ready the baggage, procuring the conveyance, etc., is a subordinate volition. Such subordinate volitions, in so far as they are regarded as carrying out the governing volition, are called *executive* volitions. The putting forth the hand to take the orange after the determination to appropriate it, is an executive volition.

It is obvious that the same volition may be in one relation a predominant volition, and in another relation a subordinate volition. The getting ready one's baggage is subordinate and executive in relation to the predominant volition to take a journey; it is itself predominant in relation to each specific volition, as going to the shop to purchase, purchasing, ordering or bearing home, etc.

The highest volition of which man is capable, and thus with him absolutely the predominant volition, which is subordinate to no other, is that which controls the entire activity of the mind so far as subject to the will itself. Such a predominant volition determines the character of the man in its largest and most proper sense. From the very nature of motive as object to the will, such predominant purpose must have for its object as motive the chief good of the soul as actually selected by it. The good so taken to be the chief good may possibly be an inferior good, as compared with some other good that might have been taken. Such is the prerogative of the will as essentially free ; it can choose the lesser of two goods. In the grand alternative of choice in which the perfecting of character and condition is presented as one of the objects and rejected or declined, the lower good is in fact chosen as the chief good. And this choice of the inferior good is the sin ; as St. Augustine in his confessions B. ii., § x., well defines :—"Sin is committed while through an immoderate inclination toward those goods of the lowest order, the better and higher are forsaken." Such sinful choice, although of a lower good, consisting in the selecting, the allowance, and enforcement of a lower appetency, yet becomes the predominant volition, and so governs and determines the succeeding acts of the moral life, and gives character to the entire current of the soul's activity.

# CHAPTER IV.

## CONSCIENCE.

§ 221. The term *conscience*, originally and etymologically synonymous with *consciousness*, denoted self-knowledge generally. But usage has greatly modified its signification, first by restricting it to matters of will or morality, and, secondly, by enlarging it to include feeling as well as knowledge. It has, therefore, acquired a new import widely differing from its primary sense.

Other expressions are in use to denote the same mental state with more or less modifications, as *moral sense, moral faculty, sense of duty* or *of right and wrong*.

The peculiar relationship of the conscience to the will, as needful condition or necessary concomitant modifying the character of its action, justifies or even necessitates the distinct recognition of it in a full exposition of the doctrine of the will.

Conscience includes three chief distinguishable elements:—(1) a discernment of right and wrong; (2) a feeling of obligation; and (3) an approval or disapproval.

The term is used sometimes with more promi-

nent reference to one of these elements, sometimes with more prominent reference to another.
It properly implies, however, all three, even when
used with such prominent reference to one, inasmuch as the three necessarily exist and imply one
another.

§ 222. 1. Conscience involves, as a chief element, the discernment of right and wrong.

We have already recognized the truth that the
idea of free personality involves the idea of being
a subject of rights and duties, that is, the idea of
morality. In other words, the fact of free choice
reveals to us at once the attributes of morality
as truly as the orange reveals to us the attributes
of form and of color. It is impossible for us fully
to contemplate such an act without recognizing
this attribute of morality, by which is understood
that the act must be considered as either right or
wrong.

This is the proper origin of the category of
morality which includes under it the specific and
alternative attributes of right and wrong. It is
true, however, that the existence of this attribute
as pertaining to free action in man may be proved
from other assumed truths. From the assumption of the being and rule of God there follows
by necessary deduction the subjection of his free
creatures to him, which subjection implies the
enforcement upon them of the observance of the
right and the avoidance of the wrong. He cannot rule without subjects; and as he is free and

righteous, he cannot be true to himself but as re-
quiring righteousness of his free subjects.

The existence of this attribute as pertaining to
free action may be deduced equally from the assumed existence of that true law, right reason
or rule, invariable, eternal, universal, of which
Cicero so profoundly and so justly discourses.
Given such a law, and it follows that action under
it must be characterized as right or wrong.

It may be proved also from universal acknowl-
edgment, from the general consciousness of men,
and especially as expressed in the language of
men.

This attribute of free action—that it is moral,
that is, either right or wrong—as necessarily pertaining to it, may be discerned by the human intelligence in every case, whether the act be one's
own, and so properly within the range of personal
consciousness, or another's and apprehended by
observation.

The fundamental element in conscience is this
discernment of the right or wrong in every free
act which of itself and immediately reveals this
attribute to every free contemplation.

§ 223. 2. Conscience further involves the sentiment of obligation.

A sense of moral freedom involves a sense of
obligation to do the right and shun the wrong.
So soon as a free choice is proposed, obligation is
felt. As every volition involves the necessity of
an alternative determination, of choosing or re-

fusing, and as there is given in this freedom the attribute of being obligatory—of constraining to the right—so the sensibility is impressible by the attribute. It is true, the mind in its sovereign freedom, may turn away to a certain degree its sensibility from the attribute: yet as the mind is in its highest nature a free and consequently a moral agent, this sense of obligation cannot be utterly prevented or annihilated.

This sense of obligation, thus necessarily springing from the consciousness of freedom, has for its objective counterpart what is fitly called "the law of God written on the heart." It is accordingly a legitimate inference from this consciousness, from this sense of obligation, that there is an outer source of this obligation; that there is a law, given to man from without himself, and inscribed on his inmost nature; and that this source is none other than God himself, who created man and endowed him with his freedom and who wrote the law in his inmost being and rules ever to sustain and enforce it.

§ 224. 3. Still further, the full contemplation of an act of free-will necessarily brings along with it a sense of approval or of disapproval.

Every such act reveals in itself this attribute of fitness to awaken this feeling, as the orange reveals the attribute of juiciness and so impresses the outward sense. Relatively to the doer, and as seated in him, the attribute is that of merit or demerit, desert or guilt. In every free act the doer feels this desert or ill-desert according as he has chosen right or wrong; and exactly correspondent to this feeling in the heart of the personal doer is the judgment of approval or condemnation, of praise or of blame, by whoever scans the act with a moral eye.

Such is the threefold function of conscience; it discerns in every free act the right or the wrong; it feels the obligation to do the right and to shun the wrong; it approves or condemns— awards praise or blame.

Conscience, it should be added, has sometimes been regarded as the seat of that pleasure or pain which attends on all mental activity, and which in moral acts and states is deepest and most intense. We speak of the pleasure of a good conscience, and this pleasure may, perhaps, not unwarrantably in less strict language, be regarded as a function of conscience. In this case we should add as its fourth function that of giving the sense of that peculiar pleasure or of pain in the doer which naturally attends all right or wrong action.

§ 225. The will extends its sovereignty over the conscience as over the entire mental activity.

It directs and controls the culture of conscience, which, like all other mental activities, is capable of culture and growth. Quickness and accuracy of moral discernment, tender sense of obligation, and ready and just response of praise or blame, are matters of culture. There is open to man a

23

path of advancement, of ascent, leading ever on
and up towards that infinite perfection which belongs to the judge and ruler of all.

The will, also, regulates and controls the conscience in respect to specific acts.  Most moral
acts of men are more or less complex, embracing
some lawful elements, some unlawful.  Morality
in this respect is like truth and beauty; it appears among men in forms complicated of the
perfect and the imperfect.  As there is some deformity in almost every beautiful form on earth,
some error in almost every truth held by men, so
there is in the life even of the upright man some
taint of imperfection.  And on the contrary,
there is no form wholly destitute of every
beauty, no error void of all truth, no sin destitute of some feature or element that is morally
approvable.  The thief may steal to procure food
for a starving family; the theft is sinful, the care
for the dependent ones is right.  The will can
thus fasten the attention more upon this or more
upon that one of these complex elements that
enter into every moral act of man, and so the
recognition of the right or wrong, the corresponding sense of obligation to choose or refuse,
and the consequent approval or disapproval may
vary.  Hence the consciences of men, however
true in themselves, differ in men of different
moral habits or dispositions in their estimate of
particular actions.  One's own conscience varies
with his moral mood.  The same action is

judged and felt by him differently at different times. His intelligence varies in quickness and keenness, and his sensibility in tenderness. But above and beyond this, his will, as sovereign, may turn the view or the sense now more on one element, now more on another. Even one's own conscience is not uniform in its action.

Nevertheless conscience remains to man the highest arbiter and ruler in all his moral life. The authority of the Divine Ruler and Judge speaks only through that. If the human conscience is not infallible, it is yet the supreme arbiter within the man himself in all morality. Man knows no higher in any department of his nature. The will itself in all its sovereignty must yield to the arbitrament of conscience; for the Creator has not with freedom granted exemption from responsibility. As the mind by the necessities of its nature, must be conscious of its own action, so the will must, to some degree at least, pass its own determinations in review before the censorship of the conscience. It may to some extent hinder, or defer, or even mar the action of conscience; but it cannot wholly silence nor so corrupt as to destroy it.

Hence arises the duty and the importance not only of training and cultivating the conscience, but also of securing it from being stifled or warped by a perverse will.

# CHAPTER V.

## HOPE, FAITH, AND LOVE.

§ 226. HOPE, FAITH, and LOVE are not only three comprehensive graces; they are also comprehensive virtues.

They sometimes appear with the sensibility or in feeling predominant and so characterizing them, and then consequently are proper graces. They sometimes, however, appear with the moral element—the free-will—predominant in its actions and so characterizing them as virtues.

As graces they come but indirectly, while as virtues they come directly under this law; but under the law of duty in both cases they are properly subjects of immediate command. The practical reason, the conscience, recognizes them as right, as obligatory, as praiseworthy, and accordingly by its voice of authority as the organ of the divine will and word, commands them. As graces, they appear characteristically as spontaneous; as virtues they appear as voluntary and free. As thus enjoined duties, in these exercises the will puts itself forth and embodies itself in the feeling as its needful body and form of expression. It selects the feeling to be moved; it directs the

awakened feeling upon its object ; keeps the feeling on its object and animates it to its proper
degree of life and tenderness, and moreover protects it from being smothered or overpowered by
any adverse feeling.

§ 227. IN HOPE, the free-will leads the feeling
of desire fed with expectation to its proper object. This object, as legitimate to the human
soul, must be a good, and in order to hope as an
enjoined virtue the good hoped for must be the
highest good which is possible in the case.

Hope, as a virtue, may be defined to be the
choice of good as the object of desire and expectation.

Hope as an enjoined duty and virtue comprises
several leading distinguishable elements and
modifications which we proceed to enumerate.

1. Hope, as a duty, implies something positive
to be done. It is not a wholly passive exercise,
a mere grace. The will is summoned to go out
and find the proper object of hope and put the
feeling in exercise. Such object in some form is
ever attainable. As surely as the activity of the
soul was ordained and fashioned and conditioned
in infinite wisdom and goodness for good as its
end, so surely is it that the duty of hope is a
practicable one under the rule of God. The
good in the nature of things connected with
right action, is in the duty of hope to be sought
and proposed as object to the sensibility.

2. In the duty of hope, the desire and expecta-

tion are to be set on this good by the sovereign direction of the will.

3. The duty of hope is both generic and specific. The whole activity of the soul is to be subject to hope in such sense that each governing purpose or choice shall be inspired by it ; the whole man is to move on in hope. And subordinate volitions are to stand in like relation to the duty of hope, receiving each its special inspiration from it. No duty can be rightly and perfectly discharged except as thus inspired by hope.

4. Hope has its limitations both as to the kind of its objects and the degree of its allowance. The one legitimate object of hope in its generic and supreme exercise, is the good for which the soul was designed and fashioned. The will is enjoined in this duty to seek out and choose this good as highest object of desire and expectation. The duty prohibits any other good to be thus taken as the object of the soul's governing hope. Among the objects of specific hope there is wide room for selection. Some objects are absolutely prohibited ; other objects are prohibited only because, in the circumstances, less worthy than others which are presented or may be found.

The highest legitimate good brings no limitation to hope in degree but such as is imposed by the capacity of the soul itself or by the due demands of other capacities in its culture and regulation. Allowable specific objects of hope are limited in their demands to their due measure of desire and expectation. These limitations vary indefinitely with condition and circumstance.

5. Finally the free-will is enjoined in the duty of hope not only to find its proper object and regulate the affection to its proper degree, but also to guard and protect it from being overborne, and also to sustain and nourish it that as participating in an active living nature it may ever grow and strengthen.

§ 228. IN FAITH, the free-will leads the natural feeling of dependence to its proper object.

Faith, as a duty, may accordingly be defined to be the allowance and regulation of this feeling on the proper object of dependence. It involves the actual exercise of the feeling in reliance and trust.

The objects of faith are all those objects on which man may in any way depend. Its highest form is in relation to God, as the creator and disposer of man. The office of faith in this its highest form, is to recognize God as the one comprehensive, legitimate, absolute ground of dependence and trust. In this highest form, faith is well characterized as " the subtle chain that binds us to the infinite." In lower and subordinate forms, faith finds its legitimate specific objects in all the beings within its reach which fill the universe of God and in all the events of his providential rule. Especially does it find legitimate objects in fellow-beings of the same rational nature. Manifold modes and degrees of

dependence determine manifold forms and measures of faith. Even the manifold capacities and
functions of the soul itself call for manifold kinds
and measures of faith as they are interlocked
with one another in manifold forms and degrees
of reciprocal interdependence. We must have
faith in our senses, our thoughts, our purposes.
The soul's true life depends on the legitimate
ministries of these functions.

Faith, as a duty, like hope, involves divers elements and modifications. It implies something
positive to be done ; it involves the fixing of the
feeling of dependence necessarily belonging to a
finite nature on its proper object or ground,
whether this object or ground is the highest and
most comprehensive as God himself, or subordinate as his creatures and ordinances ; it has its
limitations both as to object and degree ; and
requires protection and nourishment.

§ 229. IN LOVE, the free-will leads out the
natural feeling of sympathy to its proper object.

Love, as a duty, may accordingly be defined to
be the choice of the proper object for sympathy.
It involves the actual exercise of this sympathy
toward its object.

The sphere of love as a duty to man, is commensurate with the range of human sympathy.
With whatever being the human soul can be in
sympathy and in whatever way such sympathy
can be felt and manifested, toward that being
and in that way the duty of love extends.

Its highest forms are in relation to those objects or beings with which the soul is in closest, broadest, deepest relations of sympathy. No being is so near to the soul as its creator and disposer. No being can engage or reciprocate such deep sympathies. Love consequently is highest and most imperative toward him. It is supreme and comprehensive of all exercises of love toward inferior beings.

As there can be nothing more worthy to engage our sympathy, nothing in a particular being that is more worthy to enlist our highest and warmest sympathy, than the comprehensive good for which he exists, so love in its highest and most commanding form involves sympathy with this end for which the object has his being. If we reverently characterize the end of God's being as the perfectness of his infinite nature, or the perfect glory of his character and the infinite blessedness which waits on his perfect working, then our love to him must necessarily express sympathy with this end as its highest possible form. Love to God thus in its highest form is will to please him or will to glorify him. As the end of man's being is his true excellence of character and consequent highest blessedness, love to man in its highest, most generic form, is will to promote this well-being in him.

The specific and subordinate forms of love respect the manifold specific attributes and relations and conditions of other beings so far as they can enlist our sympathy.

Love, as a duty, like hope and faith, involves divers elements and modifications. It implies a positive act of will, something to be done; it involves the fixing of the natural sympathy of the soul on its appropriate object in kind and allowing to its natural expression its proper degree; it requires protection and nourishment as being subject to culture and growth.

## CHAPTER VI.

### THE GOOD—ITS NATURE AND MODIFICATIONS.

§ 230. THE GOOD is proper object of the will — it is that which the will as a function of the mind immediately and exclusively respects as the legitimate end or result of its action.

This term, like most others employed in speculations respecting the mind, is used in different meanings. The ambiguity naturally occasions in ethical discussions, in which the term is of fundamental import, serious misapprehension and error. Two different meanings have been very generally recognized, each legitimately belonging to it according to the uses and analogies of language :—1, *happiness* in the largest and most comprehensive sense ; 2, the means or conditions of happiness. All good, thus, it is held by some writers, is either happiness or the means of happiness. But to others this whole view is unsatisfactory. They hold that there is a true good to be found in mere being or condition of being irrespectively of all happiness. The works of the creation, it is said, were pronounced to be good, not because there was universal happiness nor yet because simply they stood in the relation to happiness which would bring in happiness or to that on which happiness depends. These works were good in themselves as being perfectly fashioned both in respect of their own individual natures and also in relation to all surrounding and related things, but emphatically good in respect to the special end or purpose of their respective being. God saw his works were good, answering his fair idea. They were all made for an end, each individual being and each particular function of each being; and that end, whether more comprehensive or more particular, was ever and always good. It might be true and doubtless it is true, that the designed and the legitimate result of the working of each and all would be happiness, and happiness unmixed. If such working be not happiness itself, happiness is but the sign and test of it, being its necessary effect. But irrespectively of that relation to happiness, all these works were good in respect to the end for which they were made; and this end was correspondingly good. It was good as the result of the right working of each and all existing things and good also in its relation to all other ends in the system of universal being and action. As the true respects the essence of things and signifies the congruous relationship internally and externally existing in things, and the beautiful respects their form as they interact in perfect sympathy with one another, the good respects the end of this being and interaction, and signifies that it is the fit and legitimate result of their nature and action. And so down through the history of philosophical speculation from Aristotle onward, the highest good to man, his *summum bonum*, has been held to be the highest and most comprehensive end of his being. Inasmuch as man exists but as part in a universe of being with which he must be in sympathetic interaction, his ministry to secure this end or highest good, can be neither more nor less than to perfect his own being and his relationship to the beings by which he is environed. Whatever else may be said of man's duty or man's interest, this ever remains as the fundamental truth that his good, his true good and his highest good, as the legitimate comprehensive end of his entire activity, is *to perfect his character and his condition.*

This view of the nature of the good, as the term is employed in ethical and metaphysical speculation, seems to be not only accordant with authoritative usage but also to be supported by its significance and helpfulness in resolving some of the perplexities in this field of knowledge. This use of the term seems certainly legitimate ; for what can be a truer, a more perfect good to a being than that its own being and condition should be just what it was designed and fitted to be by its creation in infinite goodness and wisdom? In the case of an active and growing nature what can be its proper highest good but the attainment of the highest perfection possible to it? Especially in the case of a rational being whose predominant attribute is that it is end-seeking, what higher end as good can it propose to itself than such perfection of its nature and condition? This is in truth his proper joy, his truest happiness, his highest blessedness, his chief glory, that he be himself in the greatest perfection of his own being and condition. This he can by his own free action, in part, at least, effect; he can, to a certain extent, by direct exertion of his free-will determine such a good for himself. Happiness is beyond his immediate control; he can reach that only through his character and condition. He can will conduct on which providence suspends all happiness for him; he cannot will happiness. His true good, in so far as he is a free being and capable of willing it, is to be what he should be. This is the only good which the action of his will can reach.

This kind of good he may be required to seek and pursue. He was made for this: if he regard his relation to his maker, he cannot but see that it is his maker's will that he seek this good directly in all his free action. This will is the supreme law of his being. It is the law written on the heart—on the inmost tablets of the soul. He is called not to happiness, but to perfect living, which is to be attested and sanctioned by the pure joy and blessedness that waits upon it. So we answer without hesitancy the question : Whence springs the sense of obligation—of obligation to do right—in the soul of man ; why should he do right ? It springs from the observed nature and condition and manifest destiny of his being. He observes powers or capacities for certain ends. He should be what he was made for and fitted for, and should therefore employ those capacities for the uses for which they were created. Especially he observes in himself as a predominant character-istic a free-will fitted to act for a certain end, in which action he secures his highest perfection—comes to be himself most perfectly. The sense of obligation comes at once on this observed character of a free being. Man should be his most perfect self. His supreme good is to be his best self.

§ 231. The field of the good which is thus the end or object in all legitimate voluntary action divides itself at once into the two realms of *the self* and *the not-self ;*—of the mind itself and the being extrinsic to the mind, with which it may interact.

In the first of these realms, that of the mind itself, the most fundamental and the most impor-tant of the activities which the will may direct and control are the instinctive motions, ongoings, trendings, which characterize the very essence of every activity in actual exertion. Whether the whole soul or only a particular function be en-

gaged, some object more or less specific must
be regarded in the excited activity, and this direction of the activity is, as we have seen, under the
control of the will.  To direct it aright, and this
can be no other than to direct it so as to secure
its highest perfection in character and condition
so far as this may depend on the particular act, is
the proper end—the true good—proposed to the
will to effect by its control.

These instinctive ongoings or trendings of the
activities of the soul appear in manifold forms
and connections and degrees and are abundantly
designated in language in a vast diversity of
terms.  Of these terms the following will serve
as  exemplifications :—like  and  dislike, relish,
taste ; disposition, inclination, propensity, procliv-
ity, bias, bent, tendency; appetency, want, desire,
avidity, craving, longing, appetite.  These all
come, so far as in exercise, under the control of
the will as exciting, maintaining, strengthening,
diverting, in all ways regulating them: and its
province is so to regulate each and all, as to secure the legitimate end of each and all, their best
condition and working, which is the true good to
them.

But the will also has the power directly to
summon forth, to incite and to direct, the several
functional activities of the soul, its thoughts, its
feelings, its subordinate purposes.  Its legitimate
end here is still comprehended in the great end
of perfecting character and condition: this is the

true good to be proposed as its end. It will of course be included in its field here to repress and to divert as well as to incite and lead.

In the realm of the proper *not-self*, the end proper to the will is that which is suitable to it as a member ministering to the body of which it is an organic part, and can be no other than the perfecting of all this body so far as it may, and particularly in the relations of the whole and every part to itself. It is a principle of all organic life that the perfect condition and working of every part is necessary to the highest perfection of each particular member. In this field, the end is more characteristically and more largely remote as compared with the end in the field of the proper self. After the control of the appetency or desire at the root of all free action, the immediate end of the will here is the working and directing of such instrumental agency as may involve and draw in that remoter end which the will may have allowed the desire or appetency to crave. For the most part, certainly, if not in fact entirely, this instrumental agency is the force or energy which works in the body and is recognized under the name of nerve-force or nervous energy. The human will acts directly on this nerve-force; evokes it, directs it to its purposed object. Its action here, as we have before intimated, is a mystery. When we purpose to walk, we seem to deliver our command immediately to the foot, and order that it lift itself and put itself

forward, and have no consciousness of any inter-
mediate agency or work between our proper selves
and the member that is ordered to move. But
science teaches otherwise. At all events the will
can act immediately only on some active nature
with which it is interacting, and this is the nerve-
force residing in the body. Through this instrumentality the will works toward its remoter end,
putting the instrumental activity to its true and
perfect use, this being in the existing relation its
proper good.

We conclude in the time-honored and time-
proved words of Aristotle. Under the assumption that the function of man is activity of soul
according to reason, he says, " activity of soul according to virtue becomes the good to man, or,
supposing a diversity of virtues, according to the
best and most perfect ; and further in a perfect
life ; for a single swallow does not make a spring
nor yet a single day. So does neither one day
nor a brief time make one happy and blessed."
Or in paraphrase :—the highest good to man is
virtuous activity of soul in a perfect life of the
best and highest particular virtues in the most
favoring conditions.

§ 232. The good which is the proper object to
the will is termed a *moral* good as distinguished
from all other kinds of so-called good. All these
may comprehensively be designated as *natural
good*. Natural good comes to man from no direct
determination of will. It is the normal result or

24

end of all activity whether spontaneous or voluntary. It may be remote consequence of free action. It includes accordingly, as a part, the happiness that naturally attends upon right conduct
or the legitimate exercise of faculties. Happiness as we have seen cannot be the immediate
object of the will, and therefore strictly speaking
it is only a natural, not a moral good. In so far
as an object or end is regarded by the free-will,
the object or end is thereby characterized as
moral ;—it is termed a moral good, or, as it may be,
a moral evil, simply because it is the immediate
object in the action of the free-will.

§ 233. Moral good or the good which the free-
will respects and effects is more direct and immediate object in character, and more indirect in
condition. The object of the will and action in
character is to be found in the specific acts which
make up character. Its object in condition is
in the adjustment of one's self or of another to
those circumstances or those relationships to
other beings and influences which help to determine character; or conversely, the adaptation of
those circumstances or relationships themselves
to the ends of character.

§ 234. Moral action, accordingly, which must
ever respect a good either in one's self or in
another, must be in its true perfection characteristically *beneficent*. All morality, all virtue must
be found in beneficent action ; in that action, in
other words, which seeks the good—the perfect

character or condition—of one's self or another. Moral action involves the three elements of an object, an agent, and an act of the agent upon the object. It may be characterized as perfect or right from regard to either element, provided only that there be ever understood a real, if un-expressed, an implicit, if not explicit, co-existence of the others. If perfect moral action be charac-terized in respect to the object, the effect on the character or on the condition as affecting charac-ter is emphasized and the action is characterized as *beneficence*. If the action be characterized in prominent reference to the agent or doer, it is the sympathetic action of the free-will in its in-teraction with other beings which is emphasized; and the action is then characterized as *love*. If the action, as being in right relation between the agent and the object, be emphasized, the action is characterized as *rectitude*. The three principles— beneficence, love, and rectitude—are co-ordinate and complementary; they all unite in every per-fect moral action; neither can exist without the others, although one may be more prominent in reality or in our thought than the others. They are in truth three different aspects of the same thing.

Inasmuch as the good admits of degrees, a per-fect choice involves the selection of the highest degree of good in character or condition which is possible. The determination of what is, in the particular case of choice, the highest, is left of necessity to the moral judgment—to the intelligence acting under the impulse and guidance of a pure morality.

It is the proper province of ethical science to unfold the nature and forms of free action adopting as its starting point the act itself of the will— a moral act rather than the agent or doers of the action, and rather than the object which the action immediately respects, just as logic starts from thought rather than from the thinking function— intelligence—or the object in thinking which is the true; and æsthetics starts from beauty or form realized in feeling or imagination, rather than from the mental function or from the beautiful or perfect in form in its own nature.

# CHAPTER VII.

## THE GOOD PRESENTED.—MOTIVE.

§ 235. By MOTIVE, as object to will, is to be understood that which the will immediately respects in its action.

The term *motive*, as applied to moral action generally, has been used in two widely distinguishable meanings, to denote both the object of the will, as just stated, and as we shall for convenience use the term except when specially modified, and also the inward spring or impulse or propensity inducing or prompting the action. This double use of course leads to a certain degree of confusion and to corresponding error. There seems, however, to be legitimate ground for each of these uses. The mind as essentially active is by the strong set of its whole nature prone to act. This natural propensity we have recognized as the rudimental principle of the class of feelings called *desires*. This prompting principle is, in a legitimate import of the word, a *motive*, as moving the mind to action. But it is a motive-spring to thought and to imagination, to the reception of truth and the love of beauty, as truly as to purpose and choice. This motive-spring or impulse,

moreover, respects an object ; and the specific object on which it fastens determines the specific
character of the motive impulse itself.    In the case
of the intelligence, thus, this specific motive-spring
is the desire for knowledge.    We have recognized
it under the form and name of *curiosity.*    The inward spring or incentive to knowledge is this desire—this curiosity.    But knowledge determines
curiosity, as knowing is the object or end of intellectual desire.    We study in order to know ;
and the attainment of knowledge or truth—knowing—is the motive to study, inasmuch as it determines and moves the desire in that particular direction.    Curiosity may thus be spoken of as the
motive-spring or incentive to knowledge, while at
the same time and with equal propriety of language, truth and knowledge may be spoken of as
the motive-object in intellectual endeavor.

In any concrete act, accordingly, in which the
will is engaged, we have both motive-spring and
motive-object.    But, it is worthy of remark, the
immediate object on which the will may act, may
be this very instinct or appetency which constitutes the motive-spring ; and the end or result of
the action of the will upon it is allowance, or in-
citement, or direction.    It is this end—the effect
to be produced in the instinctive activity of the
mind—which is here the proper motive as object
to the will.    The will itself, as an active nature,
it may also be remarked, possesses this instinct
or appetency to act ; but of this element it is sel-

dom important to take account in ethical discussions. But the distinction indicated between motive-spring as applying to the appetency upon which the will immediately acts on the one hand, and motive-object as applying to that which the will seeks to effect in regulating this instinct on the other, although it may seem at a first glance rather overnice, is yet of vital importance in some of those discussions. To motive-spring as a mere spontaneity, no moral character as right or wrong can attach ; only to motive-object as involving the free activity of the will can this attribute of right or wrong be ascribed.

§ 236. Inasmuch as in an act there must be, as alike necessary, both agent and object, there is a certain propriety in the statement that either factor determines an act of choice or volition. The will cannot allow and enforce an appetency or desire unless that appetency or desire be actually present, as the appetency or desire itself cannot be except as it is awakened by its appropriate object. This object itself may thus be truly regarded as determining the action of the will ;—the presence of the orange awakening the desire, determines my will to take it. All this, however, must be understood as allowing freedom to the will itself—the power of determining its own acts. It can will or nill ; it can allow the appetency or disallow, or even refrain from either allowing or disallowing ; it can take, or refuse to take, the orange. The will is the doer of its own acts ; it is a self-willer, a self-determiner, in the truest and highest signification of the expression. It is not another that wills in my willing ; not another being, nor thing, nor force ; it is myself. Its native prerogative of willing or nilling is never subverted, but by its own allowance. The motive, whether as spring or as object, has no such absolute control; it is occasion, or it may be effect, not proper cause of willing. The motive as spring or incentive I am ever free to resist or to allow; the motive as object to be effected by my will is the result not the cause of my willing.

§ 237. A motive-object can be such to the will only in so far as it is an end within the scope of the free activity of the will. Such an end is a proper good. The highest good to man, as we have seen, is perfect activity according to the nature and condition of his being. Every specific affection or act, that is truly legitimate in itself in the time and condition, is a true good, a legitimate motive, because a true end of man's being. § 211.

Good and will are thus seen to be exact correlatives, bearing the relation of object and subject to each other. Good and motive-object, moreover, it will be seen, are synonyms.

§ 238. Motives are of two classes—*external* and *internal.*

AN EXTERNAL MOTIVE is primarily some modification of the nerve-force on which the will acts by summoning it forth and directing it on something exterior to the mind. More remotely and so in a sense more inexactly and derivatively, the result of this action of the nerve-force—the movement of the hand, the grasping of the orange, may be regarded as the motive, but only by reason of its following the movement of the nerveforce which the will determined.

AN INTERNAL MOTIVE is the act or affection of the mind itself which the will regards; as, the exercise of the imagination, the putting forth of a thought, the allowance of a desire as determined by the will. In this class—internal motives—must be embraced all those ends which we seek in our free action in other spiritual beings; external motives being limited to those which lie in the direction of the nerve-force. Of our immediate interaction with purely spiritual natures, its extent, its modes, its processes, its results, science gives us little information that is trustworthy. What the future of experience and discovery may reveal, it would be unwise to conjecture. It is enough to say here that science and revelation agree with human experience in testifying that between the soul and its maker there may be, even as there unquestionably is, free and immediate interaction in which the creature may directly seek to move its creator and without intervention of neural energy. Man may thus find in God a true motive to its adoring and loving action.

It will be noticed that motives of different

classes may be associated in the same complex act. There may be the motive of exciting the nerve-force to take the orange associated with the motive to gratifying the appetite. Sometimes one will preside and govern, sometimes the other. I may move my arm to take the orange without the consciousness of any desire for it; and yet there may follow a sense as of the gratification of such a desire. Or I may desire the orange, and the will to gratify that may draw on the executive volition to take it. The motive with a hungry man to take food that belongs to another may be to appease his appetite; the actual determination to take it follows as a subservient motive. With a kleptomaniac the motive may be to indulge a perverse passion for appropriating as the primary and governing motive; he may use the food he has thus thievishly appropriated to satiate his hunger.

# CHAPTER VIII.

## THE GOOD PRODUCED.—DUTIES.

§ 239. The highest good in character and condition attainable in the case being recognized as the object in a perfect choice, the actual adoption of this object by the free-will in positive exertion to secure it is its truest and best action. This is true virtue. But we have recognized a sentiment of obligation as springing up spontaneously in the mind when the free-will is brought into this face-to-face relation to its object; and virtue becomes *duty*—action that is obligatory—because of the organic relationship of the will to its co-ordinate functions and to the mind itself, and of the analogous relation of the individual self to others as like parts of one moral whole —a moral universe. Moral obligation—*duty*— is founded in this organic relationship. And to duty there is the correlative—of *right*. That which is due from me to my neighbor is his right. Duties and rights are correlatives, reciprocally implying each other. If the question be raised, how do I come to see or feel this obligation— whence comes the sense of duty—the answer must be that the organic relationship indicated immediately reveals it; I discern my duty of ministry at once in this, that I am organic part of a living whole.

The fundamental fact here to be considered is just this—that the will is a part of a living whole, a true member of an organism, the life of which is sustained and nourished by the common ministry of each part. Each particular member has its own office, which office the welfare of the whole and, as involved in this, the particular welfare of itself and of each other part demands, and which office it belongs to the particular member to discharge. The will thus properly and truly owes, by reason of its own nature and its relation to the whole soul, this faithful discharge of its office, or fulfillment of its ministry. It exists for this; its end and function are fulfilled in this. I normally feel this obligation—have a sense of duty—as I perceive this relationship of function and end. To this it is to be added in the case of the will, that being free, endowed with the high prerogative of selecting and directing its ministrations, allowing ministry or refusing it as to any particular service, the idea of duty takes on a peculiar character—that of being moral and carrying responsibility with it. By virtue of its membership of a living whole, the function of the free-will is charged by its very nature with the obligation to fulfill its office toward the other members and the whole soul. Its entire office in this relation to the whole man and to the several co-ordinate members consists in summoning forth these several co-ordinate functions of the soul or of the whole soul itself as the particular occasion shall require, of directing them, sustaining them, and giving them free scope and sway, and all so as to effect this highest and fullest perfection in accordance with the end of their being, whether of the whole man or of the several members of the organism.

But the soul itself is a part of a larger whole. It exists in vital relationships to other beings around it. It is a veritable member of an organic whole, in the life of which its own life is enwrapped. The obligations of a ministering member exist here as in the former case. They are of the same general character and are comprehended in the general duty of effecting the highest perfection of every part and of the whole. Thus are indicated the objects of duty to the human soul—to self, to fellow men, and to God. These are the objects at least which most closely concern it. They are accordingly those which it is of importance to enumerate here.

The particular ways in which the will discharges the duties of its ministry have been already intimated. It will be sufficient simply to restate them. First and chiefly, perhaps, the will fulfills its duty by allowing or disallowing some particular propensity, or appetency, or drift, which we have recognized as native to the soul of man, and giving it sway. In this ministry the will forms what we call character. If it accept the highest and most comprehensive appetency of the soul's nature, and give it control over all other appetencies, the highest and best character is formed ; for, as we have seen, activity, once determined in a particular direction flows on till positively arrested. If a lower appetency be allowed to rule in place of a higher, the character is lowered accordingly. In the next place, the will determines specific imaginations, thoughts, subordinate purposes. Such movements of the soul affect, if they do not fully determine, character. They strengthen character, or impair it. In the third place, besides these immediate determinations of the will, through the rational nature of the soul, remoter ends may be proposed and accepted by the will when, if the purpose be a living one, subordinate immediate determinations are made by the will, both in the personal life and also in the life of the outer being around with which the soul is in organic interaction.

§ 240. A fundamental condition of duty, of virtue, of right action of will, is sympathy in the large sense of susceptibility of being affected by others and capacity of affecting them. Such sympathetic relationship between the different departments of the mind or self we must also suppose to be conditional to all proper personal duties. It becomes at once the fundamental duty to secure and maintain this relation of active sympathy between the subject or agent in duty and his object. Ranking with this, as a second fundamental duty, is that of securing and maintaining a practical acquaintance with the objects of duty. And still a third of the same rank of fundamental duty is that of maintaining a disposition of will to meet the calls of duty, as addressed by the several objects of duty. Such a sympathetic, intelligent, and ready disposition it is the proper function of the will as sovereign to foster and cherish. Only so can that habit of action which constitutes virtuous character be secured. Viewed in this light the duty might more properly be considered as falling into the division of personal duties as a part of personal culture. Yet as obviously fundamental and conditional to duty in the comprehensive sense it may, without impropriety in method, be presented here for distinct consideration.

§ 241. The distribution of specific duties follows most conveniently for practical uses the principle of division furnished in the objects of duty. Only in them is to be found the proper motive to the will—the good, in character and condition, of sentient rational being. We have thus as the most generic classification of specific duties the threefold division, of (1) Duties to self ; (2) Duties to fellow men ; and (3) Duties to God.

Duties to self or Personal Duties comprise (1) duties in respect to the body, of guarding, nourishing, and ruling it ; (2) in respect to external condition, including such as relate to nature or the external world, to property, to station, and to friendship ; and (3) in respect to character.

Duties to fellow men embrace the three classes of (1) duties to individuals; (2) duties in the family ; and (3) duties in the State.

Duties to other individuals, or the proper social duties comprise the three classes of duties determined by the threefold constituents of duty —love, good, right, viz.: (1) sympathy, kindness, loving endeavor; (2) courtesy, truthfulness, justice, and benevolence ; (3) sincere intent in action that is governing, unswerving, and accordant with condition.

Duties in the Family or proper Domestic Duties comprise (1) those of marriage, or conjugal duties; (2) parental and filial duties, and (3) fraternal duties.

Duties in the State or proper Civil Duties are those of loyalty, obedience, and support.

Duties to God or proper Religious Duties are those of personal piety, and of social religion.

It is the proper province of Ethical Science to unfold the doctrine of duty in its nature, grounds, and specific forms.

# BOOK V.

## THE REASON.—MIND AS ORGANIC WHOLE.

---

### CHAPTER I.

#### ITS NATURE AND MODIFICATIONS.

§ 242. IN our survey of the general attributes of mind we recognized its most essential character as activity. This activity it is impossible for the human mind to apprehend except as it is manifested in specific exertions—specific acts. The exhaustive consideration of this active nature cannot go beyond the study of these specific acts of whatever form and kind, gathering them together into classes by means of some common characteristic belonging to them, and then fixing them in their true relationships to one another and to the whole of which they are the organic parts. All these special acts, we have found, may be comprehended in the threefold functional activity of feeling, thought, will,—as it goes out toward the respective objects of these several functions, the beautiful or perfect in form, the true, and the good. This threefold diversity of function we recognized as pertaining to a simple organic whole; the threefoldness consisting with a complete organic unity which is a fundamental character of mind, never to be lost from view in the study of its nature. Another general attribute was recognized as that of finiteness and dependence. The human mind is finite—limited in its range of object and in its intensity of action. It is also dependent for its action upon objects that present themselves to it more or less beyond its control as well as upon the channels or means through which these objects gain access to it. This characteristic indicates and involves the great truth of its being a part of a larger whole—a part of a universe in fact, so that its whole life, the entire development and outgoing of its active nature, is determined, shaped, and sustained through this relationship to an environing universe of being and to the other co-ordinate parts which with it constitute and make up the whole. In this circumstance of being and life it is susceptible of indefinite growth and maintains a character of unbroken continuance. Three prominent features at once associate themselves with these general facts of observation in regard to the human mind. First, as a distinct unit among those which constitute the universe of similar life, it interacts with them, receiving and imparting, impressing and being impressed. In this interacting relationship, in the next place, it is self-conscious as well as cognizant of the objects that impress it. In the third place, it is self-determining, as it maintains by a power within itself its independent life and determines within the limits of a finite nature, its acts, its affections, its forming character.

With this general survey of the attributes of the human mind, the continued study led to a more minute and thorough investigation of the three specific modes in one or other of which its essential activity manifests itself. This investigation we have prosecuted in the last three Books. It will occur to the thoughtful student that our study of the human mind does not reach its extreme limit with this separate study of the several functional activities of the mind, even although they constitute the entirety of its nature as essential activity. There is a view of its life and history as one organic whole which is not contained within this study of particular functions. There is a life of the organism embracing all this specific action, but not embraced within it. As single, the mind is in every function—it is " all in the whole and all in every part." This is a great fact never to be forgotten. But there is a view of the whole which is more than a view of the sum of the constituent parts; for the mind is more than a mere aggregation of functions. It has a life which contains this aggregation, and what is vastly more, which converts it into one living organic whole. Each several function is other and different from what it would be if subsisting by itself, were this possible. Each member partakes of a larger life by which it is shaped and characterized, and which in its turn it helps to shape and characterize. A mere functional treatment of the human mind misses the wholeness there should be observed both in the mind itself and also in its object. Such a functional psychology gives but the anatomy of mind and leaves out the vitality of action, which is its truest characteristic.

Philosophical discussion and the language of cultivated men generally have fully recognized this fact, that the science of the several functions of an organism does not fill out the full knowledge of the organism itself. There are relations sustained by the organism as a whole, both internal toward its own members and constituent parts and also to other organisms around it, which are peculiar to it and do not immediately respect the individual members. The body has a life other and different from that which can be portrayed in the science, however perfect, of its separate organs; and the activity—the condition and working—of the several organs is affected by the condition of the whole bodily organism. Divers errors of very serious moment have arisen in mental science, it is believed, from the limitation of its sphere to the presentation of the several functions. Something more, for illustration, is meant by the phrase "rational nature" than would be signified in any expression of the combined functional activities of sense, thought, free-will. No hesitancy is felt in characterizing an act of the mind in imagination, intelligence, or purpose as rational. This implies that any specific act might be genuine and in itself altogether legitimate and complete, and yet fail of being entirely or perfectly rational. To exclude in the full study of mental activity, this organic whole of mind as a rational nature cannot fail to occasion error.

The term "reason" is synonymous with the phrase "rational nature." As a single term it is more convenient in use. For the use of it as denoting the mind as an organic whole, abundant vindication could be adduced from our best literature. It will suffice simply to cite the following from Sir William Hamilton. As his sixth special faculty under the general cognitive faculty, he gives what he calls the Regulative Faculty. This faculty corresponds, he says, to what was known in the Greek philosophy under the name of νοῦς. It is analogous to the term *Reason* as used by the older English philosophers and to the *vernunft* (*reason*) in the philosophy of Kant, Jacobi, and others of the recent German metaphysicians. It is also nearly convertible with the Common Sense of Reid and Stewart.

The designation—Regulative Faculty—happily points out a leading characteristic of what is generally understood by the phrase *rational nature* or *reason*. But the reason is more than a mere cognitive faculty. When we speak of a "rational thought" we mean something more than a well-regulated thought as a form of knowledge; something more than a thought well grounded and well formed and well adjusted in its parts and external relations, as the laws of pure knowledge prescribe. A rational thought is a thought which is worthy of a rational soul, which is not only logically sound and congruous, but is pervaded with feeling and has an aim ;—a rational thought is a sympathetic and also a wise thought. The phrase opens out to our view a field vastly richer than the merely cognitive element exhibits. Rationality is more than intelligence ; reason, more than intellect. It is also more than feeling, more than choice. It is more even, as we shall see, than mere aggregation of the three—thought, feeling, choice.

§ 243. Without further vindication of this mode of designating mind as an organism and leaving the propriety, not to say the necessity, of this distinct treatment of it to be seen in the exposition of its nature, we will in the next two chapters, present the twofold view we may take of it, first subjectively and then objectively. We follow in this the method of our treatment of the several specific functions of the mind. It is obvious that this faculty may be modified both in reference to the specific determinations of its outgoing activity from within itself, and also in reference to the specific characteristics of the general object which may address it from without.

# CHAPTER II.

## THE REASON—I. SUBJECTIVE VIEW.

§ 244. THE HUMAN REASON—the Rational Nature of Man—the Human Mind viewed as a living organism the essential nature of which is activity expressing itself in the threefold functional modes of Sensibility, Intelligence, and Will —is obviously to be viewed as no co-ordinate faculty in the rank of the special functions just named, any more than the human body is to be co-ordinated with any special function such as that of nutrition, muscular contraction, nerve-sense. It is rather to be regarded in the larger view suggested by the term of a power than in the more restricted view of a faculty. It is not a special faculty. On the other hand it acts only through some special faculty and never in its action contravenes the laws of such special faculty. Just as the body breathes only through the lungs and precisely after the law of the lungs, so the reason, the mind, as a living organism, feels only through the sensibility and according to the - laws and forms of the sensibility, imagines only through the imagination; thinks only through the intellect; and chooses only through the will.

It, however, through this diverse functional activity performs work that is beyond the reach of any of these separate functions. This work, it is to be noticed also, is not a merely combined product of two or more of these functions, as we have recognized, for example, in the sentiments in which feeling is expressed combined with intelligence or will, or as in the virtues, hope, faith, love, in which all the functions find characteristic expression. This peculiarly organic work, which is properly to be recognized as the work of the reason in distinction from that of either of the three functional activities, is at once distributed into three distinguishable fields. The first of these is its work as directed upon itself.

## I. THE ACTIVITY OF THE REASON AS DIRECTED UPON ITSELF.

§ 245. The human reason, the mind of man as a living organism, we have found to be sympathetic, conscious, free. It exhibits these several attributes in its reflex action—in its action upon itself. It is, in a true and most important sense, in sympathy with itself. It has by its very nature an interest in its own well-being. It is sensitive to the very depths of its being to whatever vitally affects this, its inner well-being. No deeper principle can be found in its nature. Absolute recklessness, absolute unconcern here is a human monstrosity, if not a contradiction.

The suicide who murders the bodily life in an inconsiderate wreck of all higher interests, has his only motive-spring or inducement to his deed of desperation in this self-regard; for why should he seek to terminate a life that does not concern him? It is the very unbearable pressure of this self-regard that drives him to this climax of madness. It is a woful mistake, but it is that of a man, a rational nature, however misled, not that of a stick or a stone. If a man is crushed, he knows that he is crushed; and more, he knows and feels that it is himself that is crushed; alas! still more, he knows that he freely crushes himself. The human reason is in vital sympathy with itself. It acts back upon itself; it feels its own presentations; its own imaginings. It holds up its ideals of life, of being, of character, of destiny, before its own capability of feeling; it receives these ideals to itself; it feels them.

It acts back thus upon itself also in full consciousness. Even when not holding up such inner work before its cognitive power in distinct form so as to be reflected upon and remembered, it yet works consciously, intelligently, observing the principles of truth, the essential nature of things in its work and conscious, too, possibly if not actually more or less, of the proper effect of its work, of its fitness to its end. Moreover, this inner work is done aimingly, in reference to some end, more or less felt and seen. Just as the total life-force in the bodily organism exerts itself on

each organ, determining in harmonious co operation, motor power and muscular power and every
organic power, upon the inner life in some particular need, so the reason acts back as a whole,
in the conspiring exertion of all its functions
upon its own interior nature. It is in the highest sense a regulative power over its entire inner
self. With a true, sympathetic, conscious, purposing interest in itself, it rules within the limits
of its nature its whole activity in reference to its
demands.

The human mind possesses, as we have seen,
the attribute of continuousness. Action, which
is its essential nature, involves continuousness.
The human reason discerning this character of
continuousness, as it must in any proper introspection, and discerning that it is to itself at least
an unending continuousness with a conscious
sense of this fact, together with the consciousness
of its being capable of an indefinite growth and
expansion, an ever growing enlargement both of
experience and of capacity,—the reason is of necessity impelled by an irrepressible ambition to
act under the law of this unlimited continuousness of its activity in this growth and drift of its
nature, in such a way as best to secure its truest
well-being and its highest perfection. The human reason beyond all question is capable of this
high, most worthy ambition. It may well be
doubted whether a mature reason ever failed at
some time to be conscious of its inspiration. It

may be smothered, it may be disregarded, it may
be resisted ; the human reason is free and is able
to sell its birth-right for the paltriest indulgence.
But this high ambition is a true belonging to the
human reason.   It is its proper work, its most
commanding and pressing work, indeed, to obey
the promptings of this high ambition and form
for itself a true character in the perfecting of its
powers and capabilities.   The destiny of the man,
thus, as mainly depending on his character, is entrusted to the care and ordering of the reason, as
its indefeasible organic trust and care.

Such is the peculiar office-work of the reason
in respect to its inner self—feelingly, consciously,
aimingly to shape out and nourish up into its
highest degree of well-being its own true nature
and thus, so far at least as depends upon itself, to
determine its final destiny.   Involved in this
work is the regulation of all specific and subordinate actions so that they shall helpfully and
harmoniously carry forward this high development into perfect character.   It is beyond the
province of any special function to effect this co-
operation, each in its turn and in its degree, in
perfect adjustment to the final end.   It is the
reason that must summon forth the particular
function, select its object, and direct the activity
upon it, regulate it, in the largest sense, as to direction, intensity, and continuance.   It is the
office of the reason to keep the several functional
activities in equipoise and symmetrical working.

Sense and imagination. intellect and will, can move only as called forth by this higher authority : they can each work only in its own respective lines according to its own laws. Only as supervised, harmonized, controlled by the reason can they effect any worthy comprehensive result.

Such is the high function of the rational nature —the reason—to regulate the entire outgoing of the mind's activity so as to effect the highest perfection of its own nature. The candid study of its nature discovers this momentous truth concerning itself. The "categorical imperative" of duty, the "moral sense" in man, comes from this study by a true rational intuition,—by an introspection into itself by the reason. The indestructible impulse in the inmost life of mind toward a comprehensive end which is to be found only in a perfect character, the irrepressible drift of the essential activity of mind toward this end, the consciousness of the power to regulate toward the consummation of it, constitute the imperative call to the duty, reveal the obligation, and press to the performance. Here is the seat and origin of conscience. Hence is the authoritativeness of its high behest that the mind make itself to be the best it can.

The free-will has a part here ; if it be not the better view to regard moral freedom as pertaining rather to the rational nature—to the reason— than to the specific function. In any view, the freedom in man remains in all this urgency of

reason and of conscience. The high end of
rational perfection may be taken or refused ; and
the refusal involving the choice of a lower aim,
does a fatal work—a work that is obviously irrep-
arable by itself.   No subsequent action of its own
can undo what is done.   It yet remains true that
in the very nature of the human reason and its
necessary outworking is revealed the fact that
the true comprehensive end of all its activity is
the perfecting of its own well-being and condition.

## II. THE ACTIVITY OF THE REASON AS DIRECTED UPON THE SEVERAL FUNCTIONAL ACTIVITIES.

§ 246. The reason finds a second field for its
work in the special regulation of the specific
functions of mental activity—the sensibility and
imagination, the intelligence, the will.   As already intimated, it selects their objects, summons
forth and controls their activity as to degree and
measure.   This is a work altogether outside the
province of the special function.

More particularly ; in the field of the sensibility
and imagination, the reason selects the objects by
which the sense is to be impressed or which it is
to impress and controls these impressions as to
their force and range.   More than this, acting in
this sphere the reason becomes a designing and
constructing power, a faculty of means and ends,
and of methods in the particular working of the

function of form, and, moreover, modifies, shapes, adapts the forming work, in reference to ulterior objects and ulterior ends. In all proper art and also in the construction of proper science, the rational imagination does its fashioning work sympathetically with all related things, in conscious congruousness as to all parts and relations, and in governing aim toward its own chosen ends, and adaptations to outer objects.

In the field of the intellect, the reason also comes in to regulate so as to effect cognitions, forms of thought and of knowledge, altogether beyond the sphere of mere intellect. Rational intelligence is true wisdom ; and wisdom and mere science of knowledge are far from being one. Prodigies of science and learning are sometimes most irrational ; the more prodigious, the more irrational. Rational intelligence acts in sympathy with all objects of knowledge and all the powers and capabilities of the soul, whereas pure knowledge is in itself hard and unyielding to exterior things. Rational intelligence, farther, co-ordinates each special knowledge with all other cognitions and also subordinates according to due rank and worthiness, fashioning all knowledge into shapely completeness and symmetry, in due dependence and relation, into a veritable body of truth with its own proper unity. It pours in upon each act of knowledge a light from the principle of knowledge, assuring it to be a work of true knowledge, comprehending all specific cognitions in their grounds, and directing all, both to their respective places in the body of truth and also to the specific ends of the knowledge or even to the comprehensive end of all knowledge.

In the field of the will, in an analogous way, the reason controls all specific exertions of choice as to object; correlates them to other exertions both of the will and of the other mental functions; brings all into due symmetrical relationship to the whole mental condition and destiny. The rational choice is put forth in sympathy with all related things and in conscious reference to all its bearings both such as are internal and also such as are external to itself.

## III. THE ACTIVITY OF THE REASON AS DIRECTED UPON EXTERNAL OBJECTS.

§ 247. The human reason has a third field of activity in the world of being properly extraneous to it. Here are comprehended the relationships of the mind to the body which it inhabits, to external nature, and to other minds.

The interaction between mind and body has already been considered so far as manifesting itself between the special functions of form, on the passive side, known as the sensibility and on the active side, known as the imagination, and their respective objects. We need here only to superadd the consideration of the activity of the proper rational nature in this interaction, beyond and outside of the action of the special function, as also beyond its regulation of the special function as already noticed. In the first place, as an organic whole in vital connection with the body as also an organic whole, its general life and action are in sympathetic interaction with the life and action of the bodily organism. Mind and body affect each other with the sympathetic sensitiveness and quick response of members of the same organic whole. The health and vigor of the one affect the health and vigor of the other. Bodily vivacity and energy awaken and sustain mental action; the weariness of the one induces lassitude and weakness in the other. Lively feeling, vigorous thought, determined purpose, quicken and strengthen the heart-throbs. "Conceit can cure and conceit can kill," is a familiar maxim in the experience of the physician. If the warm blood of youth animates the feelings and thoughts and purposes of earlier life, the established vigor of mental life protects and upholds the bodily life in later years. Sudden death not infrequently is the consequence of a sudden termination of active intellectual pursuits. Body and soul as parts of one organic whole, thus act and react upon each other; and they thus act and react because one life affects another in organic relation to it by natural sympathy. Such is the ordinance of nature. Every life is interlinked with its neighbor life. "Man's life,"

26

says Emerson, "is intertwined with the whole chain of organic and inorganic being."

In the next place, the mind as a whole, the whole rational nature acting as a single organism, interacts with the body in interchange of impression, each imparting and each receiving. In sympathy: in conscious apprehension too of what it seeks to effect, of the character of its own action, and of the effect it is to produce, as well as of the means to secure the effect; in aiming purpose, likewise, as one activity although tri-functional, the reason acts upon the body; and in corresponding sympathy, consciousness, and free allowance or resistance, receives to itself the action of the body.

This sympathetic, vital interaction between soul and body suggests, if it does not prove beyond reasonable question, that a like nature prevails in both; that in other words, the action that comes from the body on the soul is that of a being like the soul itself. The interaction is between two like energies, similarly constituted. We are safe from all reasonable question when we assume that the energy which works in the body on the mind is itself spiritual like the mind. It follows from this assumption that the activity of the human reason on the body is in fact directed immediately on another mental nature like its own; and consequently that this action on the body is exactly pictured in its action upon itself and upon its special functions, as we have just recognized it.

But this living energy of the body thus in sympathetic interaction with the reason can be no other than that which pervades the natural world around us generally. We discover the same interaction between the mind and the external physical universe as that which we have discovered between mind and body. The only difference is that here the interaction is more mediate, whereas in the other case, it was more immediate. Yet the interaction between mind and body is to a large degree properly mediate. If I press the end of my finger on yielding wax, the impress on the wax is mediately effected through the bodily organ ; but my purpose to make the impress acts in a true sense mediately as it travels along the efferent or motor nerve out through the arm and hand to the tip of the finger. And so in regard to the entire interaction between the mind and the external world, we find substantially the same character of action, only modified by the greater or less degree of immediateness in the interaction and by the respective qualities and condition of the particular objects. The reason acts in relation to these objects as joint member with them of one organic whole, affecting them in the first place by mere presence of life, and in the next place by the positive exertion of its own communicative, thoughtful, purposeful energy upon them ; and is passively affected by them in their sympathetic, truthful, and aiming work.

The result we find to be the same in its general characteristics if we push forward our investigation to the interaction between one mind and another. There is the mediateness of interaction that we have already recognized; only it is of a remote degree—a mediateness through the energy that pervades all being, and by which all interaction between different organisms is effected. I think of a man: I communicate my thought through certain nerves producing at length a sound which we call his name: the air vibrations of the sound traverse a space and reach another organism in which afferent nerves convey movements that at last effect an image in another mind; and joy, grief, fear, anger, stormy emotions, it may be, follow. I purposed them in uttering the name; and the energy there is in nature took up the purpose and conveyed it to its destination. The mind which my purpose finally reached and moved is discovered to me to be of a common nature with mine. All the properties and laws of interaction between my reason and itself or its special functions, govern here in this interaction between my reason and other natures around me. My rational activity is in harmony with that of other beings; it interacts with them; it impresses them and is impressed by them; it determines the rational tri-functional activity of others through a sympathetic, conscious, aiming action of its own.

Simple, unquestionable, comprehensive, thus, is the law of the human reason as tri-functional activity ;—it is regulative through sympathetic, intelligent, purposive exertion.

# CHAPTER III.

## THE REASON.—II. OBJECTIVE VIEW.

§ 248. THE proper function of the reason being predominantly and characteristically regulative, the object or end of its work must be precisely to perfect character and condition. This is its comprehensive work and the comprehensive effect of its work. The work is twofold, as it respects (1) character or the essential properties of its object, and (2) condition or its relation to other beings. But such a regulative work in the case of the human mind can be exerted, directly at least, only on active beings—energies, or forces, or powers. Man cannot affect any portion of matter even, except by directing some force upon it, as through some motor nerve-force. This regulative work, accordingly, of reason in any object in regard to character is simply this—to effect *that such object be at its best.* Every object, however, with which the human mind is to act, is a part of an organic whole, and cannot be at its best estate unless its environment, its condition, its relation to other objects, be the most favorable. Such then is the twofold work of reason upon its objects to make them, so far as it can, perfect in character and also perfect in condition. The objective view of the human reason as a regulative power or function covers precisely this field—the perfecting of the character and condition of the beings upon which it works. It will be sufficient, so far as the demands of our present undertaking are concerned, simply to outline in a summary way the effected object of this regulative work of the reason in this twofold direction—*egoistic* and *altruistic*—in the respective departments of its office work.

§ 249. As directed upon itself, in its proper egoistic work, the regulative office of the reason is to perfect the essential activity of the spirit— to effect that it be ever at its best, as to fullness, roundness, and symmetry, and as to direction by being expended on the highest and best objects. To this one high end its growth and culture are to be regulated, while all specific outgoings of its active nature, which must always be in harmony with the demands of the best culture, are to be kept at their best. It is, in other words, the sacred trust and office of the reason, so far as may depend on it, to render the soul a fully developed activity with its specific functional powers in perfect harmony and symmetry—a feeling, intelligent, aiming spirit, ever moving in due sympathy, enlightenment, and free determination, a spirit of love and light and beneficence. But the character of an activity must of course depend on the character of the object on which it is exerted. It is high or low, broad or narrow, noble or base, according to this object. The activity of the human soul, we have seen, has a strong and steady drift and set in the direction in which it is made to move. This drift or set works itself out in the form of desire; and the comprehensive desire as allowed by the rational free-will determines the character of the soul and is determined or characterized by the object on which it fastens. As desire, it is spontaneous and therefore is not in itself moral or immoral, until the rational free-will comes in, in its sympathetic, conscious, aiming work, to allow or disallow it. The object of the desire, whether bodily indulgence, intellectual strength, or nobility and excellence of character, cannot, as we have seen, be the immediate object of this action of the rational free-will, for that must be some activity which it is to control and regulate. It is the activity in the desire which comes under this controlling power, and by allowing or disallowing that, by fostering or repressing that, determines the fundamental and comprehensive form of character. The first, chiefest, most fundamental, and most vital work of the rational nature in forming character is found accordingly just here, in regulating this all-pervading sweep of the soul's active nature appearing in the form of desire, by directing it upon its proper object and then steadfastly sustaining it and developing it into its fullest and largest sway. The supreme

good, the *summum bonum*, to man, his chief end
and the object of his highest endeavor, is the perfection of his own being in itself and in its condition. As he constitutes a part of an organic
whole, the life of which is his life, the perfecting
of his condition is but the perfecting of his fellow members in this organic whole. This is the
altruistic part of the work allotted by its nature
to the reason as regulative.

Summarily, then, the comprehensive object
of true rational activity is the perfecting of the
natures of all individual beings in their organic
relationships to one another, beginning its radical and germinant work in regulating the fundamental drift or desire of the soul itself aright,
following it up in regulating all specific desires
and propensities and determinations, and ending
with a like work on all surrounding natures with
which it is in interaction.

The product or resultant of this rational work
would be the realized ideal of a perfect character
in each of the organic parts of the universal cosmos, both as a whole with its parts in congruous
relationship to it and to one another, and also as
a part in like congruous relationship to all other
parts of the cosmos. This realized ideal, as perfect, would of course bear the several characteristics which we have recognized, the true in essence, the beautiful in form, the good in end.
These characteristics will, in a nature finite and
imperfect as is the present lot of man, naturally be

realized with a diversity of aim and of endeavor. The essence of a perfect character will be more regarded by one part of the race, as by the Roman the *just* or *right* was esteemed the true mark of the perfect soul or the perfect act. The form of character will be the leading ideal of another part, as the noble—the *kalon*—by the Greek. The end in action will be the governing ideal in another, as *wisdom* was the comprehensive character of the perfect soul in the estimation of the Hebrew. The absolute perfection in character will be the three joined in true organic union—the true or essentially right, the noble or beautiful in form, and the practically wise in relation to the good as end. This is the comprehensive result of all proper egoistic work as regulated by the reason.

The altruistic work is perfectly analogous. It will modify itself only in reference to the peculiar character and relationships of the being on which this part of its work will be directed.

Certainly the grand center and source and all-pervading energy in this cosmical organism—the very creator and disposer of it—must be the chief object in this rational activity. The specific character of its work is determined at once by the peculiar character of the object; and the perfecting work of the reason here can be only the endeavor to secure that character and condition in all created natures which shall perfectly show forth the perfect character of the great creator and disposer in the comprehensive features of love and wisdom and beneficence conjoined in the supreme reason.

Should the question arise : of these two depart-ments of rational endeavor—the egoistic and the altruistic—which should be esteemed the higher and the more commanding; the answer is, that the two endeavors can in a perfect life never come in conflict, any more than one organ of the body in a perfect condition conflict with another. In the next place, the perfected character and condition of all related parts of the cosmos is indispensable to a like perfection in character and condition to each individual part. It is still true that in all finite natures, the objective is before and so leading to all subjective action. The human soul waits on external object to awaken it to the first going forth of its activity ; and ever, as we have seen, it recognizes its dependence on the external object for lead and guidance. In this view, it would seem that whenever there arises a doubt which should be the dominant principle in action, the presumption should favor the altruistic. It is the sad condi-tion of humanity that the proper egoistic work has disastrously prevailed, a true egoism has become a downright selfishness; and a proper counterbalancing remedy for this, would seem-ingly be found in determined altruistic work. Job's misery ceased when he prayed for his friends.

The grand result and outcome of this rational work in a rightly proportioned egoistic and altruistic endeavor will be, in the mind itself, a whole-souled and harmonious movement of all its functions in loving, wise, and purposive action toward the noblest and worthiest objects, bringing in, as the consequence appointed and assured by the supreme wisdom, love, and power, the perfect blessedness of a perfect character and condition.

This grand result and outcome in respect to all fellow-creatures must be a like loving, wise, and purposive activity going out in all opened ways toward them, modified from a proper self-love only in the respects due to co-ordinates and fellow-members of the same body.

Finally, in respect to the great Supreme, this result and outcome will be a like loving, wise, and purposive activity, going out here toward him in due reverence, submission, and trust. To perfect character and condition in the creature and subject is the one way to manifest the perfections of the creative and sovereign ruler conceived in his creative and ruling work. To "glorify God" accordingly is in one aspect the "end of man." In another aspect, the highest blessedness of which a man is capable, is a true and right end of his action, but mediately and in so far only as a consequence that is appointed in the constitution of the universe to wait on all legitimate action. While to perfect for himself this character and condition is the one immediate legitimate end of all free activity in man. Most truly says Seneca : " Man is a rational being ; therefore his good is consummated by fulfilling the end for which he was made. *Rationale enim animal est homo ; consummatur itaque ejus bonum si id adimplevit cui nascitur.*"

# INDEX.